J. Mitchell

COMEDIAN.

Late of Theatre Royal, Covent Garden, London.
Proprietor of the Olympic Theatre, New York.
August 1848.

THE TEMPLE OF MOMUS

•

Mitchell's Olympic Theatre

by

David L. Rinear

The Scarecrow Press, Inc.
Metuchen, N.J., & London
1987

Frontispiece: "William Mitchell (1798-1856)." Theatre Arts
Library, Harry Ransom Humanities Research Center, The
University of Texas at Austin.

Library of Congress Cataloging-in-Publication Data

Rinear, David L., 1944-
    The temple of Momus.

    Bibliography: p.
    Includes index.
    1. Olympic Theatre (New York, N.Y.) 2. Mitchell,
William, 1798-1856. 3. Theater--New York (N.Y.)--
History--19th century. 4. New York (N.Y.)--Buildings,
structures, etc. 5. Theatrical managers--United States--
Biography. I. Title.
PN2277.N528497 1987   792'.09747'1   85-22077
ISBN 0-8108-1850-7

TABLE OF CONTENTS

PREFACE

My curiosity in the subject of this study was piqued about twenty years ago in an undergraduate class in the history of the American theatre. Much to my dismay, I found that there weren't enough secondary accounts of Mitchell and the Olympic Theatre to put together a term paper, but what little I found only whetted my appetite for discovering more. The sage Douglas McDermott, Whose knowledge of and enthusiasm for the history of the American theatre is truly unbounded, suggested, with his wryest grin, that I might want to dig a little deeper when I developed the requisite research skills and background knowledge.

The study grew broader and deeper at Indiana University where Walter Meserve, Richard Moody, and Oscar Brockett provided support, encouragement, and seemingly impossible questions. My ongoing work on the subject has led me to the conclusion that rigorous scholarship and hearty laughter need not be mutually exclusive enterprises.

In addition to the scholars already mentioned, many people have helped along the way. Harold Nichols provided useful information from his own research. Attilio Favorini and Richard Mennen listened, laughed, and shared insights. J. P. Wearing of 19th Century Theatre Research provided encouragement by publishing an essay on the subject a decade ago. Greg Kunesh, Director of The School of Drama at The University of Oklahoma and Nat Eek, Dean of the College of Fine Arts at the same institution have provided both moral and financial support.

The support of Vice Provost Kenneth Hoving and a grant from The University of Oklahoma's Office of Research Administration provided assistance for this study's illustrations. Mary McClain of the University's Information Processing Center deserves a special thank-you for her patience, thoroughness, and helpfulness in preparing the manuscript.

I am extremely grateful to Mr. Fred Rebmann and Mr. Lou Hochstrasser of Ship Bottom, N. J., both of whom helped to "float" me through the sabbatical leave during which much of the writing was completed.

Finally, and most importantly, I am indebted to my wife, Sheila Lynch, without whose love, support, patience, encouragement, and incisive editorial skills this study would never have been completed.

David L. Rinear
Cedar Bonnet Island

CHAPTER ONE

The Olympic Theatre and Its New Manager

William Mitchell's career as a manager of New York's
first Olympic Theatre did not begin until 1839, but the man,
the playhouse, and the growing city's theatrical activities have
significant, if somewhat erratic, prior histories.

With the opening of the new Park Theatre on 21 September 1821, theatrical activity in New York rapidly developed
in the direction it was to follow for almost twenty years. The
new theatre held over two thousand spectators and contained
the box, pit, and gallery auditoriums usual in British and
American theatres throughout most of the nineteenth century.
In size and design it was not unlike the first-class playhouses
of London and the continent. The theatre in the growing city
of approximately one hundred and twenty five thousand residents, it was managed by Edmund Simpson and Stephen Price
well into the 1830s. The managers extended policies which
had their inception prior to the War of 1812.

Price, who had been instrumental in arranging George
Frederick Cooke's triumphant American tour of 1810, annually
contracted a steady stream of London's brightest stars who
habitually started their American tours on the boards of the
Park. During the 1820s such luminaries as Edmund Kean,
William Charles Macready, Charles Mathews, Junius Brutus
Booth Sr., and a host of lesser lights performed at the Park
under Price and Simpson's auspices.

Between twinklings of the seemingly ceaseless constellation of stars, the theatre's resident stock company performed
pieces from the standard eighteenth- and early nineteenth-
century repertory. Fifteen to twenty resident actors played
a full-length comedy or tragedy and an afterpiece when no
visiting luminaries appeared, and performed in support of
the stars in their vehicles when they were present. Very
few new full-length plays were produced, but fresh farces

1

from the London theatres were frequently given their American premieres at the Park as afterpieces. Nevertheless, the audience went to the Park primarily to see the actors in established vehicles, not to see new plays. Since the same standard pieces tended to be repeated ad nauseam, little money was spent on scenery, costumes, and other spectacular elements of production.

In 1826 the Park's monopoly as the city's only large playhouse received the first of many challenges with the opening of the Bowery Theatre. Manhattan Island's city had grown to about one hundred and sixty five thousand residents and some investors reasoned there was room enough for another theatre similar to the Park on the east side of town on the Bowery. The neighborhood was, at that time, a respectable and even lovely one as the name of the once tree-lined street indicates. But the Bowery Theatre's original policy of stars and a stock company in pieces from the standard repertory failed to provide remunerative audiences during its first seasons under Charles Gilfert's management.

In August of 1830 Thomas S. Hamblin assumed management of the theatre, and changed its name to The American Theatre, Bowery. He immediately began presenting spectacular, thrilling, and frequently jingoistic melodrama designed to attract the increasingly large number of workingmen living on the city's East Side who were developing a proud sense of both class and nationalism traditionally associated with the rise of Jacksonian Democracy. The Bowery soon developed its particular audience and bill of theatrical fare while the Park continued its established practices. The two playhouses, then, served separate segments of the city's population, and they really weren't in competition with each other.

A third large theatre, originally built for the exclusive production of Italian opera, opened in 1834. Although opera had been seen frequently at the Park, the city's sophisticated theatregoers were not numerous enough to support grand opera on a continuing basis and the Italian Opera House failed after its premiere season. Reopening as the National Theatre in 1836, it soon provided fierce competition to the Park for the older theatre's audience until fire destroyed the newer playhouse in the autumn of 1839.

An additional significant theatrical tradition began during the summer of 1828. The large playhouses closed during the summer months, because their gaslights and lack of adequate

ventilation made them extremely uncomfortable during the
swelteringly humid months of July and August. Additional
problems occurred during any summer that yellow fever
broke out in the city as people were terrified to congregate
in any large indoor structure.

The small city ended at Wall Street at that time.
Several New York restauranteurs opened tented refreshment
gardens in the "country" above Wall Street during the 1820s.
These pleasure gardens featured light meals, ice cream, and
occasional musical entertainment. In the summer of 1828
actors from the first Bowery Theatre, which had recently
burned down, struck a bargain with William Niblo, a famous
restauranteur of the day who was also proprietor of the largest and best known of the summer gardens, and began to play
there during the hot weather months. Niblo's Gardens soon
became New York's primary summer theatre. In the late
1830s, a permanent theatre was built on the site for the annual summer entertainments, but it did not house a year-
round company until many years later.

Several smaller playhouses opened and closed in the
city with dazzling rapidity during the 1820s and 1830s, but
by the autumn of 1837, the only theatres which were operating
on a continuing basis during the winter months were the Park,
Bowery, National, the much smaller and even less significant
Franklin, and the soon-to-be-opened Olympic.

New York's first Olympic Theatre, designed by Calvin
Pollard and built by Stacey Pitcher, occupied a lot which had
formerly housed the Broadway Circus of Simpson and Price.
Located in what was the heart of the growing city's commer-
cial district at 444 Broadway--halfway between Howard and
Grand streets--the theatre was constructed at the behest of
William Rufus Blake and Henry E. Willard, its first managers.

Because New York's theatrical entrepreneurs had enjoyed a decade of growth and prosperity by continually looking
to London for actors and plays, it is not surprising that someone would build a New York theatre in conscious imitation of
Madame Vestris' London Olympic, which had enjoyed unprecedented success since 1832. Blake and Willard's new theatre
unabashedly imitated its famous prototype. The house contained the box, pit, gallery, and dress circle seating areas
usual in British and American theatres throughout most of
the nineteenth century. But the auditorium differed from
those of New York's other playhouses in one important respect

--its size. The city's three most important theatres--the
Park, the Bowery, and the National--had extremely large
auditoriums capable of seating upwards of two thousand patrons. Available information indicates that the Olympic held
about half the patrons of the city's other theatres, with a
capacity of between one thousand and twelve hundred.[1] Although still commodious by today's standards, Lawrence Hutton
notes that New York's newest theatre was considered petite
by its contemporaries:

> Small, snug, bright, comfortable, it was all that
> a theatre should be; its interior presenting more
> the appearance of the home of an elegant lady in
> its refined tasteful surroundings, than the mere
> regulation, tinsel-ornamented 'home of the drama. '[2]

The theatre's diminutive stature was reflected by its
stage as well as its auditorium. The lot upon which the playhouse was constructed was too narrow to provide a stage
wide enough for the wing space necessary to accommodate the
shutter and groove system of changeable scenery prevalent
on the stages of eighteenth- and early nineteenth-century
theatres in this country and in England. Only painted drops
and free plantation scenic pieces could be used at the Olympic.[3]

The debt of New York's Olympic to its London name-
sake extended beyond physical similarities. Willard and
Blake, the new theatre's inaugural managers, consciously
aped Madame Vestris in the type of entertainment they presented. Playbills for the theatre's grand opening on 18
September 1837, announced: "The entertainment will consist
of the lighter varieties of the drama, combined with opera,
vaudeville, and ballet, as at Madame Vestris' London Olympic. "[4] The term "lighter varieties of the drama, " was explained on the occasion of the theatre's grand opening in an
address written by E. Burke Fisher and spoken by Blake:

> Friends of the Stage, the laughing muse is ours,
> and bids you welcome from her throne of flowers.
> She bids you hail! Not in the pensive mood, which
> palls the soul with deeds of guilt and blood. Hers
> is the power, the balmy power of Art, to sooth the
> passions, and improve the heart.[5]

Although Willard and Blake were the only managers in New
York specializing in light, short entertainment, they soon
found, as did the city's other theatre managers, that the

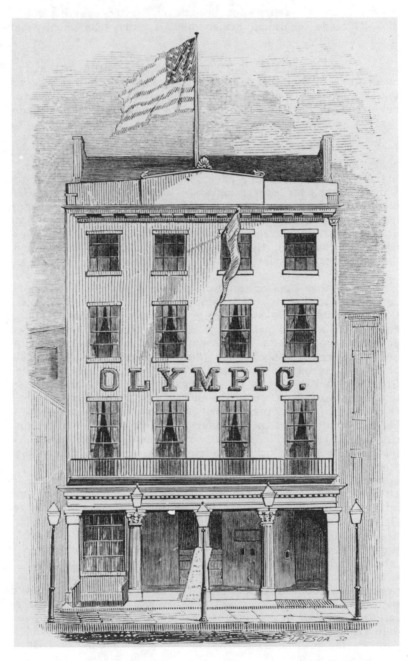

"The Olympic Theatre."   The Harvard Collection.

recent economic depression brought on by the specie panic
of 1837 made theatrical management a more than usually perilous game.

Throughout the 1820's and the early 1830's national
economic and territorial growth coupled with the city's swell-
ing population to provide a favorable environment for theatrical activity. But as early as 1830 danger signs for the ado-
lescent nation's robust economy appeared.

From 1828 on, proponents of cheap money--paper currency unsupported by specie reserves of gold and silver--
blamed Nicholas Biddle, president of the Second Bank of the
United States, for preventing state banks from issuing sufficient paper money to carry on the growing nation's expanding
business, particularly in the rapidly developing western states.
State banks that lent more money than their specie reserves
supported found that Biddle's National Bank would not accept
their bank notes at face value.

Western land speculators and businessmen, strong
supporters and allies of President Jackson, persuaded "Old
Hickory" that Biddle's policies were preventing economic
growth and national prosperity. Biddle, fearing that Jackson
and the "cheap money" proponents would muster enough support to force a change in the National Bank's specie payments
policy, nurtured a probank anti-"cheap money" opposition in
Congress and the press by making large-interest free loans
to influential congressmen, senators, and journalists. In
December of 1830 Jackson proposed that the National Bank
become a branch of the Treasury Department when its charter
expired in 1836. The carefully cultivated probank coalition
managed to get the bank rechartered in Congress during the
spring of 1832, four years prior to the expiration of its
operating charter, but Jackson vetoed the rechartering bill on
10 July and took his landslide victory in the election of 1832
as a mandate to destroy the Second Bank of the United States.
Because everyone knew that Biddle's "hard money" policy
would expire with the National Bank's charter, western banks
began issuing currency with reckless abandon. Extensive
land speculation in the west led many state banks to issue
vast amounts of paper currency unsecured by specie. This
produced a booming inflationary spiral that became nationwide
between 1834 and 1836. The government helped to fuel this
inflationary fire by increasing the amount of federal land for
sale from four million six hundred thousand acres in 1834 to
over twenty million acres in 1836. By the spring of 1836

the inflationary spiral was threatening the economy and in an
attempt to control it, Jackson issued the Specie Circular on
11 July. This executive order required that all land purchased from the government after 15 August 1836 be paid for
in silver and gold. Land prices turned sharply downward and
commodity and stock prices followed suit in the spring of 1837.
With the failure of several London banks which had over-
extended themselves in loans in the Northeast and New Orleans
the depression became national in scope and the panic hit
New York in the spring of 1837. On 10 May Philip Hone,
a leading member of New York's business community, reported to his diary, "No goods are selling, no business stir-
ring, stocks have fallen again."[6] The depression deepened
in 1839 with the failure of Nicholas Biddle's large and powerful Bank of the United States of Pennsylvania, the former
Second Bank of the United States rechartered as a Pennsylvania State bank. Economic conditions began to improve
gradually after 1845, but general prosperity did not return
until 1848 when the war with Mexico fueled the economy and
the California gold rush provided the growing nation with all
the specie it needed.

New York's established playhouses managed to maintain
operations during the first two years of what was to be almost
a decade of hard times, but the new little Olympic did not
fare as well. Its initial managers were unable to operate profitably and abandoned their fledgling enterprise in January of
1838.

Between Blake and Willard's abandonment of the Olympic in January of 1838 and May of 1839, the theatre was
operated by five different managements which ranged in dura-
tion from five days to three months.[7] No one seemed able
to make the Olympic a paying enterprise. Mismanagement
was not the sole reason for the several successive failures
of the Olympic. Because of the theatre's size, an evening's
gross receipts, at prices of admission competitive with the
city's other theatres, could not exceed $535.00. This man-
dated that operating costs be kept low and that popular traveling stars, who often demanded and received as much as
$300.00 per evening, could not be hired.

With each of the successive ill-fated managements,
the quality of both the theatre's entertainment and its patrons
progressively deteriorated. The Albion, one of New York's
leading weekly periodicals, noted that when Mitchell assumed
management of the Olympic, "its character was sunk to the

lowest pitch of theatrical degradation; ...none but visitors of
the most irregular habits and meanest condition would conde-
scend to congregate there."[8]

     William Mitchell, the man who was to make the pre-
viously ill-fated Olympic New York's most successful theatre
through most the 1840's, had vast experience as both an
actor and stage manager before becoming the Olympic's sole
lessee.

     Born to the family of a merchant ship captain in
Billquay, Durham, England, in 1798, Mitchell enjoyed a comfortable childhood before his parents decided to prepare him
for a career in commerce. To that end, he was apprenticed
as clerk in the office of a West Indies merchant at the age
of fifteen. At the end of six years as a merchant's clerk,
he gave up commerce and made the stage his profession.
In 1820 he obtained his first professional engagement--playing
on a sharing system with a minor provincial troupe in Kent.
Two years later, he joined the excellent provincial company
of DeCamp in Sheffield. This troupe was one of the best of
its kind and included several young actors who were later to
become well known in this country. Among them were Thomas
S. Hamblin, George Holland, and Thomas Flynn.

     During his theatrical apprenticeship in the provinces,
Mitchell earned a reputation as a low and eccentric comedian
of more than ordinary merit. By 1831, he was acting in
London at both the Strand and Covent Garden. His London
career was erratic and he frequently found himself playing at
the minor theatres--those playhouses which operated on the
periphery of the licensing act by presenting short legitimate
plays and musical dramas which were classified as "irregular.'
This was a dangerous business because the licensing authorities were often inconsistent in deciding which of the minor
houses were in violation of their limited licenses. Mitchell
was the victim of one of the periodic purges of the minor
houses in 1834 when he was fined £50 for being a member of
the Strand's company at a time when it was convicted of
violating its limited license. After this unfortunate and costly
experience at the Strand, Mitchell spent the next two years
at three theatres in London: the Victoria as an eccentric
comedian; the Adelphi as stage manager; and, the St. James
as principal low comedian.[9]

     Unable to achieve his goal of becoming principal low
comedian at either Drury Lane or Covent Garden, Mitchell
decided to emigrate to this country in 1836.

Upon his arrival in New York, Mitchell was immediately
hired by Thomas Flynn--with whom he had worked in DeCamp's
provincial company--and Henry E. Willard as principal low
comedian at their National Theatre. He stayed with Flynn
and Willard for the entire season, but when they gave up the
National in May of 1837, he moved to New York's Franklin
Theatre. Throughout the fall of 1837 and the spring of 1838
he played limited starring engagements at several different
theatres in New York. While this may seem surprising, it
was not unusual. During that period of time an English reputation enabled almost any British actor to obtain "star" engagements.

The autumn of 1838 found Mitchell back at the National,
then under the management of James W. Wallack, as principal
low comedian and stage manager. Mitchell profited greatly
from his association with Wallack. Although stars were
occasionally imported, the resident stock company--probably
the best in the country at the time[10]--managed to draw profitable audiences on their own. It was probably Mitchell's
experience with Wallack at the National which convinced him
that a good stock company could draw remunerative audiences.
As stage manager he contributed significantly to the estimable
reputation which Wallack's productions enjoyed. George Odell
claims, "Wallack first showed New York what was meant by
perfect stage-management, with an eye to every detail however slight; never on his stage were noticed the incongruities
of costume, scenery, etc., that, I am afraid, disfigured the
best efforts of Old Drury (the Park Theatre)."[11]

When Wallack started his third season as manager
of the National in August of 1839, Mitchell was again employed
as stage manager and principal low comedian. The season,
however, was brief: the National Theatre was destroyed by
a fire that may have been arson on 28 September 1839.
Wallack, with a strong company and no theatre, moved immediately uptown to the new theatre adjoining Niblo's Gardens.
He opened there on 30 September, a mere two days after the
conflagration which had destroyed the National. But the success which Wallack had enjoyed at the National did not follow
him uptown to Niblo's. Although the Gardens had become the
favorite resort of New York's theatregoers during the summer,
it was too far from the commercial and residential center of
the growing city to attract large audiences during the regular
theatre season. Wallack was unable to operate the theatre
at Niblo's Garden profitably and abandoned his management on
18 November 1839.

VIEW OF BROADWAY, N. Y.
between Howard & Grand Streets, 1840

With the demise of Wallack's management, his former company and staff found themselves unemployed. Mitchell probably had little difficulty interesting several of them in opening the little Olympic Theatre, which had been vacant since the preceding June, under his managerial auspices.

[opposite]: "Broadway Between Howard and Grand Streets, 1840." The Harvard Theatre Collection.

CHAPTER TWO

Establishing a Tradition

During the three-week interlude between Wallack's abandonment of the theatre at Niblo's Gardens and the reopening of the Olympic, William Mitchell was an extremely busy man. He was able to rent the theatre for only twenty-five dollars a week,[1] making a significant portion of his overhead extremely low. Traveling stars at the Park frequently earned in excess of one hundred and fifty dollars a night and some of that theatre's stock company were paid more weekly than Mitchell spent on rent. While the Olympic's rent may seem to be an incredible bargain, none of the theatre's previous managers had succeeded and the little playhouse had developed an unenviable reputation. Its owners were probably delighted to have it occupied at any price during the extremely depressed winter of 1839. Because the new manager was able to strike such a favorable bargain regarding the rent fee, he had the theatre redecorated.

Mitchell assembled an acting company of eight men and six women, all but one of whom had been performing in the theatres of New York for some time. From the remnants of Wallack's company came Henry Horncastle, Mr. Everard, James S. Browne, Mrs. Bailey, Mrs. Plumer, and Lydia Singleton. The Chatham contributed James Anderson, Mr. Russell, and Evelyn Randolph. Mrs. Jones of the Bowery and Sidney Pearson of the Park completed the list of actors previously seen on the boards of New York's theatres. Of the entire company, only Mrs. Johnson was without experience in Gotham. Mitchell hired Ben A. Baker as prompter. Richard Bengough and George Loder assumed responsibility for scenery and musical direction, respectively. Both had been formerly employed by Wallack, and Bengough's reputation as a scenic artist is attested to by the accolades which Wallack's stage appointments received from both the public

13

and the press.   Business affairs of the enterprise were
entrusted to William Corbyn, who served as treasurer.

Mitchell's initial policies were essentially those of the
several previous unsuccessful managers of the theatre.   The
small Olympic was ideally suited to intimate comic entertainment; Mitchell had a strong reputation as a low comedian;
and much of his London experience had been in short comic
plays at several of the City's minor playhouses.   Several
short pieces were to be produced each evening and the bill
of fare was to be changed frequently.   He announced to the
public:

> His arrangements, as far as they are completed,
> give a goodly token that he will be able to produce
> such a constant succession of novelties as will en-
> title him to a share of that patronage which it will
> be his constant endeavour to deserve, and his high-
> est gratification to obtain. [2]

The evening's entertainment was to begin precisely at
7:00 p. m., with the doors of the theatre opening thirty minutes in advance of curtain time.   Tickets were available only
at the theatre's box office from 10:00 a. m. until 4:00 p. m.,
except Sunday, when the theatre was closed.   Prices of admission, competitive with New York's other theatres, were:
Dress Circle--75¢ ; Boxes--50¢ ; and Pit--25¢ .

On Monday, 9 December 1839, the Olympic Theatre,
under the management of William Mitchell, opened for business with three short British farces: Frederic Reynold's
No!; William Rede's His First Champagne; and James Townley's
High Life Below Stairs.   There was nothing particularly
innovative about Mitchell's opening-night bill.   All three of
the farces were part of the standard afterpiece repertory in
New York's larger theatres and, as Odell has noted, they,
"might have been the opening attraction at any of the minor
theatres."[3]   They may have been chosen because members
of the acting company were familiar with them and they could
be readied for production with a minimum of rehearsal time.
The same bill played to a small audience on the following
evening with Mitchell, the company's best comedian, appearing in the leading roles of all three plays.   The addition of
a fourth play to the bill on Wednesday and Thursday did not
improve attendance, and it appeared that Mitchell's management of the albatross-like Olympic was to be short-lived.
In desperation, Mitchell made a policy change which usually

marked the beginning of the end for theatrical managements,
but was to help make his successful: on 14 December, he
reduced the prices of admission to 50¢ for the dress circle,
25¢ for the boxes and 12½¢ for the pit.[4] These new prices,
designed to attract additional audience members during a time
of severe economic depression, made the cost of an evening's
entertainment at the Olympic exactly half as expensive as at
the Bowery or the Park.

The course of events indicates that Mitchell's first week
in business was not successful. He had added a fourth piece
to the evening's bill and reduced prices in an attempt to attract paying patrons. His fledgling enterprise was on something less than shaky footing, but that was to change literally
overnight.[5]

On Monday, 16 December 1839, Mitchell produced his
first burlesque at the Olympic. Entitled The Roof Scrambler
and written by Henry Horncastle, a member of the acting
company, it ridiculed the popular opera, La Sonnambula. The
opera treats a heroine who sleepwalks after her true love
every evening. It was first seen in New York in 1835 at
the Park and Odell notes that the city's operagoers were,
"to adore it down to the days of Etelka Gerster, a half-
century later."[6] J. W. Wallack, Mitchell's former employer,
had produced it on 5 September 1837, the second night of
his first season as manager of the National Theatre, and
again on 10 December 1838 with Miss Sheriff singing the role
of the somnambulist, Amilie, and Horncastle and Mitchell in
supporting roles. The members of Mitchell's company who
had worked at the National were intimately familiar with the
opera and must have relished an opportunity to burlesque it.
Mitchell played Molly Brown in the lampoon--a romantic
heroine who scrambles the city's roofs trying to catch her
here-today-gone-tomorrow lover. Although it has proven
impossible to isolate those elements of Sheriff's singing and
acting style that Mitchell burlesqued, he must have managed
to parody her with much effect and tremendous humor. The
Spirit of The Times' theatre critic reported. "Never again will
we be able to listen to Miss Sheriff in the part without suffering from the remembrance of Mitchell's Molly Brown."[7]
Immediately and immensely successful, The Roof Scrambler
played each evening for the entire week and was revived ten
additional times by 6 January. It was, therefore, absent from
the evening's bill only twice between its premiere and 6 January 1840.

Mitchell knew immediately that he had a hit on his hands, for his playbill of 20 December brags of the success of The Roof Scrambler.[8] Yet because his stock company had not drawn good audiences during the first week, Mitchell had engaged George Mossop, the Irish comedian, for one week beginning 23 December.[9] Mossop's usual round of Irish characters shared the evening's bills with Mitchell's stock company hit. Reviews of the theatre's offering left no doubt that The Roof Scrambler, and not Mossop, was responsible for the increased attendance. The Spirit of The Times' critic urged his readers to go see Mitchell's lampoon since, "So happy a hit has not been made in many months in the way of fun."[10] The Mirror's reviewer agreed that it was, "a laughable piece,"[11] and reported that, "The audience seem [sic] to enjoy it highly."[12] But he found the piece offensive, noting that, "the humour was at times a little too broad; and we can imagine nothing more reprehensible in the stage appointment than the attire of the assumed female character."[13]

The Mirror's critic seems to have been the only one offended by Mitchell's portrayal of Molly Brown--the first female character he played in New York. Throughout his tenure at the Olympic, Mitchell occasionally played female roles, but only in burlesques. His farcical, low comic style of acting must have made his transvestite characters sufficiently unrealistic that they were not offensive, for he was never again chastised for playing a female role. Mitchell was not beginning a New York drag tradition. Transvestitism was not unusual in New York's theatres during the period, and it was not confined to men playing comic female characters. Charlotte Cushman had already debuted as Romeo, which she was to play extensively throughout her career, and she was soon to add Hamlet to her tragic repertory.

The audiences that Mitchell suddenly attracted to the previously ill-fated Olympic were as unusual as they were large. Among the fortunate manager's regular patrons were many representatives of New York's high society, as well as a number of actors from the city's other theatres.[14] By 28 December, a mere three weeks after the opening of the theatre, The Spirit of The Times reported, "The attendance is not only highly respectable, but the house is almost nightly crowded to the ceiling."[15] The little theatre on lower Broadway became a fashionable gathering place for New York's elite citizens within a month of Mitchell's assumption of the management.[16]

The patronage of the patricians was no accident, for
Mitchell carefully cultivated the leading men-about-town.
Through his prior association with Wallack, he knew most
of New York's leading citizens, and any "gentleman" of the
city with whom Mitchell was acquainted was given entreé into
the Olympic's greenroom. While this may have been good for
business, it almost certainly proved a nuisance to the company, and even led to accusations of backstage immorality.[17]
The privilege of greenroom entreé that the leading men-about-
town enjoyed seems to be concomitant with the rise of fashionable support for Mitchell's enterprise, and may have been an
unstated policy from the beginning of his management. It
almost certainly was a practice by the new year.

While the fashionable members of New York society
were making the Olympic dress circle and boxes a place in
which to be seen, the opposite end of the socioeconomic spectrum was busily making the pit their particular province.
Shortly after the reduction of prices, Mitchell's pit became
the favorite haunt for the newsboys, butcherboys, and apprentices known collectively to that day and age as the "b'hoys."
New York's other theatres tended to be homogenous in their
audiences. The better class of people went to the Park, and
the rude mechanicals and "riff-raff" attended the Bowery.
But everyone went to the Olympic. The pit's clientele makes
it seem possible, and perhaps even probable, that the city's
elite went to the Olympic in order to see not only the evening's bill of fare, but also the "b'hoys," for there was no
other place in the city frequented by these two extremes of
New York society.

An operatic burlesque probably did as much to win
Mitchell the patronage of high-class clientele as did the special privileges he extended them. The Roof Scrambler would
certainly have been funnier to audience members who were
familiar with the original than it would be to those who were
ignorant of operas in general and La Sonnambula in particular.
While inexpensive prices, low comic acting and the sight of
the "swells" in the dress circle may have been all the impetus
the "b'hoys" needed to throng to Mitchell's theatre, the aristocratic members of the audiences were better qualified to
appreciate the burlesque of La Sonnambula by virtue of their
probable familiarity with the opera.[18]

The ironic experience of paying a star who was being
carried by the success of a stock piece made Mitchell realize where his fame and fortune were to be earned: with

humorous burlesques produced by the stock company and not
in a succession of traveling stars. Although other comic
actors were to be engaged for limited periods throughout
Mitchell's tenure at the Olympic, only one--a former member
of the stock company--was given star billing, or presumably
star salary, between Mossop's engagement in 1839 and 1848
when Mitchell, hard pressed by competition from Burton,
hired the Yankee actors Marble and Hill in succession.

Although Mitchell's patrons through the end of December
went to the Olympic primarily to see The Roof Scrambler, the
other offerings must also have been attractive. It became
general policy to fill out the evening's entertainment with two
or three short farces on those frequent occasions when a burlesque or extravaganza served as the main attraction. After
the first week of business, during which four of Mitchell's
bills contained only three pieces, an evening at the Olympic
usually consisted of four pieces.

Mitchell himself was the company's strongest drawing
card as an actor and usually appeared in three of the four
pieces presented on any given evening, while Horncastle and
Browne most often played the leads in those plays in which
the manager did not appear. During this inaugural season,
no one actress handled all the female leading business, primarily because all of the company's women were equally
competent. The manager had consciously collected a company
of good comic actors about himself and the selection of his
personnel enabled him to develop a strong acting ensemble.
The Spirit of The Times reported, on the first day of 1840,
that the Olympic was earning money--a rarity among New
York's theatres during the depressed winter of 1840 and a
feat never before achieved in the succession of ill-starred
managements that had preceded Mitchell. The same journal
noted that the stock company was consistently good in light
comedy and farce, and that the acting of Williams, Browne,
and Mitchell seemed better appreciated in the smaller Olympic than upon the boards of the National Theatre where they
had all previously performed under J. W. Wallack's management. [19]

The observation regarding the relationship between the
actors and the smaller house suggests that Mitchell, who had
played several of the small Vestris-like minor theatres in
London before emigrating, may have been instrumental in
coaching his actors to adjust to the peculiar demands of
playing in a smaller space.

On 6 January, The Roof Scrambler was withdrawn
from production in favor of a new burlesque which proved to
be Mitchell's first dismal failure. The play, Chrononhotonthologos, 20 was not reviewed and little material is available concerning its subject matter save that contained in the playbill
for its only night of performance: "The most Tragical tragedy
that ever was tragedized by any company of tragedians."21
The cast included Browne as Chrononhotonthologos, "the King
of Queerrummania," and Mitchell as Regdium Fumidas, "a
courtier." The corpse count concluding Jacobean and early
nineteenth-century tragedies seems to have been one of the
targets of the unsuccessful burlesque, for "The Piece concludes with a Dance of Dead Bodies."22 The reasons for the
lampoon's failure are lost to history, but it was withdrawn
after one evening in favor of The Roof Scrambler, which reappeared from 7 through 18 January. It was to be seen on
the boards of the stage sporadically throughout the rest of
the season and qualifies as Mitchell's first big hit: it had
been played on twenty-four out of a possible twenty-eight
evenings that the theatre had been open since its premiere
on 16 December. While it was still drawing crowded audiences, on 10 January a new kind of piece debuted. Entitled
the Irresistible Cadets, it was actually a farce with songs
featuring the women of the company in an attractive chorus
which played on eight successive evenings.

On 15 January, with two hits running and his managerial
venture an undisputed success, Mitchell produced the play
that was to make the Olympic the most successful theatre in
New York during the season of 1839-40. The new piece, a
Henry Horncastle adaptation from Dickens' Nicholas Nickleby
entitled The Savage and The Maiden, proved to be the most
durably popular piece in the Olympic's repertory for the first
nine years of Mitchell's management.

There is no extant copy of a play with that title by
Horncastle or anyone else. Yet it may be that the play has
survived under the title, The Infant Phenomenon.

Horncastle worked in England for a number of years,
primarily in the minor theatres, before joining Wallack's
company in New York in 1837. While at the Strand Theatre
in London during 1832, he adapted a short piece from Nicholas
Nickleby and entitled it The Infant Phenomenon. Published
sometime after 1850 by Dick's Standard Play Series, the list
of characters contained in the published play is identical with
the bills for the Olympic's production of The Savage and The

Maiden. Moreover, the action in the published play progresses
in exactly the same way as reviews describe the story of the
Olympic's piece. It is highly unlikely that the same author
would treat the same subject with the same list of characters
in the same fashion in two highly distinct ways within a space
of seven years. The two pieces are apparently identical.

In the published version of the play, Nicholas Nickleby,
disguised as Johnson and traveling in the company of his
friend Smike, journeys to Portsmouth and is persuaded by
Crummles, the manager of the theatre there, to become the
house writer for his troupe of players, a company comprised
primarily of members of his family. After Nickleby's accep-
tance of Crummles' proposal, the rest of the play consists of
the following action: Crummles misnames Smike and calls him,
alternately, Tyke, Spike and Dyke; a debate with members of
the company over the merits of the youngest Crummles, the
infant phenomenon; and, a hilarious rehearsal scene in which
the "phenomenon" wards off the ill-intentioned advances of the
Savage, Folair. That is all there is to it. The published
play is but eight pages long, including copious stage directions.
Given breaks for laughter and an inordinate amount of comic
business, it is highly unlikely that the piece, or a possible
variation of it, occupied more than thirty minutes playing
time.

The cast of the Olympic's production included Mitchell
as Crummles, Horncastle as Nicholas Nickleby, Miss Randolph as Smike, Mrs. Russell as Folair and Le Petite Celeste
as the Infant Phenomenon. The piece ran for eighteen evenings. Returning to its premiere place in the evening's bill
on the very next evening, 5 February, it enjoyed twenty-seven
additional consecutive performances. Thus, it was performed
on forty-five out of forty-six evenings and enjoyed the longest
run that New York had seen of any play to that date.

The Savage and The Maiden is slightly unusual as a
first-season success at the Olympic, since it was not a burlesque. Nevertheless, there were probably some burlesque
elements in it, and perhaps even self-parody. The fact
that Mitchell, the manager, played Crummles, the manager,
and persuaded Horncastle, the resident playwright to become
Nickleby, the resident playwright, would not have been lost
on the Olympic's audience. The play's phenomenal success
was due to the performances of the company. In this respect, Mitchell eclipsed his employees: his delineation of
Crummles was long regarded as equal in hilarity to his

Mr MITCHELL as CRUMMLES

PUBLISHED BY W. CURRY

At his Dramatic Repository 499½ Broadway, New York

Nov.r 1841.

"Mitchell as Crummles in The Savage and The Maiden."
The Harvard Theatre Collection.

great rival's best role; William E. Burton's famous rendition
of Toodles. 23

     With the moderate success of The Irresistible Cadets
coupled with the prodigious popularity of both The Roof
Scrambler and The Savage and The Maiden, Mitchell was the
envy of every other theatrical manager in New York during
the season. His management was not quite two months old
and could already boast three hits, "that were like a gold
mine impossible to be played out. "24

     Attendance at the Olympic became so great after the
introduction of The Savage and The Maiden into the evening's
entertainment that Mitchell suspended the theatre's free list
a week into the popular new sketch's run. He justified this
revenue-increasing change of policy on the basis of the theatre's small seating capacity, the inexpensive admission prices,
and the amount he was spending on producing his plays and
maintaining the company. Members of the press and the
theatrical profession, however, were still entitled to free
admission. 25

     While the public was flocking to the Olympic in such
numbers that Mitchell suspended his free list, the press
lauded both The Savage and The Maiden and Mitchell's general
enterprise as an actor and manager. The Spirit of The Times
praised the new play as "more laughable even than the 'Roof
Scrambler,'"26 and also noted: "Mitchell is doing decidedly
a good business, and he deserves to do so, as he gives more
fun for the same money than any theatre ever before open in
New York."27 A week later, the same paper offered its
readers an explanation for the phenomenal success of Mitchell's
theatre, claiming that his tremendous ability as a low comedian combined nicely with his attention to the details of management. Apparently, not even bad weather could keep people away
from the city's new fun-spot. The Spirit noted, "The house
on Monday was crowded to suffocation, and even on Wednesday,
when the rain fell in torrents, it was well-filled."28

     Less than a week into the run of Horncastle's adapta-
tion from Dickens, Mitchell produced yet another new piece
which was to prove immensely popular. Entitled Olympic
Revels, and based loosely on the famous extravaganza that
Madame Vestris had produced during her premiere season
at the London Olympic, the New York version featured the
resident deities of Mt. Olympus squabbling amusingly on a
stage decorated by Bengough's elaborate scenery. The piece

ran for fourteen evenings at the same time that The Savage
and The Maiden led the bills.

During the six weeks that the theatre had been open,
Mitchell had produced four undisputable hits. All of them
had satirical burlesque elements in them, but the lampoons
were of a general nature and not aimed at specific individuals
or particular contemporary incidents. But the innovative
manager moved from the generally ludicrous to the specifically ridiculous on 27 January with the premiere of Billy
Taylor which ridiculed both the productions and the exaggerated advertising of T. S. Hamblin, manager of the American
Theatre, Bowery.

Hamblin's Bowery, known to New Yorkers of that day
and historians of the theatre as the "bucket of blood," was
famous, or perhaps infamous, for the sensational nature of
the entertainments presented there for the pleasure of New
York's less sophisticated theatregoers. Hamblin catered to
workingmen and the Bowery "b'hoys," the same class of
society that comprised the audience in Mitchell's pit. In an
effort to draw large audiences, Hamblin puffed the merits of
his productions in both the theatre's daily playbills and his
advertisements in the city's several newspapers. In January
of 1840, the Bowery's manager had reached a new height of
puffery with the announcement of his 2 January premiere of
The Fairy Spell:

> New Scenery, new dresses, new machinery, new
> music, new decorations, and new ballets; produced
> at an expense of many thousand dollars: the scenery
> painted on upwards of thirty-one thousand square feet
> of canvas--has been three months in preparation.
> N.B. In consequence of the length of time, the
> new spectacle will occupy in representation no other
> piece will be performed on the same evening.[29]

Mitchell had a great deal of fun at the expense of the
above-quoted announcement in his playbills for 27 January,
the premiere of Billy Taylor:

> New Scenery, new dresses, new machinery, new
> music, new decorations, and new ballets; produced
> without an immense expense; the entire cost being
> considerably under ten thousand dollars. The new
> scenery is painted on less than 50,000 square feet
> of canvas, and has not been many months in prep-
> aration.

N.B. In consequence of the Burlesque not being
too long, three other pieces and a variety of entertainments will also be played on the same evening.[30]

J. B. Buckstone's Billy Taylor, probably adapted by
Horncastle in such a fashion that it ridiculed specific aspects
of the Bowery and its clientele, enjoyed a twofold burlesque:
the theatre and its advertising policies. This was the first
instance of a practice that Mitchell was to follow intermit-
tently throughout his career as the Olympic's manager: his
playbills frequently indicated what was to be burlesqued in the
production which they advertised.

In Billy Taylor, William Taylor, the hero, "familiarly
called Billy Taylor, a perfect gentleman, though living in a
state of Cannibalism, viz. upon his father,"[31] was played
by Mitchell. Horncastle performed Carolus Lanternus, a
watchman, while Anderson played Old Nicholas, "familiarly
called Old Nick."[32] "Twenty stout young fellows by Messrs.
Everard and Clarke--eighteen invisible,"[33] made up a sparse
crowd.

During its six-night run, Billy Taylor attracted large
numbers of the "b'hoys" to the pit and is primarily significant
as the first of Mitchell's burlesques of other theatres, thus
establishing the policy of specific burlesque which was to
contribute greatly to the rising fortunes of the Olympic. As
Odell has aptly noted, "This sort of cool impudence made
Mitchell the idol of his patrons from the newsboys in the pit
to the elegant literati in the boxes. It was new, and it
exactly hit the fancy of the American humourists of the day."[34]

Specific mockery of Hamblin and the Bowery was
ideally suited to the tastes of both extremes of Mitchell's
audience. The fashionable members of the audience had
little use for Hamblin and his vulgar entertainments, and
savored a joke which made him the butt. The "b'hoys"
were pleased, for they frequented the Bowery when not at the
Olympic and no doubt felt they were in on the joke.

Early in the week-long run of Billy Taylor, Mitchell
showed his abilities at disciplining his vociferous pit patrons
--an ability that was to be utilized several times during his
managerial career. Apparently, the pit wasn't large enough
to hold all of the would-be spectators during one evening and
a noisy fight over seats erupted after the evening's performance began. The "b'hoys" created such a din that Mitchell,

who was performing Billy Taylor, marched to the footlights
and told them, "Gentlemen, you had better be quiet: if you
are not, I shall be under the necessity of raising the prices."[35]

Order was instantly restored. Throughout his tenure
as the Olympic's manager, Mitchell would resort to threats
of raising prices whenever the "b'hoys" in the pit got too
rambunctious. The threat must have always worked, for he
was never forced to carry it out. Although commotion in the
pit occurred frequently throughout Mitchell's management, the
wrangling never became too serious. No reports of serious
confrontations or bloodshed among the pittites exist. This is
remarkable when one considers that the rough types who frequented the place were the same ones who were to lay siege
to the Astor Place Opera House in 1849.

With three overwhelming successes and two moderate
ones in the evening's bills by 1 February, the Olympic was
the best-attended theatre in the city. Although it was smaller
than either the Bowery or the Park, it had established itself
as the most serious rival to those theatres.[36] The Mirror
noted in the middle of February: "Since the reduction of the
prices of admission, the little theatre has been filled nightly.
Light and laughable pieces--just the things for these dull and
pensive times--are well-played there. The pit is always
crowded at a shilling."[37]

Mitchell had become a theatrical force to be acknowledged. During February, even the Knickerbocker Magazine,
New York's most sophisticated monthly literary periodical,
noticed the shilling burlesque house on lower Broadway:

> There is more amusement, literally speaking, to
> be found in this nice and well-ordered little box,
> than in any theatre in the city. It is invariably
> well-filled, which evinces that the public appreciate
> the exertions of the manager, Mr. Mitchell, who
> is really one of the most laughter-moving comedians
> in town. 'The Roof Scrambler,' which ran so long
> and so successfully, has been succeeded by the
> 'Olympic Revels,' and 'The Savage and The Maiden,'
> which bids fair to be equally if not even more popu-
> lar than their attractive predecessor. Indeed, what
> could exceed the manager's admirable 'Vincent Crum-
> mles'? Success to the Olympic.[38]

The above had just appeared in print when on 3 February, Mitchell opened what was to be the sixth success of

the season. Once again, it was a general operatic burlesque
--probably written by Horncastle for the occasion--and once
again Mitchell played the starring role. Entitled The Revolt
of The Poor House, it ridiculed the popular Revolt of The
Harem. The press did not review the new piece, since they
were still ecstatically commenting on The Savage and The
Maiden. Yet the new operatic burlesque was moderately
successful: it ran uninterruptedly for eleven performances.

        The manager continued his phenomenal February suc-
cess with yet another new piece. On the thirteenth, he presented what was to be the first in a long line of successful
Shakespearean travesties. The text was a standard treatment
of Hamlet written in England in 1828 by Poole. On the occasion of the new lampoon's Olympic premiere, Mitchell in-
serted an "apology" and justification for burlesquing the Bard
in the theatre's playbill:

                        TO THE PUBLIC

        Whilst the beauties of poetry shall continue to de-
        light the world, the works of the immortal

                        SHAKESPEARE

        will be read with enthusiasm by every man, woman,
        and child with a

                        SOUL ABOVE BUTTONS

        and so unapproachable are they in their beauty,
        truth, and excellence, that it would be absolutely
        ridiculous to suppose that any injury could be done
        by a harmless burlesque....

                        HAMLET

        Although the public have doubtless seen many very
        laughable burlesques of this same play in the large

                LEGITIMATE TEMPLES OF THE DRAMA

        But then the difference is they try to make you
        weep and cannot, we try to shake your sides with
        laughter and do it. [39]

        The Hamlet Travesty played on eight consecutive

evenings. Then, after a two-day respite, it was reinserted
into the evening's entertainment on 23 February and played
nine additional times. It too was something of a hit, playing
on seventeen out of a possible nineteen evenings.

The reception of the first night's audience assuaged any
misgivings Mitchell may have had about travestying the Bard's
work. An announcement of the second night of the play's
performance mocked the pretentious billing many minor league
tragedians of the day received in puffed-up advertisements
and playbills:

> The first appearance of that not at all celebrated
> tragedian
>
> MR. MITCHELL
>
> in the arduous, overpowering, philosophical and
> awfully tremendous character of
>
> HAMLET!
>
> may be looked upon as an era in the dramatic an-
> nals of the present generation and then again may
> not. To say that in his embodyment of his art, he
> displayed the solemnity and slow-coach style of
>
> JOHN PHILIP KEMBLE
>
> the overpowering majesty of TALMA, the grace
> and dignity of YOUNG, the head and front of
> HAMBLIN, the manly form and spirit of FORREST
> with the fire and energy of the TWO KEANS would
> perhaps be considered as going it a leetle too
> strong--but it is not so, for it is a fact susceptible
> of the most ample proof that he did things which
> none of the above CELEBRATED ARTISTS ever
> attempted. [40]

As was most often the case with the Olympic's lampoons, the attractiveness of the Hamlet Travesty was not
in any inherent quality of the piece as dramatic literature,
but the performances of the company, especially Mitchell,
who was an excellent mimic. Throughout his career, he
excelled in burlesquing the general style and idiosyncracies
of some of the most famous actors of his day. The Hamlet
Travesty provided Mitchell with an opportunity to parody the

acting styles of Charles Kean and W. C. Macready, even
though the latter had not appeared in America for twelve
years. In fact, it would have been impossible for Mitchell
to have witnessed the work of the eminent tragedian anyplace
but in England. Charles Kean, however, had been in America
during the preceding fall. Mitchell had ample opportunity to
observe his acting closely, for Kean had appeared under
Wallack's auspices at the theatre at Niblo's Gardens on 28
October while Mitchell was still Wallack's stage manager.
Kean was probably the weakest of that period's Shakespearean
stars of the first magnitude and tended to take himself very
seriously. For these reasons, he was an ideal object for
Mitchell's ridicule. The success of the Hamlet Travesty re-
inforced what must have become apparent to Mitchell by that
time: there was much money to be made in burlesque during
the depressed winter of 1839-40. The Spirit of The Times
commented on this lucrative trend in its review, noting that,
"The manager appears to have opened a new vein, and so
successfully has he worked it thus far, that it would seem to
be exhaustless."41

        The review also indicates that one of Mitchell's strong-
est assets as a manager was his ability to use his actors to
best advantage. Because his company was not founded on the
then-current practice of dividing lines of business among the
performers, he could use any actor in any role. This he
often did. It was not unusual for Horncastle or Everard to
play the lead in one piece and a supernumerary in another on
the same evening. Through the efforts of Horncastle as adap-
tor and playwright, Mitchell was able to have many of the
Olympic's plays custom-tailored for his company. In this
respect, he was the first manager to select his repertory
with his stock company in mind. The triumph of this experiment, even in his first season, speaks for itself.

        To follow the Hamlet Travesty, Mitchell produced
another burlesque which relied on mimicking a specific actor
for its appeal. The new piece, a musical parody of Lord
Byron's Manfred, entitled Man-Fred opened on 24 February.
It was the Olympic's third consecutive burlesque in which the
object of ridicule had been specific rather than general, for
it satirized the former opera company which had played under
Wallack at both the National Theatre and the theatre at Niblo's
Gardens.

        During the previous October, Wallack had produced
the opera Amilie at Niblo's. Mitchell, as stage manager, was

in the position to have observed the performances of all of the
principals very carefully. Each member of the cast of Man-
Fred mimicked a member of the cast of Amilie, and this
burlesque mimickry provided the prime attraction of Man-Fred.
The Mirror selected Lydia Singleton, who affected the mannerisms of Miss Sheriff, the female principal in the opera,
for special commendation: "Miss Singleton's imitation of Miss
Sheriff's manner was wonderfully true, and consequently extremely ludicrous."[42]

The production is also significant for the establishment
of another trend which was to become commonplace at Mitchell's
theatre. It marked the first time that Bengough, the scenic
artist, provided elaborate drops of "well-known localities"
in the city as part of the setting. Unfortunately, descriptions
in the playbills and reviews in newspapers and weekly periodicals are not specific enough to determine which localities
the scenery represented. It seems, however, that the success
of the production was partially due to the settings, which
were far more elaborate than anything previously seen on the
Olympic's stage.

The policy of providing elaborate scenery for plays
which the manager hoped would have long runs is not surprising. If a new piece was intended to be presented on a
large number of successive evenings, Mitchell could justify
the expenditure necessary to stage it lavishly. Conversely,
the attractiveness of lavish scenery usually helped to promote
a longer run than that which could be expected if older stock
scenery was used. Mitchell appears to be the first American
manager who realized that elaborate scenery could increase
the attractiveness of a new piece sufficiently to extend the
length of its run.

Man-Fred, which opened on 24 February and remained
in the bills nightly until 24 March, ran for more consecutive
evenings than any of Mitchell's previous hits. After its
twenty-seven night run, it was frequently reinserted into the
evenings' bills during the remainder of the season.

With such a number of successful pieces in his repertory, Mitchell did not premiere any new plays until the
end of March. He merely alternated his previous hits in
the evenings' bills, and people continued to flock to the
Olympic to see them. On 30 March, however, he presented
the American premiere of Gilbert A'Beckett's popular farce,
The Unfortunate Miss Bailey.

MR MITCHELL AS MAN-FRED.

I'll jump at once, why should I further stop,
What is a bruise to me or what a whop;
They'll take me to the hospital I knows,
And there they'll feed me well—so here I goes!

"Mitchell as Man-Fred." The Harvard Theatre Collection.

This was the first of A'Beckett's plays to be produced
under Mitchell's management. During ensuing seasons
A'Beckett's pieces were to form a sizeable portion of the
Olympic's repertory, and for good reasons. During the 1830s
and 1840s A'Beckett, one of the original members of the staff
of Punch, earned a highly enviable reputation in London as
both a witty playwright and a hilarious journalist. Most of
the fifty to sixty pieces for the theatre which he wrote either
single-handedly or in collaboration with such other literary
lights as Douglas Jerrold and Mark Lemmon were short, light
comedies and spectacular extravaganzas. Their reliance on
wit and spectacle ideally suited them for production at Mitchell's
theatre.

Featuring Lydia Singleton in the title role, The Unfortunate Miss Bailey was performed on only three consecutive
evenings. But it was seen an additional twenty-six times
during the remainder of the season and was second only to
The Savage and The Maiden as Mitchell's most popular farce
during this inaugural season. Mitchell's Olympic, it was
becoming clear, was not destined to be a mere meteorite in
the heavens of New York's theatres. With the added attractiveness of the new farce, The Spirit of The Times, noted
on 4 April: "No establishment of this kind in this city has
ever been better patronized for such a length of time."[43]

April of 1840 saw another successful burlesque on the
Olympic's boards. Entitled Asmodeus In New York, or The
Devil's Diary, it premiered on 13 April and ran for twenty-
seven evenings, one calendar month. In the piece, Mitchell
played Asmodeus, a little devil who roams through the confused and depressed New York in the spring of 1840 and makes
his own contributions to the general chaos. Unfortunately,
the play has not survived, and reviews of it are not specific
in identifying Mitchell's targets. Yet the piece marks another
first for the Olympic: the objects of the Aristophanic manager's wit were not theatrical, but rather political and social.
The Spirit of The Times indicates that local characters and
politicians were the butt of Mitchell's new joke, which treated,
"a great variety of interests and well-known characters."[44]
The Spirit's reviewer loved the new piece and invited those
of his readers who were "fond of fun and broad slashing cuts
at the times to join the crowd that nightly applaud the truth-
fullness of the representation."[45]

Through the remainder of April, Asmodeus shared the
evening's bill with three other pieces--another of Mitchell's

big hits of the season, and two short farces. The initial
campaign at the Olympic was rapidly drawing to a close, and
the number of proven pieces made it unnecessary for Mitchell
to produce any new material. So popular was the established
repertory that the little theatre was crowded nightly while the
big playhouses--the Park and the Bowery--were virtually
empty. 46

        Since the premiere of The Roof Scrambler in December,
Mitchell had consistently packed large audiences into his little
bandbox of a theatre on lower Broadway, but his competitors
at the city's larger playhouses had not been as fortunate.

        As early as 7 September--two weeks into the season
--The Spirit of The Times reported that the Park had, "been
doing the poorest business the past week, almost ever known. "4
Hard-pressed by competition from James W. Wallack and able
to contract only second-rate stars, the Park's attendance was
abysmal through November. Even after Wallack was burned
out of business at the National things did not improve at the
Park. A starring engagement by the popular dancer-
pantomimist Madame Celeste brought about a temporary improvement over the Christmas holidays, but business slipped
badly upon the conclusion of her limited visit. Things went
from bad to worse with the death of Stephen Price on 20
January 1840. He had been the managing partner responsible
for contracting the greater and lesser London stars who
traipsed across the Park's boards annually. This left the
surviving partner, the aging Edmund Simpson, with full
responsibility for contracting stars and managing the internal
affairs of the theatre. Odell notes that Price's untimely
death occurred, "when the Park was in throes of great
financial distress. "48

        Although Fanny Elssler's triumphant engagement at
the Park at the end of the season caused a temporary flurry
of activity at the old playhouse, the season's overall business
was so bad that Price was forced to mortgage several of
his real estate holdings to pay off the theatre's creditors at
the season's conclusion. 49 Without a steady succession of
stars of the highest magnitude and with prices twice those
of the Olympic during the depressed season of 1839-40, the
Park simply had been unable to earn money.

        Bad times came to the Bowery a bit later in the sea-
son than they did to the Park. Hamblin was initially able
to attract his usual loyal audiences with new sensational

melodramas. Business was especially good during the second week of December when Edwin Forrest, always a favorite
of Hamblin's rough-and-ready pit patrons, played a nine-day
engagement. Forrest was followed by Charles Kean, whom
Hamblin had enticed to play at the Bowery when the earlier
fire, which had burned Wallack out of business at the National, had terminated Kean's engagement there.

But without any stars or new melodramas after the
first of the year, Hamblin's business fell off rapidly. During February he turned the Bowery into a freak show by
hiring first Hervio Nano and then Messr. Behin. Nano, billed
as the Human Fly, was a deformed grown man with a strong
torso and arms and the legs of a two-year-old who could
crawl up and across the ornate bas-relief proscenium arch
of the Bowery. Behin was a Belgian giant, over seven feet
tall, who starred in the nineteenth-century equivalent of our
contemporary Conan and Hercules films. Even these curiosities failed to draw and Hamblin was forced to close from 10
through 16 March. He reopened with another limited engagement of Forrest. Odell suggests that only Hamblin's pride
and the belief that things couldn't possibly get any worse kept
the Bowery in business through the late spring of 1840.[50]

Before Mitchell's inaugural campaign drew to a close,
one other event provided him with a grand opportunity to
display his abilities at topical burlesque. This was the
"Elssler madness."

Fanny Elssler may have been the greatest sensation to
appear on the American stage during the early 1840s. A
dancer of international reputation, she drew capacity audiences
wherever she appeared. When it was announced late in April
that she was to dance at the Park in May, there was a mad
rush to procure tickets. Consequently, her entire engagement
was sold out a week in advance of her debut. Her first
appearance, eagerly anticipated by New Yorkers, was announced for 14 May. It was this intense public interest in
the forthcoming appearance of Mlle. Elssler which provided
Mitchell with an occasion nonpareil upon which to exercise
his burlesque wit. A notice in his playbill for 11 May, three
days prior to Elssler's premiere at the Park, read:

> Notice--The intense excitement created by the forth-
> coming debut of the Divine Fancy Elssler renders
> it highly probable that myriads of people will be
> unable to gain admittance to the Park on the first

three-hundred and sixty-five nights of her performance. Now this is to give notice that great numbers of the disappointed may find much consolation
in their grief by repairing immediately to--The
Olympic. 51

Although the notice is not specific, it does suggest that Mitchell was preparing some sort of production which would lampoon Elssler.

For her premiere at the Park, Elssler danced her
most famous ballet, La Tarantula. On the day of her debut,
the following appeared in the Olympic's playbill:

TERRIFIC ANNOUNCEMENT!!

The public are respectfully informed that Mr.
Mitchell

HAVING ARRIVED FROM EUROPE

four years ago--has, with very little difficulty,
prevailed upon himself to appear on

MONDAY NEXT

in a new pantomime ballet entitled

LA MUSQUITOE [always sic]

which never was performed at

L'ACADEMIE ROYALE DE MUSIQUE AT PARIS

and it is very probable never will be

PERFORMED THERE 365 SUCCESSIVE NIGHTS!

VIVE LA DANSE, VIVE LA MUSQUITOE, VIVE LA
BAGATELLE!52

To understand the extent of Mitchell's burlesque of
Elssler's performance--which was the stunning success that
everyone expected it to be--it is necessary to outline briefly
the plot of Elssler's La Tarantula. 53

Luigi and Loretta are in love and wish to marry, but

Loretta's mother has arranged for her daughter to become the
bride of the wealthy Dr. Ormeoquaco, who had lost his wife,
whom he supposes dead, to a pack of bandits. Luigi rides
off with a group of peasants to track down the brigands, and
Loretta, in order to stall the doctor until Luigi returns to
rescue her, feigns madness as the result of the supposed bite
of a tarantula. The ploy works: Luigi returns with Ormeoquaco's presumedly dead wife; and Luigi and Loretta live
happily ever after.

Fanny Elssler's big moment in the ballet was the
frenzied dance brought on by the supposed bite of the tarantula.
As announcements of her performance stated: "This ballet is
founded upon the supposed properties of the tarantula spider,
whose bite is said to throw the patient into a fit of dancing
delirium, in which the sufferer expires from exhaustion."[54]

Mitchell opened his burlesque of La Tarantula on 21
May, a week after Elssler opened at the Park. He probably
went to see her at the Park in order to be able to mimic
her dancing adequately. Moreover, the week's lag time would
have enabled his upper-class patrons to see the genuine article before Mitchell produced his lampoon. The playbill for
the opening night of Mitchell's La Musquitoe included this
announcement, in keeping with the point of departure for
Elssler's ballet: "The ballet is founded upon the well-known
properties of the musquitoe, whose bite renders the patient
exceedingly impatient and throws him into a fit of scratching,
slapping and swearing deliriums, technically termed the
'Caecothis Scratchendi.'"[55] In Mitchell's treatment of the tale,
Low-retta, played by the manager, loves Low-Dicky, but is
prevented from marrying by her mother, who has other ideas.
The doctor of this piece has lost his wife not to a pack of
bandits, but rather to a fleet of shad fishermen. The locale
has been transplanted from Sicily to Hoboken, and the musquitoe fulfills the function of the tarantula. The burlesque
ran for the final nine nights of Mitchell's first season, which
ended on 30 May 1840.

In a period of five months, Mitchell had managed an
extremely successful season and established the Olympic as
the most popular theatre in New York. Starting with the
notion of playing three or four short pieces nightly and
changing the bills frequently, he came to realize the possibility
of playing what was for that day long runs of his popular productions.

The experience of having a stock piece, The Roof
Scrambler, as the prime source of attraction while Mossop
was playing as a guest star also showed Mitchell that he could
manage a successful theatre without the aid of star performers. Odell has noted that "Mitchell was to find--and he was
almost the first of his time to find--that the public was weary
of stars, however good, in the old, old round of the legitimate or in farce and extravaganza repeated ad nauseam from
playhouse to playhouse."56

By retaining Horncastle as both an actor and company
playwright, Mitchell could have many of his plays custom
tailored for his stock company. Scenery also came to play
an important part in the success formula of the Olympic, for
with the ever-increasing length of the initial runs of his burlesques and extravaganzas, it was possible to have new and
elaborate settings to support them.

In spite of these contributing factors, Mitchell himself
was the greatest reason for the Olympic's first-season success.
He was in effect, his own resident star, for all of his hits,
save The Irresistible Cadets, featured him in the leading role.
Toward the end of the season, The Mirror noted the success
of the Olympic and attributed it primarily to the manager's
ability as a comedian: "If nobody played in it but Mr. Mitchell,
the manager himself, it would deserve to be filled every night,
as it is; for Mitchell is one of the best low comedians that
ever appeared on the American boards--in certain characters
the very best...."57

During the summer of 1840, Mitchell managed his
only summer season at the Olympic. The brief season ran
from 10 June through 4 July and was unsuccessful for two
reasons: the small Olympic was hot and could not be adequately ventilated to provide patron comfort against the
scorching New York summer; and, perhaps more importantly,
Mitchell's audiences migrated uptown to the cool shade and
ice cream of Niblo's Gardens as New York's theatre audiences
had for some years past.

The brief summer season is, however, important for
two reasons: it introduced to Olympic audiences Mary Taylor
and Mrs. Timm, both of whom were later to be favorites
at the theatre during the regular season; and, it provided
Mitchell with another opportunity to demonstrate his tremendous talent for topical burlesque.

During the late spring of 1840, a storm began to brew
in the editorial columns of the city's several newspapers. It
all started when the generally despised James Gordon Bennett,
flamboyant editor of the upstart Daily Herald, exposed the
corruption of the Schuylkill Bank in Philadelphia, questioned
the honesty of all of the Eastern Seaboard's large banks, and
came out in favor of inserting provisions into the bankruptcy
bill then before Congress designed to protect small businessmen, as well as wealthy speculators and bankers. The city's
other editors, most of whom were on very good terms with
the financial barons of Wall Street, resented Bennett's insinu-
ations that all banks and bankers were corrupt and disagreed
violently with his position regarding the bankruptcy bill.
There were, however, other reasons why the older editors
disliked Bennett and his newspaper.

The Herald was only five years old, but Bennett's
sensationalism had already cut heavily into the circulation of
New York's older dailies. Additionally, Bennett's quick tongue
and sarcastic wit had made him many enemies, among whom
were several of New York's most prominent newspaper
editors, including Park Benjamin of the Evening Signal,
Mordecai Noah of the Evening Star, and James Watson Webb
of The Morning Courier and The New York Enquirer. Because of the ill feelings between Bennett and the city's other
editors, it is not surprising that what began as a legitimate
editorial debate over the bankruptcy bill and the trustworthi-
ness of the large banks soon degenerated into the worst kind
of name-calling. Webb, Noah, and Benjamin allied, along
with all the other editors in the city, in a concerted effort
to drive Bennett and the Herald out of business. Don Seitz,
one of Bennett's biographers states that by the end of May:

> Bodies of self-constituted vigilantes went about
> the city making demands on advertisers to forsake
> the Herald's columns or suffer in consequence.
> Men of standing in church and trade united in the
> effort to efface the effulgent journal. The city was
> in turmoil and the excitement spread over the
> eastern part of the nation.[58]

During the first week of June, pressure was brought
to bear on the city's theatre managers by the anti-Herald
forces. The managers were not-so-politely informed that
if they did not cease advertising in Bennett's paper, none
of the other dailies would run their advertisements or review their productions. It speaks well for the moral fibre

of the city's theatrical managers that T. S. Hamblin of the
Bowery, who had publicly caned Bennett and long held a
personal grudge against him, was the only manager to be
intimidated. [59]

While the Olympic was closed betwen 30 May and 10
June, editorial invective became particularly vicious in the
city's newpaper war. Benjamin called Bennett (in print) a
"profligate adventurer, " a "venomous reptile, " and the
"prince of darkness"--to list only a few of his choice phrases.
Noah's appellations were not quite as colorful; the best he
came up with was "turkey-buzzard."[60] Bennett, it must be
admitted, kept cool under fire. On 4 June, he announced,
"We can waste little time on these asses, "[61] but that was
the single instance upon which he stooped to the low level of
invective that his detractors used. He did promise, however,
with a note of elegant sarcasm: "If Webb, Noah and the
Holy Alliance behave well during the present week, I'll send
each of them a bottle of wine and a piece of cake. "[62]

Given Mitchell's proclivity for burlesque, this "war"
could not be ignored. His brief summer season opened on
10 June and featured revivals of the previous regular season.
But the hostilities in the city's editorial columns posed a problem. As a caterer to the fashionable gentlemen of the city,
Mitchell probably had at least a passing acquaintance with all
the belligerents. He obviously could not advertise in the
Herald and exclude the other papers, nor could he patronize
the other dailies and eliminate his customary advertisements
in Bennett's news sheet. Consequently, he pursued what was
probably the wisest course of action and ceased buying space
in all of the city's papers. In lieu of buying advertising
space, he began printing his own reviews and editorials in
which he had a great deal of fun at the expense of everyone
involved in the slanderous editorial war. In his playbill for
13 June, he stated that he had always considered himself on
good terms with all of the city's editors, but because of the
current hostilities among them, he was forced to adopt a
new policy:

> That from this day until peace is restored in the
> editorial columns, the Olympic Advertisements,
> Puffs (?) and criticisms, instead of appearing in
> any of the newspapers, shall be home-made, pub-
> licized each day in the form of a bulletin at the head
> of the bill, with occasional 'Extras, ' 'Double
> Sheets, ' 'In Advance of The Mail' and 'Late and
> Important From The Interior' of the theatre, etc. [63]

Two days later, on 15 June, Mitchell published the
first number of his Olympic Advertiser at the top of his playbills. The "paper," approximately thirty lines in length,
contained a masthead which looked suspiciously like that of
the Herald. The first edition published a review of Mitchell's
performance of Low-Retta in La Musquitoe and mocked the
encomiums the press had heaped on Elssler's performance in
La Tarantula a month earlier: "He launches at once and un-
hesitatingly into the intricacies of the dance, his sylph-like
form glides, floats, sinks, swims and undulates in poetic
motion, while now with a precision truly electrifying his tiny
fairy feet keep time with the music."64

Early nineteenth-century newspaper reviewers had other
excessive quirks. Touring stars tended to repeat roles from
their established repertoires throughout their careers with
few new additions. Audiences had seen stellar performers
in their best roles over a period of years and critics had
reviewed their efforts extensively. In an effort to find something new to say, the city's art reporters frequently compared
the stars unfavorably with other performers in the same role,
especially if the star being reviewed was disliked by the
paper and its primary readers for social or political reasons.
Bennett's Herald, the self-styled champion of the working
classes, invariably puffed the native American tragedian
Edwin Forrest--hero of the "b'hoys" who frequented the
Bowery and Mitchell's pit--at the expense of the favorite of
New York's upper-class theatregoers, the English tragedian
William Charles Macready. Webb's papers, The Morning
Courier, and The New York Enquirer drew their readers from
New York's "better" classes and consistently praised Macready,
frequently at Forrest's expense. It was this propensity of the
city's less-then-objective theatre critics that Mitchell satirized
in the second number of his "paper," which appeared on 16
June:

> Mitchell played Molly Brown in the Roof Scrambler.
> His performance of the character is so well known
> and has been so much praised that it may appear
> somewhat strange, captious and hypercritical in us
> to find fault with it; but we have a duty to perform,
> and we shall not flinch from it. We know that the
> eyes of the world are upon us!!! and look for
> strict impartiality, and a fearless exposure of an
> actor's faults. Therefore, we say, and we challenge
> any of our contemporaries (hem) to disprove our
> assertion, that Mr. Mitchell has neither the soul-

thrilling pathos of Malibran, the naivete of Sheriff,
nor the pure contr'alto of Poole; then how dare he
assume so delicate a character as that of Molly
Brown! We have not yet done with Mr. Mitchell.
We have strong suspicions that...but of that anon.[65]

Interestingly, although the first two numbers of the
new daily commented on things theatrical, the rhetoric was
a slightly exaggerated version of the gusty prose which had
been bandied about by the combatants in the newspaper war.
Not every edition of Mitchell's "paper" concerned itself with
burlesquing theatre critics.   On 24 June, he included an
editorial which ridiculed both the frequent accusations that
Bennett was heavily in debt as a result of his high living
and Bennett's defense of his credit: "It may well be stated
here, that the only bills sent into Wall-Street by Mr. Mitchell
are Play-bills; and his high standing there may be ascertained
by the avidity with which they are sought after."[66]

The Olympic Advertiser was published only twice after
25 June. It was the only daily in the newspaper war of 1840
which was neutral, and it was the only one which did not survive.

Mitchell's "paper" is significant as an extratheatrical
lampoon, for he produced no theatre piece which burlesqued
the newspaper war. His use of the Olympic's playbills for
a satirical comment on a public affair which was of general
concern to his fellow New Yorkers indicates both his ingenuity
and his eagerness to extend the medium of his Aristophanic
wit beyond the boards of his theatre.

On 4 July, one week after the last number of the
Olympic Advertiser appeared, Mitchell ended his brief summer season. His tradition of future management was established, for he was to pursue, if in a somewhat modified
form, the policies which had proven successful during his
first regular season for the next decade. His unsuccessful
summer venture amply demonstrated that the Olympic was not
well suited to attracting remunerative audiences during the
hot weather months. He never played a summer in his
theatre again, but closed annually at about the same time
that Niblo opened his Gardens for the amusement of New
York's theatre patrons during the summer.

CHAPTER THREE

A Continuing Tradition, 1840-41

During August of 1840, Mitchell assembled personnel for his second Olympic campaign. Ben Baker, William Corbyn, George Loder, and Richard Bengough retained their respective positions as prompter, treasurer, musical director, and scenic artist. Having learned the previous season that his managerial fortunes were tied to long runs of burlesques and extravaganzas, Mitchell announced, during the first week of his second season, that a new burlesque would be produced every two weeks.[1] To improve the visual elements of his "novelties," Mitchell added two new specialists to his staff: Taylor, a man whose first name and previous experience has proven impossible to determine, became the first resident costume designer in a New York theatre; and, Burns, whose first name and background have proven equally elusive, was hired as stage machinist.

Although his premiere season had been extremely successful, Mitchell must have been less than satisfied with his acting company, for it was significantly revamped. Of the original men only Horncastle, Russell, and Edwin remained. Six new actors were hired. George Graham had come from Boston to perform at the Chatham during the previous season. William Horton, primarily a singer, had no previous New York experience. One of three minor actors working in New York named Clarke joined the company along with one of three utility actors named Roberts. The final new male recruit, John Cunningham, first appeared in New York at the Bowery during the previous May.

The list of actresses was even more drastically altered. Of the previous season's women, only Lydia Singleton returned. Sarah Timm, who had joined the company during the summer after six years as a utility actress at the

Park, was among the actresses hired for the fall campaign.
The Park also lost Julia Turnbull, a utility actress in Simpson
and Price's stock company for six years. Mrs. Watts, who
had worked at the Bowery, Franklin, and Chatham since 1835
was another new aspirant for Olympic applause. Mrs.
Baldock, another new recruit from the Chatham Theatre, joined her
husband--George Loder, the Olympic's musical director--at
the beginning of Mitchell's second season. The list of new
actresses was completed by Mrs. Streebor and Miss Randall,
neither of whom had prior professional experience in New
York.

Oddly enough, two actors were given limited engagements at the beginning of the new season. Charles Howard
played with the company from 7 September through 23 September; and George Mossop, the Irish Star of the year before,
appeared from 9 September through the seventeenth of that
month. The reason for Mitchell's decision to hire these men
for limited engagements is not clear, but it is interesting
to note that neither of them received star billing in the
theatre's playbills or in newspaper advertisements.

Although admission prices remained what they had
been since 14 December of the previous year, two innovations
regarding spectator accommodations were instituted: a few
private boxes which rented for $5.00 per evening had been
installed over the summer; and, an undetermined limited
number of season tickets, presumably for the dress circle,
were made available.[2]

At the threshold of his second season as the Olympic's
manager, Mitchell was in both an enviable and a difficult
position. He had managed the most successful theatre in the
city during the previous season and could be virtually assured
that his regular patrons would initially support his new campaign. At the same time, it was entirely possible that his
enterprise would fall from the public's fickle favor if the
quality of his new productions fell below the high level that
his audiences had come to expect.

On 7 September the second season opened with three
pieces. The Son of The Sun, a mythical extravaganza by
Gilbert A'Beckett with new scenery by Bengough and costumes
by Taylor, started the evening's entertainment. It was followed by an anonymous farce entitled Mr. and Mrs. White,
and the bill concluded with a "local sketch" entitled Sparring
With Specie. Of the three pieces, Sparring With Specie,

which played only three times, was the least successful and
the most interesting.

With the election of 1840 looming, it is not surprising
that an issue much debated by any number of candidates for
public office would find its way into one of Mitchell's burlesques. The issue was the rival claims of the "hard money"
men--who favored specie reserves for all bank notes issued--
and "soft money" men who felt that the country could be
relieved of the ravages of depression only if a large supply
of "cheap" money, paper currency not based on any metallic
standard--was made available.

These rival positions provided the material for Sparring
With Specie. The play has not survived, but the playbills
indicate that it was a martial piece in which the forces of
the specie army and the forces of the shinplaster army met
and did battle. Specie's warriors consisted of President
Eagle, Vice President Dollar, Shilling Usher, Mrs. Half
Eagle, and Mrs. Half Dollar.[3] This general staff commanded
a "strong force of Fips, Cents, Half-Cents, and Mills."[4]
Leadership for the rival shinplaster forces fell to General
Postnote, "a most promising character,"[5] Major Newark, and
Captain New York. Their field troops consisted of "a squad
of many light characters, sometimes 'Good for a Drink' and
quite often 'Good for Nothing.' "[6]

Although Mitchell had burlesqued matters of public
interest during his first season, he had not taken a stand on
any inflammatory issue through his ridicule of it. His lampoons had not supported or attacked any person or cause, but
rather playfully ridiculed the affectations of human nature.
Available material regarding Sparring With Specie indicates
that for the first time Mitchell was acting as a polemicist:
he favored a "hard money" policy. The play's failure,
attributable in part to its point of view, prevented Mitchell
from ever taking a stand on a controversial issue through his
burlesques again. But public reaction against the new play
went far beyond the inside of the theatre. Mitchell's position must have raised the ire of some of the city's fiery
proponents of a cheap money policy, for on the day after
Sparring With Specie opened, the following announcement
appeared in the Olympic's playbills: "$10 Reward will be
paid on the conviction of any person or persons wantonly
and maliciously destroying the bills of this theatre."[7]

This marked the only occasion during Mitchell's

career as manager of the Olympic that the theatre's bills
were torn down. The vandalism was almost certainly the
work of those who disagreed with his position on economic
policy. On the day after the previously quoted reward notice
appeared, Sparring With Specie was withdrawn from the bill
and never appeared again.

The Son of The Sun, more in keeping with the tradition Mitchell had established during his first season, was
only moderately successful. It played nightly for a week and
reappeared ten times by the end of October. It must have
been an attractive piece, for in spite of the adverse reaction
to Sparring With Specie, the opening week of the new season
drew "houses full to the ceiling. "8

Although The Son of The Sun and the anonymous Vaga-
bond, which opened on 14 September and ran for a week,
were minor successes, neither was popular enough to establish itself as a long run. Thinking that material from Dickens' novels, which had served so well in The Savage and The
Maiden, could be tailored into another popular hit, Mitchell
brought out Nicholas Nickleby on 21 September. Hurriedly
written and briefly rehearsed, it lacked the quality of its
Dickensian predecessor and received only four performances.
Hence, the last two weeks of September featured revivals of
the first season's successes--The Savage and The Maiden,
The Roof Scrambler, La Musquitoe, and the Hamlet Travesty.
These, however, played to only mediocre houses. It seemed
as if the manager were buying time until he could find a new
burlesque which would draw large audiences.

While Mitchell was attempting to develop a new lampoon that had the potential for a long run, he relied on the
American premiere of recent British farces to fill his theatre.
Both The Female Brigands, similar in format to The Irresistible Cadets, and Gilbert A'Beckett's The Turned Head opened
on 5 October. They were in the bills nightly through that
week. Another offering, Charles Dibkin's The Quaker, drew
well during early October. It is significant as Mitchell's
first operetta, a type of entertainment which he was to produce with some success in later seasons.

It was not until 15 October, five weeks into the season, that Mitchell produced a new piece that approximated
the popularity of several successes of his premiere campaign.
The new extravaganza, entitled 1940!, or Crummles in Search
of Novelty, was written by A. Allan who had contributed

greatly to the Olympic's fortunes the previous season with
Asmodeus in New York. In the new piece Mitchell portrayed
Crummles, his famous character from The Savage and The
Maiden, who abandons the management of the Portsmouth
Theatre, assumes that of the Olympic, and announces novelty
as his prime attraction. But none appears, as indeed none
had been forthcoming at the Olympic for five long weeks.
After an invocation to fancy, the demigoddess herself visits
the Olympic and conducts Crummles on a voyage of discovery
during which he learns what things are to be like one hundred
years hence. The first stop on their futuristic itinerary is
a visit to Tatter's salesroom in 1940. This scene was extremely topical to Mitchell's audience, because the Olympic
was located next to Tattersall's, one of the most famous
"dry goods" stores in New York during the 1840s. From
Tatter's they journey uptown to Niblo's Gardens for a brief
look at the summer season of 1940. Following these two
expeditions is a march of miracles in which hypothetical im-
provements in railroads and canals are presented for the
audience's edification. The piece ends in an elegant mer-
maid's cove of 1940.[9] Descriptions of the extravaganza
indicate that the spectacle, primarily Bengough's scenery,
was the main reason for the play's run of thirty-five nights.
Additionally, Mitchell proved exceedingly clever in producing
a successful extravaganza based on his problem of finding
novelty that would pack the Olympic. And pack it he did.
The immense crowds that 1940! drew were far beyond the
theatre's seating capacity. On 21 October, the sixth night
of the play's run, the house was crammed to suffocation and
more than five hundred would-be spectators were turned
away.[10]

On 16 October, the day after the long-sought hit opened
Mitchell lost the services of the most valuable member of his
company, Horncastle, who defected to the National Opera
House. Horncastle's resignation must have been amicable,
for two of his new operatic burlesques were to be produced
at the Olympic after he had quit the acting company.[11]

Two-and-a-half weeks into the run of 1940! Mitchell
opened what was to be the second hit of the season. The
new piece, an operatic burlesque by Horncastle entitled
Buy It Dear 'Tis Made of Cashmere, featured Mitchell and
Mrs. Timm burlesquing the then popular opera, La Bayadere
or The Maid of Cashmere.

New York's theatregoers had first seen Scribe and

Auber's operatic ballet spectacle, La Bayadere or The Maid of
Cashmere at the National Theatre in October of 1836, where
Mitchell was a member of Willard and Flynn's stock company.
Wallack produced the piece at the same theatre during November of 1837 and again in November of 1839. It long served
as a vehicle for Madame Celeste, one of New York's favorite
touring stars. Mitchell, Horncastle, and other members of
the Olympic's company who had served under Wallack at the
National were extremely familiar with both the opera and those
touring stars for whom it was a vehicle.

     Opening on 2 November Buy It Dear ran, mostly in
conjunction with 1940!, for thirty performances until 5 December. Three days after its premiere, Mitchell suspended
the free list. This time even actors from other companies
were excluded and only the press remained entitled to com-
plimentary admission. Within three weeks, the Olympic's
fortunes had changed drastically. Until the debut of 1940!,
Mitchell had been unable to provide the kind of extremely
popular pieces that his audiences had come to expect. Then,
within two weeks, he had two hits running simultaneously.
By the end of the first week of November, Olympic attendance
equaled the high points of its first season. This was no
mean feat, for the 1840-41 season "was one of the most depressing in the history of American Theatricals,"12 and only
one other theatre in the city was able to maintain continuous
operations throughout the season. In spite of its diminutive
size, the Olympic was earning more than any other theatre
in the city by the middle of November.13

     Buy It Dear ran until 5 December and from that date
through the fourteenth of the month Mitchell revived some of
his first season's successes. On the fourteenth, however,
he produced another new extravaganza, Stars At The Astor,
which ran for fourteen nights. The new novelty concerned
itself not with the Astor Place Opera House, which would
not be built until 1847, but rather with the Astor House
Hotel, the temporary home of most theatrical stars visiting
New York. The piece may have burlesqued the guests who
frequented what was at the time the city's finest hotel, but
the playbills and brief notices in the press do not provide
enough information to determine the exact thrust of the piece.

     Not all of Mitchell's offering through the fall had
been light and frivolous. 1840 was a presidential election
year and the wily manager attempted to capitalize on patriotic sentiments with The Home of Liberty, which debuted on

29 November. The rude mechanicals who frequented Mitchell's
pit were almost invariably volunteer firemen and frequently
members of semisecret political societies. The appeal to
that segment of the audience featured Bengough's tableaux of
famous patriotic scenes and proved successful enough to run
for thirteen nights. There was no lampooning in the piece
for although the press passed over it in silence--perhaps because it was patriotically trite--the playbills indicate that it
was a rather serious affair.

        With Stars at the Astor in the bills after 14 Decem-
ber, Mitchell refrained from producing any new pieces until
Christmas Eve when he brought out another operatic burlesque.
Horncastle's The Cat's in The Larder, or The Maid with a
Parasol burlesqued the opera La Gazza Ladra, or The Maid
of Peliseau.

        The city's opera buffs had first been delighted by
Rossini's opera at the Park in January of 1839, but they
knew the libretto of the new Italian piece well: it has the
same plot line as the venerable extravaganza, The Maid and
The Magpie. Mitchell's familiarity with the new object of
his burlesque wit dates from June of 1839, when the National
Theatre's stock company supported Sheriff in Wallack's well-
received production of the opera.

        Like several of its Olympic predecessors, The Cat's
in The Larder had no specific production or opera company
as its object of ridicule. It was almost as successful as
1940! and Buy It Dear, running for twenty-seven nights before being withdrawn from the bills and reappearing an additional eighteen times during the remainder of the season.

        The hard work that Mitchell demanded from his com-
pany in the process of playing four pieces nightly and rehearsing new ones at the same time is humorously alluded
to in the playbill for the opening night of the holiday entertainment:

>   He [Mitchell] hopes by keeping his company busily
>   engaged at rehearsal in the morning, study in the
>   afternoon, and the performance of four pieces every
>   evening to subdue their musical ardour sufficiently
>   to prevent any serious effect on The Currency of
>   The Country or The Chinese War.14

        It is not surprising that Mitchell would produce a new

extravaganza during the holiday season.   He had worked in
the British minor theatres and found the Boxing Night pantomime tradition adaptable, with some modification, in America.
During the previous season, The Roof Scrambler had packed
them in during the good cheer time of year, and The Cat's in
The Larder did even better during the week between Christmas
and New Year of 1840-41.   During the first four nights of its
performance, the Olympic was crowded beyond capacity: approximately 5,000 people saw the new play.[15]

        While Mitchell had been drawing large audiences to
the Olympic to witness his light bill of fare, the city's large
theatres had found it impossible to operate profitably during
this dreadfully ill-paying season.   The Bowery was the first
to flounder: it was used as a circus from early October until
the middle of April.[16]   The Park and the rebuilt National
Opera House struggled valiantly to meet expenses throughout
the fall, but found it an impossible task.   On New Year's
Day, 1841, the National closed its doors and remained dark
until the middle of February.   The Park soon followed and
was dark from 8 January until 17 February.[17]   Aside from
the Olympic, only Thorne's Chatham, which had adopted
Mitchell's policies and prices, managed to weather the cold
theatrical winter of 1840-41.

        Because of the closing of the city's three largest
theatres, Mitchell had his pick of many unemployed actors
during January.   But the heavy reliance on operatic burlesque as an emerging Olympic staple required that any new
recruits be possessed of better-than-average singing voices.
On 9 January, a little more than a week after the National
closed, he hired three of that defunct company's best performers.   Horncastle, who had defected in October, returned
to the fold along with two popular female vocalists: Mrs.
Russell and Kate Horn.   Their Olympic employment began
on 11 January.

        The night that the three refugees from the disbanded
National's company began playing for Mitchell also marked
the premiere of what proved to be the second dismal failure
of the season, a travesty of Othello.   It was reasonable to
assume, based on the success of the Hamlet Travesty during
the preceding season, that a well-rehearsed Shakespearean
travesty would draw good houses.   But this assumption proved
invalid and Othello enjoyed only one performance on the
Olympic's stage.   Mitchell played Othello, "Moor of Venice,
formerly an independent nigger from the republic of Hayti,"[18]

and Cunningham did Iago, "once a native of the Gaultan
Mountains, County Tipperary, province of Munster, and
Kingdom of Ireland."[19]

   Although Othello failed for reasons lost to history,
Mitchell did a booming business through the month of January. On the fourteenth, he again suspended the free list,
and The Spirit of The Times noted, two days later, that the
Olympic was crowded nightly, even though no new plays
worthy of note had appeared since Christmas Eve.[20]

   But a new kind of piece was forthcoming shortly.
During the bleak months of January and February, Niblo's
and the Park resorted to the performance of instrumental
concerts in an effort to earn some little amount toward the
management's overhead. Niblo's was the first in the field
with these Concerts de la [sic] Hiver. Opening at the Garden's
recently winterized theatre on 2 January 1841, the evening's
entertainment consisted of an eighteen-piece German band
supporting well-known local vocalists in songs from the standard popular repertory. The concerts provided something
of a Beer Garden atmosphere where patrons could enjoy
a hot bowl of Niblo's famous turtle soup with their music
on a cold winter's evening. The musicales must have been
at least moderately successful, for they were continued until
26 February.

   The Park had floundered desperately during the autumn
and early winter, and Simpson was forced to close the venerable old playhouse on 7 January 1841. Noting the week-long
and apparently successful operation of Niblo's concert series,
he, too, decided to go into the concert business, but in a
fashion more in keeping with the Park's reputation as the
city's "better" playhouse.

   Simpson premiered his series of Concerts de la Hiver
on 14 January 1841. For the ridiculously low admission
price of 25¢, patrons were treated to three-hour concerts of
works by Strauss, Mozart, Rossini, Weber, and other serious
composers performed by a forty-five piece orchestra which
was declared by The Spirit of The Times to be the best ever
heard in the city.[21] But Simpson's concerts had neither
vocalists nor turtle soup, and people stayed away in droves.
Thinking, perhaps, that New York's "better" citizens were
afraid to attend because the price of admission was within
the means of the "rabble" who frequented Hamblin's Bowery
and the Olympic's pit, on 25 January Simpson raised prices

to 50¢ for the dress circle and pit while reducing them to $12\frac{1}{2}$¢
for the gallery. This change in policy, justified because the
receipts had proven insufficient to keep the concerts open,
segregated the audience and provided the better classes with
some insularity from the lowlifes. But the manager's move
proved ineffective and the concerts sustained their final note
on 4 February as a financial failure.

In response to the new entertainments offered by his
unfortunate fellow managers, Mitchell resorted to specific
burlesque for the first time that season on 25 January with
his Concerts d'enfer. This hellish entertainment lampooned the format of the offerings at the Park and Niblo's
with squabbles among Loder's musical corps and slightly
off-key instrumental offerings. As part of the nightly entertainment at the Olympic, they were in the bills for eighteen
consecutive evenings. Mitchell may have earned more from
his burlesque of these concerts than the Park and Niblo's
did from the original versions.

On 15 February, the day after the concerts were withdrawn from the bills, Mitchell produced another specifically
pointed burlesque. Written by Horncastle and entitled The
Humpback, it ridiculed Sheridan Knowles' popular play, The
Hunchback. Mitchell played Wily Waters and lampooned the
acting style and mannerisms of John Vandenhoff, one of the
London stage's lesser luminaries whose style was reminiscent
of J. P. Kemble and whose limited fame was eclipsed by that
of his son George. Mrs. Timm mimicked the stage's most
famous Julia, Fanny Kemble, who had retired from the profession five years earlier. An immediate and immense success, the new piece drew crowded audiences for twenty-one
consecutive performances. The Spirit of The Times, which
had been ignoring the Olympic through much of the season,
reported that Mrs. Timm "is a clever imitation of Fanny
Kemble in 'Julia' ";[22] while, "Mitchell gives imitations of
Mr. Vandenhoff, and hits off many of his peculiarities, with
a truth which calls out bursts of laughter."[23]

But as the popularity of The Humpback waned during
early March, attendance at the Olympic fell off and Mitchell
seemed unable to find a new novelty to fill the breech. The
Spirit of The Times noticed that although there had been no
new pieces and a slight decline in attendance, "the audience
in the dress circle of this theatre is quite the most fashionable that can be collected in any theatre in this city."[24]

Although this is the first notice of the makeup of the
Olympic's audience during the season, one assumes that the
fashionable segment of New York's society, as well as the
"b'hoys," had been attending the theatre throughout the fall.
If the patronage on the part of either group had changed radi-
cally from the prior season, the press almost certainly would
have noticed it.

Early in March, Mitchell produced another operatic
burlesque to entertain his audiences who had exhausted the
drawing power of The Humpback.   Authored by Horncastle
and entitled Mrs. Normer, its object of ridicule was the
opera Norma, which had enjoyed some popularity in Philadelphia during the preceding season. Featuring Mrs. Timm,
who was by this time playing all of the leading female burlesque and extravaganza roles, it lacked the drawing power
of the season's other operatic burlesques and received only
twenty-three performances.   Perhaps, as Odell has suggested, the opera's lack of popularity mitigated against the
success of the burlesque. [25]

Realizing that Mrs. Normer did not have the hoped-
for box-office appeal, Mitchell produced another "local extravaganza"--probably written by Allan--entitled China, or
Tricks upon Travellers on 15 March.   It ran for twelve
evenings before being withdrawn.   The play featured Bengough's scenery, Loder's music, Taylor's costumes, and
Burns' machinery--with tableaux and stage arrangements by
Mitchell.   The subject matter of the new burlesque was the
disparaging remarks made about Americans and their customs
by such belittling English travelers as Mrs. Trollope, Basil
Hall, Fanny Kemble, and Captain Marryatt.

Throughout the 1820s and 1830s many British public
figures entertained their country's reading public with travelogues of distant ports which had piqued the national curiosity.
Interest in America and its citizens was running high, and
several prominent figures from the world of letters and the
stage augmented their incomes with breezy descriptive accounts
of America and all things American.   Unfortunately, the
younger nation's democratic institutions and homespun manners were often perceived as hopelessly coarse by refined
British travelers with aristocratic inclinations.

The first of many British travelers to paint a not-
very-flattering picture of life on the western shores of the
Atlantic was the famous London comedian, Charles Mathews,

Sr. During his 1822-23 starring tour of this country he
gathered material for one of his famous solo performances
which were known generically as Mr. Mathews At Home.

        Mathews found conditions in the new world deplorable
and went out of his way to say so. Frances Hodge notes that
Stephen Price, co-manager of the Park Theatre, was forced
to accompany him on his tour, "to insure that his discordant
comments would fall on sympathetic ears and not on those of
an oversensitive public."26

        Upon returning to London in 1824, Mathews performed
his Trip To America in which he created the first stage
yankee, Jonathan W. Doubikins. The piece contained many
satirical observations on American life and when reports of
it reached America the press damned Mathews' perceptions
as both untrue and unfair. Many Americans believed that
their young nation had been treated badly by Mathews, who,
in addition to having been lavishly entertained by the Americans, had taken large numbers of yankee dollars home with
him.

        When he returned to the United States for another
professional tour in 1834, American theatre audiences decided that they would judge the rumored insults to the
national character for themselves, and Mathews was forced
to play Trip To America in every city he visited in order to
quell disturbances that threatened to turn into riots. The
Americans laughed as heartily as their transatlantic cousins
had, and found the material inoffensive enough. But the
tempest of imagined insult had raged in the teapot of national
pride for over a decade.

        The most famous of the many British commentators
on things American during the 1830s was undoubtedly Frances
Trollope, whose Domestic Manners of The Americans was
so insulting that it produced the epithet "Trollope." Initially
used to describe any boorish individuals, the name later
specified only women of questionable character. Una Pope-
Hennessey argues, convincingly, that "No English name has
ever been held in greater execration among Americans than
that of Fanny Trollope."27

        Mrs. Trollope's two-and-one-half year stay in
America was one long disappointment. She attempted to
found a business in Cincinnati importing luxury British items
for the upper-class citizens of that city on the Ohio River.

Her book's assessment of the manners and tastes of the
Americans may be colored by her disappointment over the
native lack of interest in her goods.

      With the publication of Trollope's book, Americans
became gun-shy regarding well-known British travellers.   They
feared, justifiably, that honest attempts at civility and frank
discussions of politics would be represented as barbaric
domestic customs and dangerously anarchistic political sentiments in yet another sensational exposé of the savage life-
style of the United States.

      Additional fuel was added to the fire of national insult
with the publication of Fanny Kemble's Journals in 1835.
Kemble had commenced a two-year starring tour of this
country with her father, Charles, in 1832.   She subsequently
married the Philadelphian Pierce Butler and remained in this
country when her father returned to England in 1834.   As
the popular and talented youngest member of a distinguished
British theatrical family dynasty, Fanny was entertained by
the leading citizens of all the cities in which she and Charles
performed.   In the course of pocketing over six thousand
pounds from her American engagements, she caused some re-
sentment on the part of her hosts for the manner in which
she insulted the national character prior to the publication of
her infamous journal.

      During the winter of 1833 she is reported to have con-
fided to a riding companion in Washington D.C., whom she
supposed to be an Englishman, that she had not met one lady
or gentleman fit for her to associate with since coming to
America.[28] The American press reported the reputed insult
and many people felt that she had rubbed salt into the fresh
wounds of national outrage resulting from the publication of
Trollope's book a mere six months earlier.

      Scorn was heaped upon indignity with the publication
of her Journal in 1835.   Having been entertained by the leading citizens of the eastern seaboard's cities in which she and
her father performed, it was a bit naive for her to ridicule
their dress, manners, table appointments, and cuisine, assuming that the objects of her patronizing sarcasm would not rec-
ognize themselves merely because she had deleted their names.
Most of those Americans who had parted with their money to
see her perform must have had their faith in a divine national
providence restored when it became common knowledge that
her marriage rapidly soured and she was destined to live
miserably ever after.

The final famous British critic of American life prior
to Mitchell's burlesque was Captain Frederick Marryatt. A
legitimate naval hero, Marryatt had earned an estimable reputation as a novelist during the 1830s. Although critics
found his work less significant than that of Dickens and others,
the British and American reading public bought large numbers
of his adventure yarns. He was a popular if not critical
literary celebrity when he arrived in New York on 4 May
1838. Unlike his fault-finding predecessors, Marryatt was
not interested in the domestic manners and fashions of the
Americans. His stated purpose in crossing the Atlantic for
an extended visit was, "to examine and ascertain what were
the effects of a democratic form of government and climate
upon a people which, with all its foreign admixture, may
still be considered English."[29] Marryatt represented a
greater danger than earlier British critics of American life
for two important reasons: he was the best British writer
to ridicule America during the 1820s and 1830s; and, his
concern with things political caused him to focus on the excesses and eccentricities of democracy as practiced in this
country. Not American manners, but the very American
political system came under his scrutiny.

In his A Diary in America, with Remarks on Its Institutions, Marryatt found the American system wanting. He
believed that democracy as practiced here would prove an
eventual failure and be replaced by some other form of government. Many of his observations are astute and amusing.
On his experience in Washington he noted, "Of talent and
intelligence there is a very fair supply, but principle is not
so much in demand."[30]

The publication of Marryatt's Diary late in 1839 was
the immediate precursor of Mitchell's new lampoon.

China, or Tricks Upon Travellers supported all things
American at the expense of the series of distinguished British
detractors. The new lampoon featured Horncastle as Captain
Narrowfat, Mrs. Timm as Fanny Buskin, Edwin as Toby
Grebwill, and Mitchell as Mrs. Trail-up. In spite of the
humorous possibilities inherent in the new piece's subject
matter, The Spirit of The Times reported that it "did not
appear as ludicrous as several previous efforts of its author."[31]
Nevertheless the reviewer noted that the audiences enjoyed
the new offering immensely and that, "The Olympic has been
uniformly crammed when we have visited it this week, and
everybody is saying, 'what a fortune Mitchell must be making.'"[32]

On 26 March, the day before China closed, another new
extravaganza, without burlesque elements, debuted. J. R.
Planché's Puss In Boots, with scenery by Bengough, ran for
ten performances before being withdrawn from the bills. As
the third consecutive minor success that Mitchell had produced, it demonstrated that the Olympic was having trouble
finding pieces which would draw good houses for more than
ten to fifteen consecutive performances during the spring of
1841.

Puss In Boots is, however, important as the first of
Planché's pieces that Mitchell produced. In ensuing seasons,
Planché's works were to form a sizeable portion of the New
York Olympic's repertory. During his eleven-year career,
Mitchell produced more of Planché's farces and extravaganzas
than any other manager in America. The reason for Mitchell's
extensive reliance on Planché's works is that the plays are
written in a fashion that brought out the strengths of the
comic acting ensemble Mitchell was building at the Olympic.

James Robinson Planché is among the most interesting
figures of the mid-nineteenth-century British theatre. Earning his initial fame as an antiquarian and historian of heraldry,
Planché's historical interests took a decidedly theatrical turn
in 1823 when he designed the costumes, armor, and heraldry
for Charles Kemble's landmark production of King John at
London's Covent Garden Theatre. This production began
the nineteenth-century vogue for producing Shakespearean
drama with costumes, properties, and scenery historically
appropriate to the period about which the plays are written.

Although Planché had been writing plays since 1818,
his career as a dramatist did not become his primary interest until 1832, when he penned Olympic Revels, the extravaganza that opened Madame Vestris' famous management
of London's Olympic Theatre. Throughout Vestris' tenure as
manager of the London Olympic, Planché served as a house
writer and contributed many short farces and extravaganzas to
the theatre's repertory. The London Olympic's company,
like its New York counterpart, relied on several good comic
players rather than a single big star. Thus, pieces custom-
tailored for Vestris' company suited the strengths of Mitchell's
company nicely.

When Vestris abandoned her management of the London
Olympic in 1838 to tour America with her husband Charles
James Mathews--son of the famous London comedian who had

incensed Americans with his assessment of the national char-
acter--Planché began to write for Ben Webster's company at
London's Haymarket Theatre. Webster's company also relied
on the efforts of a group of players rather than a series of
stars.

When Vestris and Mathews tried their hand at management again in 1847 at the Lyceum Theatre, Planché took up
his former position as Vestris' house writer. The pieces that
he custom tailored for those excellent London comic companies
invariably received their American premieres on the boards of
Mitchell's theatre because they were extremely compatible with
the abilities of the New York Olympic's company.

On both 7 and 11 April the theatre was closed on
account of the death and funeral of President William Henry
Harrison. When it reopened on the twelfth, the audience
was greeted with yet another operatic burlesque from the
pen of Horncastle. Entitled Sam Parr With The Red Coarse
Hair, it burlesqued the French comic opera, Zampa, or The
Red Corsair by Herold and Melesville, which had been recently
produced at the Park. Mitchell and Mrs. Timm played the
leading male and female characters. This new piece, like
most of the others of that season, featured costumes by
Taylor, scenery by Bengough, machinery by Burns, and stage
arrangements by Mitchell. The playbill for its premiere was
reminiscent of those of the Olympic's first season by virtue
of its puns: "The chorus having bored the conductor considerable [sic] during rehearsal have been well drilled in return."33 Mitchell also made fun of his own propensity for
keeping operating expenses at a minimum; "The piano forte
has at the lavish expenditure of one dollar been put in tune."34
Sam Parr, another minor success, was in the bills for fourteen performances out of a possible fifteen playing nights.
Like most of Mitchell's other burlesques that season, it was
general in nature and did not mock any particular production
or any specific performers of opera.

The Olympic had no long-running hit during the remainder of the season, but two productions are of special
interest. The first, Sleeping Beauty, opened on 19 April.
It was the second of Planché's extravaganzas produced during
that season, and the playbill for its opening night announced
that it would be produced "exactly as performed at the Theatre Royal Covent Garden."35

The second interesting production was not a play at

all, but a series of four tableaux which featured the scenic
art of Bengough. Entitled The Tableaux of the Tyrol, this
entertainment opened on 10 May and featured four new drops
in front of which Mitchell arranged his company who were
dressed in appropriate costumes by Taylor. The scenes
represented were: Morning at the Tyrol; Noon at a Rocky
Defile; Evening on the Plain of Sorento; and Moonlight over
Rome.

Things Italian were much on the minds of Mitchell's
fellow New Yorkers during the spring of 1841. Guisseppe
Mazzini, the intellectual leader of the Italian unification
movement, was living in London and influencing the founding
of a Young Italy movement in New York. New York newspapers, most notably The Sun and The Evening Post were
supporting the ideals of the movement which had as its goal
the expulsion of foreign leaders and a unified Italy. Additional interest in and sympathy for the Italians' quest for political self-determination had been generated by the recent
publication of Catherine Sedgewick's Letters From Abroad to
Kindred At Home. An author of liberal political sentiment,
she generated American sympathy for the Italian people and
their political quest. [36] The Countess of Blessington's popular Idler In Italy, a travelogue devoted to the scenic splen-
dor of the peninsula had also recently been published. She
earned rave reviews in New York's literary periodicals.
Thus Mitchell's tableaux managed to capitalize on both the
political and travelogue interest in Italy which was at a high
point during the spring of 1841.

Although New Yorkers had been used to seeing moving
dioramas like William Dunlap's Trip to Niagara for almost
fifteen years and panoramic paintings for longer than that,
The Tableaux of The Tyrol is the first set of tableaux
vivants to be produced in any New York theatre. These
living pictures differed significantly from their panoramic
and dioramic counterparts: the audience did not become part
of the environment, but witnessed the two-dimensional painted
scenery which set off the three-dimensional performers
costumed in an appropriate fashion from the outside. This
trend of three-dimensionalizing famous historical scenes and
paintings of public interest as tableaux vivants became increasingly popular during the next decade. It may have
been given additional impetus by the fascination with and
popularity of the daguerreotype, which had been vastly improved in the spring of 1841. The Tableaux of The Tyrol
as a new form capitalizing on public interest in Italy proved

successful enough to be included as part of the evening's entertainment from the tenth through the twenty-second of May.
In a sense The Tableaux of The Tyrol marked the culmination
of a trend which had been developing throughout the season.
Bengough's scenery and Taylor's costumes contributed increasingly to the success of Mitchell's burlesques and extravaganzas throughout the fall and winter. With the tableaux,
scenery and costumes were undisputably the most important
elements of the production.

        Mitchell concluded his second season, which closed on
5 June 1841, with a two-week revival of 1940!, Sam Parr,
Buy It Dear, and Puss In Boots--the most successful pieces
of the year.

        On Wednesday, May 19, the manager took his end-of-
season benefit performance. The Spirit of The Times testi-
fies to the appreciation his patrons showed for the pains he
took for their amusement. Although it was a rainy May
night, the standing-room-only crowd was packed to the rafters
and, "more people were turned away from the box office,
unable to procure tickets, than entered the house."37

        The second season of his management of the Olympic
is not as interesting as the first. The Olympic's burlesques
lacked the topicality of many of his major successes of the
theatre's premiere season. Only three specific burlesques
were produced: The Humpback, which held the acting of
Fanny Kemble and John Vandenhoff up for ridicule; the Concerts d'Enfer, which burlesqued the winter concerts at the
Park and Niblo's; and, China which satirized British detractors
of American life and manners. The primary reasons that the
burlesques produced during Mitchell's second season were less
specific than their predecessors had been was that there were
fewer theatrical events worthy of ridicule. During the preceding season he had lampooned Hamblin, who was closed for
most of the 1840-41 season; the National's opera company,
which disbanded in January of 1841; and traveling stars who
appeared at the Park, which was dark for part of the 1840-41
season and starless for most of it. But five of the fourteen
most frequently played pieces during the second season were
general operatic burlesques, and all five were penned by
Horncastle.

        Mitchell came to realize, during his first season,
that he could operate profitably by frequently repeating his
popular burlesques and extravaganzas. This realization de-

veloped into a greater reliance on spectacle and a conscious effort to produce long-running hits during the second season. Thus, the second campaign's major successes enjoyed more consecutive performances than their counterparts of the premiere campaign: 1940! was given thirty-five consecutive performances; Buy It Dear, thirty; and The Cat's in The Larder, twenty-seven.

In one important respect the second season was less demanding on Mitchell than its predecessor had been. He was able to act less frequently because Mrs. Timm came to share the brunt of the acting burden with him, making her the first of the Olympic's female favorites. Since she was able to play the female burlesque roles, Mitchell created no new transvestite characters and confined his female characters to Molly Brown in The Roof Scrambler, and Low-Retta in La Musquitoe, both of which were popular vehicles from his first season.

The manager's course of action had proven to be the correct one, for he was, without a doubt, the most successful theatre manager in New York City during the extremely depressed season of 1840-41.

CHAPTER FOUR

A Season of Farce and Scenery

When Mitchell opened his third season in September
of 1841, a change in policy attested to the Olympic's newly
acquired position as a dominant force among places of amusement in New York City. Prices remained the same, and a
"limited number" of season tickets were again sold. But for
the first time, tickets could be obtained elsewhere than at the
theatre. The playbill for the opening night of the season,
13 September, announced: "For the convenience of strangers
and travellers--Box tickets for this theatre may be obtained
on application at the bars of all the principal hotels of the
city."[1] The Olympic was no longer merely a favorite haunt
of the "b'hoys" and New York's fashionable society: it had
become part of the itinerary for travelers and tourists who
were visiting the city. Mitchell's Olympic was one of the
places to see when in the growing metropolis.

The Olympic's personnel had changed little over the
summer. The principal nonacting positions were filled by
the same persons who had held them previously, and only
one change was made in the stock company: Cunningham
left and was replaced by John Nickinson, who was rapidly to
become a favorite at Mitchell's little theatre. The company's
stability is less surprising than it might appear when one
remembers that all of New York's other theatres except the
Chatham had been closed for extended periods during the preceding season. Employment at the Olympic offered a job
security which had not recently been available at any other
theatre in the city.

In the playbill for 13 September 1841, the opening
night of his third season as sole lessee and proprietor of
the Olympic, Mitchell assured his patrons that he would
continue to work within the tradition that he had established
at the Olympic with his "hits at Men, Manners, and things

61

in General. "[2]   Three new pieces, Edward Stirling's Out of
Luck, an English farce receiving its American premiere on
that occasion, and two new plays by Horncastle--Old Olympians
and Bob Bang--made up the evening's entertainment.

Neither of Horncastle's new plays proved attractive and
both were dropped from the bills after their initial performances.   Bob Bang is the more interesting of the opening
night's failures.   The play specifically burlesqued Price and
Swarthout, two prominent Wall Street businessmen who had
gone belly-up and lost large sums of small investors' money. [3]

A member of the season's opening-night audience noted
that the new lampoon factionalized those in attendance.   The
upper-class patrons in the boxes and dress circle found the
burlesque's pointed barbs at the Wall Street bankers, "pretty
hard on 'em, and ... too personal. "[4] The "b'hoys" in the pit,
however, loved the piece's point of view.   They began to
cheer and stomp with delight at the new lampoon and their
supportive sentiments were soon answered by hisses and boos
from the "swells" above them.   The louder one group cheered,
the louder the other group hissed until the din was enormous.
Mitchell, sensing an imminent and potentially violent outbreak
of civil war between his polarized patrons, stopped the play,
came to the edge of the forestage, and announced: " ' Ladies
and gentlemen, this is a theatre and not a newspaper office,
and personalities should have no place in it.   Ladies and
gentlemen, I assure you that this piece shall never be played
again upon the boards of this theatre.' "[5] The manager realized that he had made a mistake analagous to the production
of Sparring With Specie on the previous season's opening
night: he had burlesqued an event in such a fashion that his
lampoon divided the socioeconomic classes of his theatre into
partisan groups.

Realizing that strong partisan feelings on the part of
his heterogeneous audience would do the managerial coffers
little good, Mitchell immediately withdrew the piece, even
though he had spent a lavish sum on the six new drops
which Bengough had painted in the anticipation that Bob Bang
would serve as a long-running opening hit of the season.

Because of the failure of Horncastle's two new plays,
Mitchell was forced to present revivals of his previous season's successes, just as he had relied on hits of his first
season during the early weeks of his second campaign.   Sam
Parr, Mrs. Normer, and The Humpback were all pressed

into service by 20 September. On that date a new "fairy
burletta" by Horncastle, entitled The Wreck of The Isle of
Beauty, was produced. In spite of six additional new drops
by Bengough--a rocky shore and view of the wreck; a romantic landscape and waterfall; a lake by sunset; the seashore;
a woody ravine; and a view towards Staten Island from the
Battery--it proved to be the season's third failure and dis-
appeared from the bills after only five performances. Obviously, Mitchell was not doing well. Within one week twelve
new drops by Bengough and three new plays by Horncastle had
been put in view of the Olympic's patrons, but neither the
talent of the scene painter nor the wit of the resident playwright had been able to provide the manager with an early
season hit.

　　　　The season's first moderate success premiered on
27 September. An English farce by J. S. Faucit entitled
The Aldgate Pump, it relied not on topical burlesque elements
or elaborate spectacle, but rather on the acting ability of
Mitchell and Mrs. Timm. Faucit's phenomenally popular
farce had premiered at London's New Strand Theatre the
preceding June and run for fifty consecutive evenings. In
the Olympic's production, Mitchell played Broomy Swash, a
street sweeper assigned to the area of London around the
Aldgate Pump. Mitchell's Broomy Swash was a philosophizer
on mud and a low comic extortionist. The play concerns itself with a series of intrigues and romantic assignations
which are to be worked out at the Aldgate Pump. As each
of the main characters comes to the pump, Swash sweeps
mud all over them if they fail to give him money. During
one particularly hilarious scene, the romantic hero is wooing
his beloved while Mitchell's character sweeps street mud all
over his trouser cuffs and comments negatively on the hero's
romantic rhetoric. Mitchell's portrayal of Swash soon became one of his most popular characters and was to serve
him well throughout the rest of his tenure as manager of the
Olympic. After playing for nine consecutive performances,
the new play was revived an additional twenty times during
the remainder of the season.

　　　　By producing elaborate spectacles which contained little
in the way of topical burlesque interest and even less in the
way of dramatic import, Mitchell had been depending too
heavily on the efforts of Bengough, Burns, and Taylor in his
quest for successful entertainments. That this policy was
ineffective is shown by the failure of the season's first two
extravaganzas and the apparently unexpected success of The

Aldgate Pump. Early in October The Spirit of The Times
noted a general decrease in attendance at the Olympic and
blamed it on Mitchell's recent overreliance on spectacle and
failure to produce good new plays. The reviewer advised the
manager: "Let him rely less upon his stage appointments
and fine scenery. These are great accessories, but they
are merely accessories, and the public have now become so
familiar with them at the Olympic that something more is
required to draw money."[6]

    Mitchell was almost certainly aware of the validity of
the observation and recommendation contained in The Spirit
of The Times. On 4 October he brought out another new
farce which featured himself and Mrs. Timm. Entitled A
Lady And A Gentleman in a Peculiarly Perplexing Predicament, and written by Charles Selby, it also relied exclusively
on comic acting ability for its attractiveness. Receiving
eight consecutive performances through 12 October, it was
seen twenty-three additional times during the season, and
proved to be very popular in benefit bills for performers at
the city's other theatres.[7]

    It was also early in October that Mitchell entered the
field of opera production for the first time. Beginning on
11 October, Henry and Harriet Wells, a brother-and-sister
team noted for their singing and dancing abilities,[8] played a
week-long engagement at the Olympic in the principal roles
of La Bayadere. Although only the first act was performed,
the production was not a burlesque or self-parody but a rather
successful attempt at legitimate opera with the regular members of the Olympic's stock company supporting the visiting
performers. On 17 October, La Bayadere's place in the
evening's entertainment was taken by Mitchell's successful
burlesque of the preceding season, Buy It Dear, which had
the very opera it succeeded as its object of ridicule. For
the most part, the actors played analagous roles in the legitimate opera and the burlesque of it.

    While La Bayadere graced the Olympic's boards,
Mitchell was provided with a new object for topical burlesque.
Edmund Simpson, the manager of the Park, had modified his
policies to such a degree during the fall of 1841 that they
suspiciously resembled those of Mitchell. In September,
Henry Placide, the Park's leading genteel comedian, had returned to America with a copy of a good new five-act comedy
by a young Irish playwright named Dion Boucicault. The
play, London Assurance, had been written for Madame Vestris

and produced by her at Covent Garden with immense success
during the spring of 1841. The new play and its London success appealed strongly to Simpson who had lost much money
during the very depressing season of 1840-41. Also, he could
rely heavily on elaborate stage appointments and his strong
stock company to make his production of London Assurance
financially successful. On the day of the American premiere
of the play, Bennett's Herald noted: "Mr. Simpson has expended quite as much money to place it on the American
stage with every advantage as was done by Madame Vestris
herself. We see no exception to the cast for tonight, and,
if the actors exert themselves, it may prove a new era in the
existence of 'Old Drury.'"[9] The Spirit of The Times also
anticipated success for the new comedy: "A greater effort
has been made to do justice to the comedy at the Park than
on any occasion for several years."[10]

Opening on 11 October, the Park's production of
London Assurance was an unqualified success and played
every night for an unprecedented three weeks in a theatre
which had been specializing in star performers and frequent
changes of bill for twenty years. On this occasion, however,
the production's strong points were the overall quality of
the stock company and the magnificence of the scenery--both
of which had become commonplace at the Olympic.

Mitchell seized the excitement generated by London
Assurance to launch a few light fusillades at the expense of
Simpson and the Park's production. The following announcement appeared in the Olympic's playbills on 12 October 1841,
the day after London Assurance opened at the Park:

> To the public: the manager of this popular estab-
> lishment, determined that he will not be excelled,
> has been going into the furniture and upholstery
> business with a perfect looseness in order to prove
> that:
>
> OLYMPIC ASSURANCE!!
>
> is just as good and quite as amusing as
>
> LONDON ASSURANCE!!
>
> He therefore respectfully announces that the scene
> of the highly popular piece called 'A Lady and
> Gentleman In a Peculiarly Perplexing Predicament'
> will be presented this evening with the STRICTEST

FIDELITY, APPROPRIATENESS, AND SUPERIOR
EXECUTION OF SCENIC ILLUSION, and all that
MAGNIFICENCE OF STAGE APPOINTMENTS which
nightly elicits the APPROVAL AND ADMIRATION
OF THE BEAU MONDE of this METROPOLIS while
it exists in an equal degree THE ENVY OF ALL
EUROPE.[11]

In addition to the obvious burlesque of Simpson's production, the notice also seems to contain a note of sarcasm,
no doubt the result of Mitchell's perturbation at Simpson's
ability to generate a great deal of public enthusiasm on his
first attempt at instituting policies which the Olympic had
developed and practiced for two seasons. In parodying the
elaborate drawing room furnishings which were used for the
Park's production of London Assurance, Mitchell's playbill
announced the specific accoutrements to be used for his own
production:

THE SCENE rather an old 'en by Bengough but
COVERED with PAPER HANGINGS by BROWN of
CANAL STREET. THE IMPERIAL HEARTHUG...
neat as.... IMPORTED THE STATUARY... by COF-
FEE of CANAL ST. THE WHITE DIMITY.... from
.... VANN'S CHEAP STORE MR. MITCHELL'S
COSTUME.... by.... CHAS. COX of FULTON ST.
MRS. TIMM'S COSTUME.... by... MRS. MANVELLS
MISS SINGLETON'S APRON.... by.... MISS SINGLE-
TON'S AUNT MRS. TIMM'S NIGHTCAP.... by....
MRS. TIMM THE BED....... FROM THE PATENT
FEATHER DRESSING CO. THE YARD AND A HALF
OF RAG CARPET... OF AMERICAN MANUFACTURE
THE SECOND HAND FENDER... from... O'DOLLEY's
OF CENTRE ST. THE CHICKEN... POSITIVELY
REAL AND ROASTED FROM FULTON MKT.[12]

Olympic Assurance was not a new play, but merely
new appointments for A Lady and A Gentleman. Suitable
interpolations into the text may have been added to accen-
tuate the burlesque which the new scenery produced. The
significance of the Olympic Assurance is that it amply demonstrated Mitchell's eagerness and ability to burlesque a
theatrical event of general public interest, and the Park's
production of London Assurance was the first such event to
take place in the city of New York for quite some time.

Although the manager's two new farces proved to be

moderately good drawing cards through most of October, he
was unable to produce a new piece which had a long run. The
season had started slowly, much as his second season had;
and it took him even longer than it had the year before to
find the first substantial success of the season. It was not
until 25 October, seven weeks into the season, that the Olympic's audiences saw the successful production of the kind of
piece they had come to expect on the stage of their favorite
theatre. On that date Horncastle's Mephistopheles; or, The
Three Wishes opened. Capitalizing on the interest in and
familiarity with the Mephistopheles legend which had characterized innumerable earlier extravaganzas, the Olympic's
"local extravaganza" featured Mitchell in the title role, "a
branch devil from the blue blazes joint stock company, "13
and eight new drops by Bengough: a sculptor's studio at
Ravenna; the exterior of Drury Lane Theatre in London; the
interior of a picture gallery at Pall-Mall; Middle Row at Hol-
born in London; La Porte St. Denis at Paris; a chamber in
a hotel in Paris; the hall of Neptune's palace; and the interior of Neptune's palace. Premiering on 25 October, the
new play ran for twenty-four consecutive evenings. Like
some of its unsuccessful predecessors, it relied heavily on
Bengough's scenery for its appeal, but it was successful
where they were not, presumably because the play itself had
some merit, was lengthily and carefully rehearsed, 14 and
gave Mitchell an opportunity to display his considerable talents
as a low comedian.

As was true during the two preceding seasons, success followed success rapidly after the initial hit was established on the Olympic's stage. On 22 November, Mephistopheles was withdrawn in favor of a new piece, Planché's
Riquet With The Tuft, which featured Mitchell and Mrs. Timm
in the principal roles for twenty consecutive performances.
Planché's extravaganza had first appeared at Madame Vestris'
London Olympic on Boxing Night, 1836. The trifle's main
character is a love-struck deformed hunchback, who is a
prince by birth. Bald, with the exception on one tuft of
red hair, Prince Riquet proves that beauty is only skin deep
and eventually wins the hand of the fair Esmerelda.

Ten days later, a satirical farce entitled Saratoga
Springs was produced. Unfortunately, the play has not survived, and the press did not completely detail its course of
events. During its thirteen-night run it amused audiences
with its pointed jibes at the protracted vacations that the
upper-class citizens of New York were wont to take at that

newly fashionable watering spot.   Mitchell and Mrs. Timm
again played the leading characters, Mr. and Mrs. Timothy
Tapewell, which rapidly became two of their most popular roles.

On 6 December, with both Riquet With The Tuft and
Saratoga Springs in the evening's bill, Mitchell suspended the
free list for the first time that season.   This suggested, as
it had during the two preceding seasons, that the Olympic was
doing a "land office" business.

Even though four of his five most popular new pieces
of the season were farces which did not depend on scenery
for their attractiveness, Mitchell seemed determined to follow
the policy of relying primarily upon spectacle that The Spirit
of The Times had warned against.   On 13 December he
brought out a new series of "tableaux Vivans" [sic] which
featured more elaborate scenery by Bengough, additional new
costumes by Taylor, and stage appointments by the manager.
The new spectacular offering consisted of three unrelated
scenes: Diana and her nymphs bathing; Napoleon's bivouac;
and, Cleopatra in her galley.   Suffering the same lack of
public interest as The Wreck of The Isle of Beauty, the
tableaux were withdrawn after only eight evenings.   Try as
he might, Mitchell was unable to establish the same kind of
vogue for the tableaux vivants among New York's theatre
patrons that had captured the imagination of their London
counterparts.   Those tableaux which were to prove successful almost invariably treated patriotic scences, well-known
paintings, or scenes described in the popular travelogues of
the day.   Unrelated spectacle suggested by classical mythology
did not fare well in New York's theatres.   It seemed that
each time Mitchell relied upon Bengough's scenery to the exclusion of topicality or broad farcical humor, the public re-
jected his offering.   Revivals characterized the repertory
until Christmas Eve, when Mitchell produced another new
burlesque which, like many of its predecessors, was general
rather than specific in nature.   The anonymous Eliza Cluppins,
or The Bones of The Unburied One ridiculed "gothic" melodrama.

A fascination for what came to be called "gothic"
melodrama developed at the turn of the century with Matthew
"Monk" Lewis's phenomenally popular The Castle Spectre.
Almost immediately those London theatres operating on a
limited license and specializing in the production of spectacular melodrama began to produce a host of ghostly and
ghoulish imitations of Lewis's famous prototype.   Featuring

medieval castles, bodies rising from graves, long-concealed crimes, and all manner of scary supernatural claptrap, "gothic" melodrama rapidly developed a large following among lower-class London theatregoers. The American version of the tradition developed most fully at Hamblin's Bowery Theatre during the 1830s, where many of the blood-curdling thrillers from London received their American premieres.

Featuring the manager and Mrs. Timm, as almost all of the new plays did that season, <u>Eliza Cluppins</u> was the prime attraction through New Year's Eve. The Albion's review of the new burlesque defended it from those who damned it as, "the acme of ridiculous trash,"[15] arguing that topical burlesques could be fairly criticized only when and if their object of ridicule were understood and kept in mind: "...for unless the object be kept in view, it is insufferably vulgar, but with that understanding, its humour is restored."[16] The critic's point of view regarding the new lampoon is interesting, for it marks the first time that the New York press suggested that Mitchell's burlesque novelties should be evaluated by standards differing from those applied to the more traditional types of plays performed at the city's other theatres.

Throughout January, the bill of fare at the Olympic was characterized by two things: a revival of several successful burlesques and extravaganzas of past seasons; and, the emergence of the only member of the company ever to play anything comparable to the lines of business cherished by the actors of the city's other theatres.

During the 1840s, local-color characters in low comedy came to be very popular in both America and England. The two character types most often successfully portrayed were the Yankee and the Irishman. While America produced all of the Yankee actors except Charles Mathews--as well as some delineators of Irishmen--the greatest Irish actor of the period was Tyrone Power. Winning the hearts of the Americans on two different tours of this country, he popularized the Irish characters as a staple of American comedy.

Social conditions in New York City favored Power's portrayal of Irish characters. Between 1836 and 1842 the annual number of Irish immigrants increased from 12,645 to 51,542.[17] Most of the newcomers arrived in New York because passenger agents in England and Ireland made favorable deals with the Irish-Americans who had already captured Tammany Hall and could "vote every immigrant almost as

soon as he landed. "18   This influx of the genuine article
from the Emerald Isle during the late 1830s and early 1840s
piqued curiosity about Ireland and all things Irish thereby
providing a favorable environment in which Power and other
actors established an audience for their Irish characters.
But Power was unable to prosper from the taste for Irish
comedy he helped to create, for in 1841 he was lost at sea
while aboard the ill-fated steamship President on a voyage
from America to England.

Aware of the growing taste for "Irish pieces" in
American audiences, Mitchell had hired George Mossop, a
minor comedian who specialized in Irishmen, as his first
and only "star" during the Olympic's premiere season.

After Mossop's departure, Mitchell avoided the production of Irish humor plays, chiefly because there was no one
in his company capable of playing the Irish roles well.   During Mitchell's third season, however, Cunningham's replace-
ment in the company, John Nickinson, expressed a desire to
learn the business of Irish characters and the manager encouraged him to work on several of the standard Irish vehicles.
On 10 January 1842, Nickinson appeared in his first Irish
piece at the Olympic, The Happy Man, a thinly disguised
version of the late Power's popular vehicle, Paddy Murphy. 19
That Mitchell permitted and perhaps even encouraged Nickinson in his attempt to learn the "Irish business" indicates
that the manager had finally become aware that his audiences
were more receptive to farce than to spectacular entertainments.   Nickinson proved to be extremely popular in The
Happy Man, appearing in it twenty times between its debut
on 10 January and the end of the season.   In praising his
portrayal, The Albion stated that he had "gone further to
reconcile us to the loss of Poor Power than we could previously allow ourselves to imagine."20   Thus, through Nickinson, Mitchell became the only manager in the city who
could claim a resident Irish-character actor among the
members of his company.   Yet Nickinson was not exclusively
or even primarily a specialist; he was called upon to play
support to Mitchell in other farces, extravaganzas, and burlesques more often than he played his newly developed line
of business.

While Nickinson drew large audiences to the Olympic
to see his Irish characters, New York's other theatres suffered another bleak February.   The Park closed as a playhouse from 26 January until 21 February and the Bowery

ceased operations from 9 February through 14 March.   Since
the rebuilt National had burned down the preceding spring,
Mitchell's only competition during February of 1842 was the
Chatham, which had relied exclusively on variety entertainments through the first half of the season.   Mitchell seemed
immune to the problems that plagued New York's other managers, and continued to do his usual lucrative business
through the dead of winter.   On 5 February The Albion commented on the Olympic's usual succession of good houses
and reported to its readers: "This little bijou is always
so well filled that it would be an act of economy to stereo-
type the fact."[21]   The Spirit of The Times noted, on the
same date, that with the closing of the city's other playhouses, business at the Olympic had gone from good to excellent: "This house, which has always been well patronized,
is now nightly crowded."[22]

        It was Mitchell, as an actor as well as manager, who
bore the prime responsibility for the Olympic's success during midwinter.   His name continued to appear in large type
at the head of each play in which he appeared, suggesting
that in spite of the popularity of Horncastle, Mrs. Timm,
and Nickinson, he was still functioning as something like a
resident star.

        With the large New York theatres closed, almost
everything Mitchell produced drew good houses.   On 10 February he brought out what proved to be his greatest success
of the season, a burlesque of Richard III entitled Richard
#3.   Playbills announced the new lampoon as the work of
O. E. Durivage,[23] but there is no record of any contemporary raconteur with those initials.   Perhaps the playbills contain a misprint and the author is F. A. Durivage.   Francis
Durivage, author of many humorous articles in literary
periodicals of the day which appeared over the pen name
"Old Un," was the nephew of Edward Everett.   He was
later to achieve some fame as a colleague of Steel Mackaye
and proponent of the Delsarte acting system.   He would have
been in his late twenties in 1842, and is probably the author
of Richard #3.   The new play was unlike Mitchell's previous
Shakespearean travesties.   The others had stayed rather
close to their models in plot and character, and a good deal
of their humor resulted from the specific burlesquing of
Shakespeare's verse and well-known contemporary actors.
Richard #3 was a different matter entirely, for there was
"little attic wit in it."[24]

"Mitchell as Richard #3."   The Harvard Theatre Collection.

The piece dealt with the conflict over who was to be
the new driver of omnibus #3. Mitchell played Richard, "Cad
to omnibus #3 afterward its driver."[25] Henry King, "an old
omnibus driver,"[26] and Richard's predecessor, was portrayed
by Nickinson. Bucky Gammon, acted by Horncastle, was
another omnibus driver who aided Richard in his evil machina-
tions to attain possession of old #3. Two other drivers,
Richmund--played by Graham--and Stand and Lie--played by
Edwin--were engaged in the frivolous action. The play proved
extremely popular, running for twenty-nine consecutive evenings before being withdrawn. The Albion suggested that the
antics of Mitchell and the others were "beyond measure the
most humorous that ever convulsed a laughing audience here."[27]
A week later the same journal predicted: "Richard #3 is so
completely the rage here that we may look for its continuance
during the remainder of the season."[28]

On 23 February, with Richard drawing crowded houses
nightly, Mitchell made a valuable addition to his stock company,
the vocalist Mrs. Mossop. Performing previously under the
names Miss Kent and Mrs. Henry Knight, her comic versatility and popularity were so strong that the press suggested
that Mitchell intended to make the Olympic the "real Theatre
Comique of America."[29] During her first week at the Olympic, her name appeared in large type at the head of the daily
playbills, but she was thereafter listed merely as a regular
member of the company.

Richard #3 and the newly acquired vocalist continued to
be the main attraction at the theatre until 7 March when Cin
derella, a musical extravaganza in the comic operetta tradition, debuted. In the new piece, one character, the Prince
de Joint of Veal, was a caricature of the Prince de Jon de
Ville, who had visited the Olympic several times during his
stay in New York. This new musical, which is significant
as the first of Mitchell's successful extravaganzas in which
the manager himself did not appear, shared the bills with
Richard #3 for the first eight of its nineteen consecutive
performances. Reviewing the opening performance of the
new musical entertainment, The Albion reported that when
the duet "Sir a Secret," sung by Edwin and Nickinson, was
loudly encored, Nickinson "lost the key and sang in one different from that which was played by the orchestra."[30] The
audience found the off-key repetition hilarious, and even the
hapless Nickinson finally gave up and joined in the general
laughter. The Albion's critic found the incident, "...a good
joke--for once--but it must not be repeated."[31] Although the

reviewer was inclined to forgive Nickinson's vocal mistake,
he found some of the contents of the new extravaganza in
questionable taste, noting that "Many of the jokes in this
piece are broad, some perhaps too broad,..."[32] Nevertheless, the audience enjoyed it immensely and the offended
critic grudgingly admitted, "We may truly consider the piece
as a decided hit."[33]

            While large crowds continued to throng to the Olympic,
the citizens of New York were experiencing the most exciting
event of the year: a visit from "Boz."

            Charles Dickens, frequently known during his lifetime
as "Boz," spent a little over five months of 1842 on a tour
through America.   He landed in Boston on 22 January and
remained there until 5 February.   From 5 February through
the thirteenth of that month, he made his way to New York
via Worcester, New Haven, and Hartford.   The excitement
that New Yorkers felt about the impending arrival of Britain's
most famous living writer was immense.   His works were
well known in America--probably much to his irritation, since
the American versions were mostly pirated in both their original form and as stage adaptations.   The fashionable citizens
of New York, seeking to impress the literary lion on his
first visit to these shores, arranged two festivities in his
honor: a dinner at the City Hotel, sponsored by the city's
leading citizens; and a ball at the Park Theatre, arranged
by "a committee of gentlemen at the Astor House."[34]

            On 14 February, the day after Dickens' arrival, the
"Boz" ball took place at the Park.   The pit had been floored
over and such a great deal of money and energy was spent
in preparing "Old Drury" for the festive occasion that the
decorations surpassed anything previously attempted in New
York.[35]   The committee of gentlemen from the Astor House
in charge of arrangements disposed of three thousand tickets
at the sum of ten dollars each.   Every would-be attendant
was carefully scrutinized with regard to respectability and
previous social standing.[36]   Moreover, extensive "rules"
for the event were published in the city's daily newspapers
for an entire week before the occasion.   The ball proved to
be the social event of the season and was repeated on the sixteenth and again on the eighteenth for the amusement of New
York's less wealthy and presumably less sophisticated citizens.
On the latter two occasions, the price of admission was two
dollars per couple, and a dollar for an extra lady.

On the date of the last "Boz" ball, the dinner at the
City Hotel took place, along with much toasting and testimon-
ializing. After the dinner, Dickens remained in the city
through 6 March, and spent much of his time visiting prisons,
charitable institutions, the notorious slum section of "five
points, " and the city's theatres.

His comments on New York's playhouses show that it
was evident, even to an outsider, that the Olympic was the
most prosperous theatre in New York during the depressed
winter of 1842:

> There are three principal theatres. Two of them,
> the Park, and the Bowery, are large, elegant and
> handsome buildings, and are, I grieve to write it,
> generally deserted. The third, the Olympic, is a
> tiny show-box for vaudevilles and burlesques. It
> is singularly well conducted by Mr. Mitchell, a
> comic actor of great quiet humor and originality,
> who is well remembered and esteemed by London
> playgoers. I am happy to report of this deserving
> gentleman, that his benches are usually well filled,
> and that his theatre rings with merriment every
> night. 37

Dickens' pleasure at Mitchell's good fortune may have
resulted more from his fondness for the man than his concern
over the fortunes of the theatre on this side of the Atlantic.
According to one source, 'Dickens was an old friend of Mitchell's, Mitchell having been a poor actor in London when
Dickens was a poor reporter. "38

Throughout his stay in New York, "Boz" was daily besieged by invitations from prominent citizens to share their
tables. The press took such an inordinate interest in what
he did and with whom he spent his time that Dickens wrote
to his friend John Forster in London that if he dropped a
letter in the street it would be related in the papers on the
following day. 39 Public curiosity in his daily itinerary continued until he left the inquisitive New Yorkers on 6 March.

Through March, Mitchell relied on a revival of 1940!
while rehearsing a new burlesque of the manner in which
Dickens had been idolized by the press and New York's leading citizens. The Olympic's repertory drew its usual crowded
houses, while at the Park, according to The Spirit of The

Times, "The receipts for the past week can scarce exceed
the gas bill. "40

On 11 April, almost five weeks after Dickens' departure,
Mitchell produced his comment on the way his fellow New
Yorkers had received the literary hero. The inordinate
amount of time that lapsed between Dickens' departure and the
premiere of Mitchell's burlesque can only be explained in
terms of the labor expended to write and rehearse the new
sketch, and the effort required to produce new scenery for it.
The new skit, Boz, or The Lion Lionized, featured Horncastle as Dickens. Its seven scenes consisted of: The Dock,
Boz's landing; The Lion at the Carlton (where Dickens stayed
while in New York); The Lion besieged (the numerous dinner
invitations and constant retinue of admirers); Sam Weller a
lion as well as his master; The Lion at feeding time (a burlesque of the dinner given in his honor at the City Hotel);
four tableaux from Dickens' work, which included two from
The Old Curiosity Shop and one each from Nicholas Nickleby
and Oliver Twist; and, the Lion at the show (a visit to the
Olympic). The new sketch was extremely popular and ran
for twenty consecutive evenings. It was frequently revived
during the remaining month of the season.

The object of Mitchell's burlesque was not Dickens,
of course, but the way in which he was fawned over by the
press and the fashionable members of New York society.
No doubt many of the gentlemen of the city who frequented
the Olympic had been in the presence of the immortal "Boz,"
and some of the theatre's regular patrons had probably served
on the committees which made the preparations for the ball
and the dinner at the City Hotel. The sophisticated segment
of Mitchell's audience was, in a very real sense, the new
burlesque's primary object of ridicule. Apparently, Horncastle's portrayal of Dickens was unusually realistic in its
makeup and detail. One account claims that Dickens saw the
burlesque and was so impressed with the actor's likeness of
him that he gave Horncastle the hat and coat he wore upon
his arrival in New York. 41 Another source claims, "Horncastle looked so much like Boz in his stage rig that one night
General George P. Morris and Fitz Greene Hallack had quite
a talk with Horncastle for Dickens. "42 Dickens is claimed
to have been in on the fun of Horncastle's convincing characterization: "Once an 'interviewer' wanted to see 'Boz,'
and 'Boz' asked Horncastle to take his place. Horncastle
received the reporter in the green-room, and answered all
his questions so politely that the newspaper man went and

wrote a two column article about 'A Confidential Chat with
Charles Dickens. ' "[43]

While it has proven impossible to verify these anec-
dotes, their very existence suggests that Horncastle's portrayal
of the literary lion was, in all respects, unusually realistic
for the early 1840s.

Boz was the last significant new piece to be produced
during the 1841-42 season. Although Mitchell did attempt
an interesting production of The Beggar's Opera in which all
of the female roles were played by men and vice versa, the
piece was performed only twice. While the last month of the
season saw no new pieces on the boards, the theatre continued to draw large audiences with revivals of the most popular pieces from the repertory. Late in May, The Albion reviewed the history of the theatre and Mitchell's management
of it in an attempt to explain its anomalous success. The
journal noted that the Olympic's history prior to Mitchell's
assumption of its management had been an unfortunate one.
Both its entertainments and its audiences had deteriorated
until it became the worst theatre in the city and had, "sunk
to the lowest pitch of theatrical degradation."[44] No previous
management had been able to make the little theatre a paying
proposition and, by December of 1839, it became a general
assumption that no one could. The odds against success
were overwhelming: "To attempt a reform and rennovation
[sic] of such a place was literally to attempt the cleansing of
the Augean Stables. "[45]

Not only had the prior history of the playhouse boded
ill for Mitchell's venture, his choice of repertory was historically ill advised. No theatre in New York which had specialized in three or four light comic entertainments on each evening had ever been more than marginally successful, and that
for only a brief period of time. It seemed that the best that
small theatres devoted to comedy--The Franklin, Richmond
Hill, and the Lafayette--had been able to achieve was an
"ephemeral prosperity."[46] Yet by playing the kind of repertory that had never been more than marginally successful
in the worst theatre in town, Mitchell's management had become spectacularly successful. Neither bad weather nor the
generally depressed state of affairs at the city's other theatres
had any effect on the Olympic's popularity. How was the
manager able to overcome incredibly long odds and establish
the Olympic as the most exciting and successful theatre in
the city? The Albion suggests two reasons. First, Mitchell's

perseverance and taste had been extraordinary. According
to the columnist, anyone else would have been, "worn out
with fatigue and anxiety in less than a twelve month."[47]
Second, the members of the stock company had established
themselves as local favorites. New York's audiences had
proven ready to support a comic ensemble company rather
than the endless succession of greater and lesser luminaries
who had traipsed across the boards of the Park and the Bowery for years. Appreciation for the Olympic's actors was
attested to by the excellent benefit nights that the company's
members enjoyed during the closing weeks of the season.
The article concluded by noting that the Olympic's success,
although unlikely, had proven phenomenal.

Two weeks later, the same periodical evaluated several
members of the company who, in their respective positions,
aided Mitchell in making the Olympic a successful venture.
The commentary is interesting, for there are few extant as-
sessments of the overall competence with which the Olympic's
personnel carried out their respective tasks.

Horncastle was described as "a substantial prop"[48]
of the Olympic's fortune because of his acting, singing, and
writing abilities. The commentator noted that Nickinson, in
addition to being the best performer of Irish characters in
America, was "a clever representative of comic character
in general."[49] Mrs. Timm was praised for her versatility
and it was suggested that "her loss, for any cause, would
be most sensibly felt."[50] Only Lydia Singleton, whom the reviewer mentions as an Olympic favorite, was thought to be
less than adequate. The writer suggests that her personality
was solely responsible for her popularity.

The actors were not the only members of the theatre's
staff singled out for commendation. The critic took special
note of Bengough's contributions: "The specimens which he
has given of his art during the past season have been sufficient to stamp him a man of genius and skill."[51]

By singling out individual members of the company
for praise a mere two weeks after reviewing the general history of Mitchell's management of the Olympic, The Albion
tacitly indicated that the theatre's success, despite Mitchell's
Herculean efforts, was the result of a team effort. New
York's other theatres were not noted for their team efforts.

The season closed on 6 June. On that evening Mitchell

took a benefit which he advertised in the following exuberant
manner:

GRAND COMPLEMENTARY BENEFIT GIVEN BY

MR. MITCHELL TO HIMSELF

THE SEATS OF THE PIT WILL BE COVERED
(with people [perhaps]) THE DRESS CIRCLE WILL
BE FILLED (if enough tickets are sold to fill it)

THE UPPER BOXES (will positively be above the
dress circle) The arrangements will not be under
the direction of A Committee of Gentlemen at The
Astor House.

Observe that all pipe laying is finished opposite to
the theatre--they will therefore to prevent confusion
set their company down with the horses heads in
front, and their tails behind.[52]

The last two items in the advertisement are jibes at
the Boz ball. The superintendent of carriages for the ball,
in an attempt to control traffic, posted rules requiring:
"Carriages will come into line with the horses heads towards
Chatham Street, and take up in the opposite direction."

Mitchell's third season at the Olympic was similar to
its predecessors in some ways, but differed from them in
others. The theatre's personnel had remained remarkably
stable, with only two changes in the acting company from
that of the immediately previous season. The stability of
personnel from season to season was to continue for the
next six years. Another tradition which was firmly established by the end of the third season was the closing of the
Olympic early in June when New York audiences started to
migrate uptown to Niblo's Gardens for their summer entertainment.

An analysis of the Olympic's playbills shows that there
were only eleven pieces which received upwards of twenty
performances. Of these, two, Mrs. Normer, and Crummles
In Search of Novelty, where revivals from the preceding year.
Farce had superseded both extravaganza and burlesque as
Mitchell's most popular form of entertainment. There is
every reason to believe that this change in the most popular
type of entertainment was not planned by the manager. Early

in the season he produced three successive extravaganzas which
relied extensively on Bengough's scenery for their appeal.
They all failed. The Spirit of The Times noted Mitchell's
early season reliance on spectacle and warned against it. At
about the same time he was chided in print, he brought out
two new farces which proved to be extremely successful: The
Aldgate Pump; and A Lady And A Gentleman In a Peculiarly
Perplexing Predicament. Three other successful farces
rapidly followed, and all but one, The Happy Man (Nickinson's
Irish vehicle) featured Mitchell and Mrs. Timm.

Although five of the most frequently performed new
plays of the season were farces, the three pieces which received the greatest number of performances were burlesques.
Richard #3 played forty-five times; Boz, which opened only
seven weeks before the end of the season, was given thirty-
four performances; and Mephistopheles graced the Olympic's
stage thirty-three times. Of these three pieces, the last
two mentioned did rely heavily on Bengough's scenery for their
attractiveness. In Mephistopheles and Boz, Mitchell used the
new scenery to good advantage, but the burlesques themselves
must have been substantially better than some of the season's
earlier offerings which were just as spectacular but not
nearly as popular. The practice of embellishing a good piece
with elaborate scenery rather than relying on elaborate
scenery to carry a weak piece indicates that Mitchell came
to realize, during the course of the campaign, that he could
not rely primarily on paint and canvas to fill his theatre.

Another interesting change from the first two seasons
is the absence of any new operatic burlesques in the repertory.
Horncastle's burlesques of operas had been the most popular
type of entertainment during the Olympic's first two seasons,
and it is strange there were no new pieces of that genre produced during the third season. The almost total absence of
operatic burlesque in future seasons suggests that Mitchell,
for whatever reason, consciously moved away from their production as an Olympic staple during the season of 1841-42.

While the general state of theatrical affairs was not
quite as depressed in New York as it had been during the preceding year, it remained rather bleak. Both the Park and
Bowery had closed for about a month in the dead of winter,
and the Chatham, which relied heavily on variety entertainments, was Mitchell's only competitor to remain open throughout the entire season. So, while Mitchell's policies regarding

the type of entertainment which he produced changed slightly, his position as the most successful theatre manager in the city of New York did not.

CHAPTER FIVE

The Coming of the Palmy Days, 1842-44

While Mitchell and his employees vacationed from June through September of 1842, the Olympic was refurbished. New decorative painting by Staats, crimson damask hangings over the boxes, reupholstering of the seats in the boxes and dress circle--executed by the New York firm of Burns and Tranque--plus new cornice gilding by Marcher, increased the attractiveness of the little theatre and the comfort of its audience.

Several important changes in the theatre's personnel made the Olympic's production staff and acting company even stronger than they had been previously. Blackburn replaced Taylor as costumer, and Loder's orchestra increased from four to six members. A piano forte was no longer part of the musical ensemble, and the new instrumentation included two violins, a cello, a double bass, a clarinet and a flute. The acting company also changed. Horncastle again left and two new singers, James Dunn and William Rosenthall, were hired. Another actor of very limited experience, Charles Walcot, also joined the company. Walcot wanted to work for Mitchell so much that he offered to play for a month with no salary. Mrs. Timm, who had known the aspirant in Charleston before he became an actor, convinced Mitchell to give Walcot a four-week trial.[1] The neophyte proved himself by rapidly becoming one of Mitchell's most popular and useful performers. In later seasons, he was also to function as one of the theatre's resident playwrights. Three new actresses--Mary Taylor, Constantia Clarke, and Louisa Cooper--filled the ranks of the stock corps. Miss Cooper had no professional experience prior to joining the Olympic's company. Mitchell knew Mary Taylor's work, for she had debuted under Wallack at the National Theatre in February of 1838 during Mitchell's tenure as stage manager of that theatre. When the National burned down, she joined the

stock company at the Park as a member of the chorus and
sometime walking lady. Constantia Clarke, although quite
young, was a seasoned performer. The daughter of John H.
Clarke, a veteran stock actor, she had occasionally played
juvenile roles, where her father was acting, since her infancy.
Her first full-time employment was at the Bowery theatre
during the 1841-42 season where she played "an astonishing
number and variety of characters."[2]   Clarke and Taylor were
to become the most popular actresses ever to tread the boards
of the Olympic and soon developed vociferous rival followings
among the theatre's patrons.   Although both had prior professional experience, niether boasted much of a professional
reputation before throwing in their lot with the Olympic's
manager.

Some contracts between Mitchell and his actors for
this season and its successor have survived and provide a
great deal of information concerning the conditions under
which Mitchell employed his performers and the salaries
which they received.   Since all of the agreements are the
same in format, an examination of one of them is sufficient
to establish the general terms of employment agreed upon by
Mitchell and his thespians.   Lydia Singleton's contract reads:

> I Lydia Singleton do hereby engage and bind my-
> self to give my services as an actress and vocalist
> in Mr. Mitchell's company for the ensuing season,
> commencing sometime in September next at a Weekly
> Salary of Ten Dollars and a half of the receipts
> (after deducting one hundred Dollars for expenses)
> on one Night of the Season as and for a benefit--
> I further agree to be in all respects governed by
> the usual rules of the Establishment.[3]

Several important conditions, not in general practice
at the city's other theatres, are implicit in this contract.
There were no lines of business divided among the members
of the troupe and, consequently, every performer was required to perform any role which might be assigned to him
or her.   Furthermore, all were required to sing if called
upon to do so.   Other implicit conditions of the contract are
contained within the phrase, "usual rules of the Establishment."
Unfortunately, these have proven undeterminable. One can
only surmise that they deal with fines and punishment for such
infractions as rehearsal tardiness, inebriated performance,
and unprofessional conduct at the theatre.

While most of the actors had some sort of benefit stipulated in their respective contracts, the salaries which they received were by no means lavish, even for those depressed times, and varied widely according to the popularity and usefulness of the individual performer. Lydia Singleton, who had been with Mitchell since the beginning of his management, received $10.00 weekly, plus half the receipts above $100.00 on her benefit night. Sarah Timm, who had been the Olympic's hardest worker and most popular actress during the two previous seasons, earned $25.00 weekly plus a clear third of the receipts on her benefit night. Eliza Mossop drew $20.00 weekly plus a half benefit over $100.00. Mrs. Watts, who had proven herself a useful supporting actress, earned only $12.00 and was entitled to a half benefit over $100.00. Louisa Cooper, one of the new recruits, was given only $5.00 weekly, with no benefit stipulated in her contract. Mary Taylor, another new member of the company, was awarded $10.00 weekly and denied a benefit in her contract. Yet she proved to be so popular during her premiere season at the Olympic that she did receive a benefit in April.

Mitchell's agreement with Constantia Clarke has been lost, but it is reasonable to assume that, during her first season, she earned about the same as Mary Taylor.

Among the men, Thomas McKean drew the lowest salary. He received $6.00 weekly for acting, and an additional $6.00 as wardrobe keeper. He was not entitled to a benefit. William Rosenthall, another new member of the company, also earned $6.00 weekly. He, too, was denied a benefit. James Dunn, another new member of the corps, earned $8.00 weekly, and was given a half benefit over $100.00. J. M. Field, who played a month-long engagement with Mitchell beginning late in September, earned $25.00 weekly as an actor and dramatist, plus one third of the gross receipts on the night of his benefit. While these may sound like attractive terms of employment for Field, ownership of any plays he was to write for the Olympic fell to Mitchell, and he was not even to be given the traditional author's benefit.

The contract book does not contain all of the agreements between Mitchell and the members of the stock company. It is necessary to estimate several salaries in order to approximate what it cost the manager to maintain his company each week. Five of the company's women are not mentioned. All were veterans of at least one Olympic season, but none

were as popular or useful as Lydia Singleton, who earned
$10.00 weekly. It seems reasonable to assume that they
were in the $6.00 to $8.00 a week category and $35.00 is
an appropriate estimate of their combined weekly salaries.

It is more difficult to estimate the salaries of the
seven men for whom no contracts have survived. Davis,
Barnett, and Clarke were certainly lesser lights, and probably worked for $8.00 weekly. Everard and Graham usually
played important supporting roles. They were in the same
category of usefulness and popularity as Mrs. Watts, who was
paid $12.00 weekly, and they may have earned that amount.
Baker, the prompter, was an important individual who also
acted, and probably earned top wages--$25.00 weekly. Nick-
inson, who played the Irish roles and frequently appeared in
leading roles in other pieces may have earned $15.00.[4]

With the information contained in the contract books
and estimates of the salaries of those perfomers for whom no
contracts are extant, it is reasonable to approximate Mitchell's
weekly expenditure for his company's salaries at about $250.00.
The Olympic's rent was $25.00. Salaries for supporting
personnel including Loder, his musicians, Bengough, and
Blackburn was likely about $125.00. Adding $25.00 weekly
for advertising and running expenses bring the total of
Mitchell's operating expenses to $425.00 weekly. After
having reduced prices during his second week in business,
the financial capacity of the Olympic must have diminished
from approximately $535.00 to below $300.00, or a clear
third benefit would not have been more advantageous than half
the receipts above $100.00. When the Olympic drew well,
which it usually did, Mitchell may have cleared over $500.00
weekly.

The manager's expenses for maintaining the finest
stock company in New York were not very high. Yet it must
be remembered that for the two preceding seasons only the
Olympic and the Chatham had remained open through the depressed winter months, and, at the Chatham, stars and variety
acts played an important part in the regular bill of fare.
Mitchell, then, was the only manager who relied exclusively
on his stock company, and employment at the Olympic provided job security unavailable at any other theatre in the
city. Actors were almost certainly anxious to work for him
during those hard times and were no doubt satisfied with their
salaries which, if not sumptuous, were sure to be paid weekly.

Mitchell's fourth season opened on 17 September 1842, with three new pieces, none of which proved popular. But a notice of the first week's business in The Albion, praising the abilities of the inexperienced Walcot, indicates that Mitchell, much like Augustin Daly years later, had an ability to detect talent in little-known performers and train them to a high degree of professional competence: "A new actor also appeared in the person of Mr. Walcot; and, judging from the one specimen of his quality on that evening, we are disposed to speak of him as an actor of considerable comic talent."5

Although the acting company appeared stronger than it had ever been, the opening week of the season was not without its problems. Redecorating the theatre may have been a mistake, since the new damask hangings seem to have impaired the less-than-optimal acoustical qualities of the Olympic. The Albion noted: "Something there is, however, either in the construction of the building, or in the arrangement of the interior, which utterly kills all musical sound. The tones of the instruments fall dead and 'tubbish.'"6 The acoustics must have been improved, for on only one other occasion did the press complain about not being able to hear well in the Olympic.

As had happened during the two preceding years, Mitchell found it impossible to come up with a long-running hit during the first month of the new season. Remembering the success of his several farces of the prior campaign, he premiered three new pieces of that genre, featuring Mrs. Timm and himself, during the first two weeks of the season; but, none of them proved to be more than marginally successful. Yet he was playing to such good houses that he was not compelled to revive previous Olympic hits as he had been forced to do during the early weeks of previous seasons. Of his established repertory, only Crummles In Search of Novelty and Olympic Revels were revived.

Excepting his roles in the three new farces, Mitchell appeared only infrequently during the early part of the season and concentrated his energies on the rehearsal of new plays. His absence from the boards of the Olympic was made possible by the increased strength of the acting company.

On 3 October 1842 Mitchell produced the first of the season's new extravaganzas, John Brougham's Jupiter Jealous. Brougham, an Irish actor and playwright whom Mitchell may

have known in London, had recently arrived in New York.
He made his American acting debut at the Park Theatre on
the evening following Mitchell's American premiere of Jupiter
Jealous.   Having been a member of Madame Vestris' companies
at both the Olympic and Covent Garden, Brougham was known
primarily as an Irish comedian in 1842.   He probably supposed
that he would do well in America because no outstanding performer of Irish characters had played in New York since
Tyrone Power's untimely death in March of 1841.   Brougham
was to have a long and prosperous career in this country as
a playwright; as a comedian with Burton, Wallack, and Daly;
and as manager of his own playhouse, Brougham's Lyceum.
But in October of 1842, he was just another traveling star
with London credentials.

Like several of its Olympic predecessors, Jupiter
Jealous relied extensively on Bengough's scenery for its appeal.   The manager, however, did not appear in this treatment of the petty jealousies of the Olympic deities which, as
the season's first moderate success, ran for eight consecutive
evenings.

The theatre's first major success of the season premiered on 12 October.   The new piece--the grand opera,
Amilie--was certainly atypical.   Perhaps the manager had
been thinking of producing opera over the summer.   New
additions to the acting company--including three performers
whose experience had been primarily as singers--and the addition of two instruments to the Olympic's orchestra indicate
that Mitchell planned to present musical productions of a
higher level of sophistication than had been the norm at his
theatre.   At any rate, his first endeavor into the field of
legitimate opera since the Wellses starred in La Bayadere in
September of 1841 was immensely successful and attests to
Mitchell's ability not only to evaluate precisely the abilities
of his personnel, but also to estimate correctly the potential
taste of his audience, for grand opera was a radical departure
from the type of entertainment associated with Mitchell's
previously successful repertory.

New York's opera buffs had first seen Rooke's Amilie,
or The Love Test, at Wallack's National Theatre on 15 October 1838.   During that autumn, Wallack had specialized in
the production of opera to the delight of both his audiences
and his treasurer.   Odell notes that of the several operas
Wallack produced that season, Amilie was not only the most
popular but also the great sensation of New York theatre-

goers during the autumn of 1838. [7] The opera was revived a
year later at the beginning of the season that saw the destruc-
tion of the National Theatre by fire. Although it had proven
immensely popular and highly lucrative, it was not to be seen
in New York again until Mitchell's production of it at the
Olympic three years later.

The opera ran for nineteen consecutive performances.
Its popularity was due, in some measure, to the efforts of
the newly strengthened orchestral department and Bengough's
seven new scenes. For the first act, he painted the exterior of the church of the village of Winklern with a distant
view of the mountains on the river Erspach, and an exterior
of the Golden Grapes with distant romantic Alpine scenery.
The second act displayed, in addition to the second scene of
the first act, the vaulted retreat of the hunters. Act three's
scenery consisted of three scenes at the Chateau de Rosen:
the garden, the antechamber, and the grand hall. But Bengough's drops and Loder's orchestra were not the only outstanding components of the production. The Spirit of The
Times expressed surprise at Mitchell's decision to produce
Grand Opera, since the Olympic had become the most successful theatre in New York by operating within a repertory
characterized by short farces, topical burlesques, and musical extravaganzas. Why would Mitchell attempt Grand Opera?
The critic noted that the opera chosen was a favorite among
New York's theatregoers, and that the previously most successful production of it had occurred at the National Theatre.
What the critic fails to note, or to remember, is that Mitchell had stage-managed that production, Bengough had designed it, and over half the members of the Olympic's company had been in it. Small wonder that Mitchell believed he
could produce it successfully at the Olympic, for his personnel comprised most of the people responsible for its success upon the boards of the National Theatre four years
earlier. The manager must have been a bit apprehensive
regarding his first foray into the field of operatic production
for the review notes that Mitchell had "for a long time
been making arrangements to astonish the public by producing
it with all its original beauty and effects. "[8] The Olympic
had been duly noted by the press for the unusual care with
which pieces were rehearsed, and to exceed even his own
rigorous, lengthy, and careful rehearsal schedule suggests
unusual caution on the part of Mitchell. The Olympic's production was unlike previous versions of the opera seen in
New York in one important respect, it had no star. That
liability was, according to The Spirit, converted into an

asset. By relying on the strengths of his company he was
able to offer his patrons a version of the opera which earned
great praise: "We have rarely witnessed a performance that,
taken as a whole, was more pleasing."[9] The reviewer went
on to rave about individual members of the company. Taylor,
Singleton, Mossop, Raymond, and Walcot were commended.
But the greatest praise was reserved for Mrs. Timm.
Sarah Timm, not noted for her trained singing voice, played
Amilie, the title role which had previously been performed
only by traveling stars. The reviewer noted, "Indeed, we
had no idea she could execute the music so well."[10] Mitchell's attention to detail had paid off, for the choruses were
lauded as "full, and perhaps the most effective and faultless
part of the whole performance."[11] No single member of the
company was criticized for ineptitude and the reviewer's
only complaint was "the want of volume of voice in nearly
all the performers."[12] He excused that fault as a result of
opening night jitters, and predicted that once the company
felt comfortable enough to sing the opera with greater confidence, Mitchell would "not have a vacant seat for a month."[13]
The Albion's critic concurred with his colleague from The
Spirit of The Times, and argued that Mrs. Timm was definitely the great attraction of the opera inasmuch as she
"never sang so well or with so much feeling."[14] Reviews
of the opera clearly indicate that one of the primary reasons
for its success was the care with which Mitchell rehearsed an
and directed the production. It truly seemed that no type of
dramatic entertainment was beyond the capabilities of the
Olympic's company or the imagination of its manager.

    After the first few performances, as the actors be-
came more confident in their roles, the opera increased in
popularity. On 28 October, 1842, almost three weeks into
its run, The Albion reported that it was increasing in its
attractiveness.[15] It proved to be such an overwhelming success that for its first ten performances Mitchell broke with
his three-year-old tradition of presenting at least three separate pieces nightly and presented only the opera and an
afterpiece. The vocal strain on the company, who were not
used to the rigors of operatic performance, may, however,
have contributed to the manager's abbreviated bill.

    Once the season's initial hit was established, success
followed success with amazing rapidity, as it had during the
three preceding seasons. On 7 November, Mitchell brought
out two new pieces, both of which proved extremely popular.
A new extravaganza entitled Giovanni in Gotham, possibly

written by Walcot, transferred the Don Juan legend to New
York and made the legendary lover a fashionable gentleman
of the city. New York's audiences were accustomed to seeing dramatic treatments of the Don Juan legend. A pantomime ballet entitled Don Juan, or The Libertine Destroyed,
had proven to be one of Madame Celeste's most durable vehicles
during her starring engagements at the city's various theatres
since 1834. Opera buffs had seen Mozart's Don Giovanni at
both the Park and National theatres, and Mitchell had produced an earlier Don Juan extravaganza on New Year's Day,
1840, entitled Don Giovanni, or The Spectre on Horseback.
But the most popular and durable theatrical treatment of the
Don Juan legend had been Giovanni in London, an imported
extravaganza which had first been seen at the Park Theatre
in 1827. It was among the most frequently produced of all
the extravaganzas from the London stage, and had been seen
annually at one of the city's theatres for fifteen years. It
was this specific text that Walcot burlesqued in his new version of the tale.

        Like Amilie, Giovanni in Gotham had an initial run of
nineteen performances. On the same evening that it first
appeared, Mitchell produced the American premiere of the
new British farce by Charles Selby entitled Boots At The
Swan, a play which was to join the ranks of The Aldgate
Pump and Saratoga Springs as one of the manager's most
popular acting vehicles. Selby's farce had premiered the
preceding July at London's New Strand Theatre. Mitchell's
role, Jacob Earwig, was a deaf Yorkshireman who served
as boot polisher and general factotum at the Swan Hotel.
Henry Higgins, one of the hotel's guests, enlists Earwig as
a complotter in a scheme to attain permission from his
beloved's parents to marry her. The plot almost doesn't
work because Earwig's deafness makes it impossible to understand what Higgins wants him to do, and he almost invariably
does something hilariously wrong. The role provided much
opportunity for Mitchell's considerable low comic abilities.
Although it enjoyed an initial run of only a week, the new
farce was played an additional twenty-six times during the
remainder of the season.

        These three new offerings drew sellout houses nightly.
The Albion, commenting on Mitchell's managerial zeal, noted
that he was "for ever on the advance, for ever seeking, aye
and finding novelty."[16] The same journal marveled at the
range of comic variety to be found at the Olympic when four
pieces returned to the evening bills: "During the last week,

the house has nightly contained a crowd of laughers, who
have been well nigh convulsed over four pieces, all exceedingly
comic, but all of different comic peculiarities. "[17] On 21
November, with the three new pieces still drawing crowded
houses, Mitchell produced yet another American premiere
which was to prove popular with his audiences.   Entitled
John of Paris and written in 1816 by I. Pocock, this short
comic opera provided the manager with a tremendous acting
vehicle in the low comic role of Pederigo Potts.   Reviewing
the play, The Albion commented on Mitchell's style of acting,
which would probably have been called "mugging" by a later
generation of critics: "By-the-bye, Mitchell is a desperate
gag, but he does it so facetiously and so neatly that this very
fault is the principal charm of his comic acting."[18]   Mitchell's
role, which was the prime attraction of the new opera, did
not require singing.   Apparently, the multidimensioned Mr.
Mitchell had no musical ability, for he never sang in any role
he played.[19]

        Because farce and opera were proving great drawing
cards, few new burlesques or extravaganzas were produced
at the Olympic during the fall.   On 30 November, Mitchell
premiered yet another recent British farce, Dion Boucicault's
Curiosities of Literature.   Boucicault's one act had premiered at London's Haymarket Theatre the previous September.   Concerning itself with a young writer who manages to
overcome his competition in the eyes of his beloved's father,
it was successful enough to run uninterruptedly for ten evenings.   The success of Mitchell's farces during that fall can
be largely attributed to their newness: he was producing the
American premieres of more British plays than any other
manager in New York.

        While Mitchell continued to draw large audiences to
the Olympic with a succession of new farces and extravaganzas
produced in the excellent manner that his patrons had come
to expect, New York's other theatres were not faring nearly
as well.   Simpson opened the Park Theatre on 29 August with
a reduction of prices: 75¢ for the Dress Circle; 50¢ for the
second and third circle; 37$\frac{1}{2}$¢ for the pit, and 12$\frac{1}{2}$¢ for the gallery.[20]   The city's oldest playhouse continued to rely on
traveling stars supported by the resident stock company in
front of old and shoddy scenery.   George Vandenhoff, who
made his American debut at the venerable playhouse on 21
September 1842, notes that the theatre was not operating
profitably, and full salaries were seldom paid to the theatre's

personnel.21 Simpson struggled through the fall, but was
forced to close the theatre on 2 January 1843 and did not
reopen until 13 March.

The Bowery, like the Park, continued the policy of
hiring traveling stars and supporting them with a stock company that was mediocre at best. Although Hamblin managed
to keep his doors open throughout the season, Odell suggests
that it was a losing battle: "The prosperity of Hamblin's
season may be gauged by the necessity for absurdly diminished
admission prices."22 The only other consistently operated
theatre in the city during the season of 1842-43 was Thorne's
Chatham, which had adopted admission prices and a repertory
similar to those of Mitchell. But as Odell noted, "Thorne
floundered because--well, because Thorne was no Mitchell."23
The generally bleak state of New York's 1842-43 theatre
season is best summed up in Odell's choice of title for his
consideration of that season in his Annals of The New York
Stage: "Theatre In Misfortune."

While his competition was struggling, Mitchell continued
to prosper. If his patrons had been pleasantly surprised on
the evening of 12 October, the night Amilie was first presented,
they must have been flabbergasted on the evening of 8 December. On that occasion Mitchell broke with all of the previous
tradition he had established at the Olympic by producing a
serious play. The new piece, another American premiere,
was written by Mark Lemmon and entitled Grandfather Whitehead. Lemmon's one act had received its world premiere in
London a mere nine weeks prior to Mitchell's production of
it at the Olympic. Starring the venerable comedian William
Farren, the London production earned the actor critical
acclaim for portraying the pathetically senile title role in
such a fashion that, "The audience sympathized with the assumed character in all his troubles and delights, as their tears
testified."24 A seriously sentimental play written expressly
for a leading London comedian, Grandfather Whitehead provided Mitchell with an opportunity for displaying surprising
acting versatility in the touching title role. His performance
was described as being "beyond all praise,"25 and the play
remained in the Olympic's manager's repertory for about a
year, until Henry Placide made the role his most popular
vehicle.26

Although Mitchell produced no new pieces during November and early December, audiences continued to flock to
the Olympic. It seemed as if the manager was consciously

refraining from producing new works until the ones in the
repertory exhausted their drawing power. This notion is
substantiated by The Spirit of The Times, which observed
that the Olympic had become so eminent among New York's
theatres that Mitchell was no longer forced to present a constant rapid succession of novelties in order to draw large
audiences.[27]

        During the first two weeks of December the Olympic
continued to be crowded and Mitchell produced no new plays.
But on 19 December, Sleeping Beauty, a new extravaganza
featuring Bengough's scenery was given its first performance.
It, however, proved extremely unsuccessful and was withdrawn
after only three performances. The same date saw the premiere of a new Irish vehicle for Nickinson, Tyrone Power's
Paddy O'Rafferty, which was repeated frequently throughout
the season. The city's theatregoers were experiencing a
resurgence of interest in Irish characters spurred by John
Brougham's performances at several of New York's theatres
during the autumn of 1842. Mitchell, through Nickinson's
ability at that line of business, was attempting to capitalize
on that newly reawakened interest.

        While farce and opera had been replacing burlesque
and extravaganza as the Olympic's staples, Walcot had been
steadily rising in the estimation of the audience. On 26
December Mitchell produced the first play in which this
relatively inexperienced actor played the leading role. Planché's
Captain of The Watch, like most of Mitchell's new plays that
season, received its American premiere on the Olympic's
stage. This particular offering from the pen of Planché is
slightly unusual as one of Mitchell's productions. Originally
written for Vestris' and Mathews' Covent Garden company
in the fall of 1841, it is a two-act comedy of manners rather
than a one-act farce. Set in the Restoration England of
of Charles II, the action involves a romantic plot in which
the Captain of the Watch, Walcot's role, is smuggled into
a cloistered garden by a maid so that he can woo the object
of his affection. Containing no low comic characters and a
great deal of witty and sophisticated reparteé, the play provided Walcot the opportunity to demonstrate that he could play
Charles James Mathews roles very nicely. The play rapidly
became a popular vehicle for Walcot, who was to have a
long and distinguished career in New York.

        One of the reasons that Mitchell had not produced
many new pieces during the month of December was that he

was busily preparing another opera for production during the
holidays. On 29 December his playbills announced to the
Olympic's patrons:

> In consequence of the triumphant success which
> attended the production of Amilie and the very flat-
> tering approbation bestowed on it the manager is
> induced to produce Auber's splendid opera called
> Fra Diavolo which will shortly be presented for the
> first time in this theatre... Mr. Mitchell and every
> member of the company will appear.28

Auber's Fra Diavolo had received its New York premiere at the Park Theatre in 1831 and rapidly became a favorite among the city's opera afficionados. Produced annually
in at least one of New York's theatres from 1831 through 1839,
its most noteworthy production occurred at Wallack's National
Theatre in February of 1839, where Mitchell was stage-
managing and many of the Olympic's company were performing.

Mitchell fulfilled his announced intention to produce
Fra Diavolo on 4 January. The opera was produced uncut,
with all of the original music. The robber hero, Fra Diavolo,
was played by Mrs. Timm, who had the best singing voice of
all the Olympic's actresses and a range close to the tenor
requirements of the role. Lord Allcash was sustained by
Walcot, and Mitchell played a nonsinging role, Beppo, who
was something of an heroic brigand. Like Amilie before it,
Fra Diavolo initially ran with only an afterpiece. But after
six performances, a second farce was added to the evening's
bill. The opera enjoyed sixteen consecutive performances,
and seems to have been only slightly less popular than Amilie
had been. The Albion, in its initial review of the production,
commented on Mitchell's apparent ability to produce any type
of dramatic entertainment successfully. Noting that "some-
how, he continues to succeed in all he undertakes,"29 the
reviewer marveled at Mitchell's ingeniousness in casting the
opera: "Only think of his assigning the part of Fra Diavolo
to Mrs. Timm, and taking that of Beppo himself! Not in
burlesque either, but in 'right earnest.' Well, the audiences
are delighted, and his house is crowded--but this last of
course."30 The reviewer suggests that only Mitchell could
successfully escape failure with casting described as "operatic
perversions."31 The critic does not explain what he means
by the term "perversions," but it must have been Mitchell's
casting of Mrs. Timm as the robber-hero. His reliance on
the stock company to the exclusion of traveling stars may

have been thought of as additionally perverse in the sense
that it contradicted all previous operatic tradition in the growing city of New York.   That the term is more an assessment
of an untraditional solution to operatic production problems than
a pejorative assessment of quality becomes clear in a second
review of Fra Diavolo in the same journal three weeks later.
The reviewer, presumably the same one who had written
the initial notice of Mitchell's opera, explains in some detail
how Mitchell solved the problem of casting the opera within
the limited musical means of his stock company.   Noting that
it was a bold attempt to try the opera "with resources so
apparently limited as those of the Olympic,"32 the critic
praises Mitchell for his casting and directorial ingenuity.
In the opera, Beppo, the character Mitchell played, is the
only bass and the character has little function or interest
save for his musical contribution to the opera.   Mitchell
was no singer and gave the bass part to the character Gia-
como.   According to The Albion's critic, "to compensate he
turns the mere ruffian brigand into a sort of hero; and, in
the closing scene, he invests the character of Beppo with an
interest and dignity which are quite touching."33   The reviewer
marveled at what he described as Mitchell's "tact" in making
these alterations in the text, and goes on to praise the recently recruited Walcot as Lord Allcash, noting, "he acts it
infinitely better than any artist in this country."34

By changing the singing parts assigned to characters
in the opera, Mitchell was making directorial decisions which
had no precedent in New York and could be easily described
as "perversions."   It is really not surprising that he would
convert Beppo into a touching and sympathetic nonsinging role
when one considers his inability to sing and his recent success as the sentimental and touching Grandfather Whitehead.
His approach to the production of Fra Diavolo amply demonstrates an ability to make textual alterations designed to
maximize the effectiveness of the Olympic's stock company
at a time when such creative direction was unusual, especially
in the field of opera production.

Fra Diavolo served as Mitchell's prime attraction
through most of January and finally relinquished its place
in the bills to a new piece, Beauty and The Beast, on the
twenty-eighth.   This musical burlesque of the melodrama
Selima and Azor featured new scenery by Bengough and
played on fourteen consecutive occasions.   With its production,
Mitchell could boast of two big hits, back to back, within a
month.   In its review of Beauty and The Beast, The Spirit

of The Times lavished praise on the stage arrangements and
Bengough's scenery: "It is produced in better style than we
ever recollect having seen at this house before, famous as
Mitchell always is in giving his pieces the aid of proper
scenery and decorations."35 But the same review implies
that the month between the opening of Fra Diavolo and the
premiere of Beauty and The Beast may not have provided
the company with sufficient time to rehearse the new piece:
"With the improvement which is nightly visible in the general
performance, we predict a long and successful run of 'Beauty
and The Beast.'"36 Although the new musical may have
been underrehearsed when it opened, it captured the public's
fancy. The Albion, noting the success of the new musical,
marveled at Mitchell's apparently infallible ability to produce one hit after another: "Hardly has be spread wide the
fame of one favorite before he brings out another, and each
challenging the precedence over its predecessor."37

        During the run of Beauty and The Beast Mitchell pro-
duced two additional English farces which had not been seen
in this country. 2 February 1843 marked the premiere of
George Godwin's The Last Day, featuring Everard and Walcot.
Six days later Mitchell starred in another new piece written
by T. J. Dibkin and entitled The Auctioneer. Neither of
these farces proved remunerative. The Last Day lasted for
only three days and The Auctioneer went off the block after
only five evenings.

        From 8 February through 1 March, Mitchell was un-
able to find a new hit. Three consecutive performances was
the best that any of his new offerings--W. B. Bernard's
Woman Hater, R. N. Peake's £ 100 Note, and the anonymous
Mr. Liston--achieved during that three-week period. Nevertheless, his audiences continued to be large. In reviewing
business at the Olympic during the first week of March,
The Albion succinctly stated the shortcomings of the recently
produced Bluebeard: "...there was not sufficient depth of
humor in it to sustain it during the usually long run of performances for which the greater number of pieces produced
at this house are so remarkable."38 The same notice complained that Sarah Timm had become sloppy in her work to
the point that she was, "in danger of injuring her professional
reputation."39 In a correctively critical vein the reviewer
noted: "She bawls rather than speaks, and it is really quite
necessary that she put herself under greater restraint in her
comedy. Mrs. Timm has been a very substantial support to
this house, and we trust that she will take in good part a

"Mrs. Timm in Beauty and The Beast." The Harvard Theatre
Collection.

hint which is in accordance with widely expressed opinion."[40]
Perhaps the rapidity with which new pieces were being rehearsed and produced during the spring of 1843 made it impossible for Mrs. Timm to be as careful as she had previously been, or perhaps she felt that Mitchell's ability
to bring out a seemingly endless succession of hits insured
that she would be well accepted by the theatre's patrons regardless of the fine points of her performances. In either
event, she must have taken the criticism seriously, for no
member of New York's reviewing corps saw fit to mention
the problem again.

    March at the Olympic began with a ten-day run of a
new piece entitled Anthony and Cleopatra. It was a curtailed
travesty of Shakespeare's play featuring Walcot and Mrs.
Timm in the title roles. Another moderate success of early
March was Planché's The White Cat, which opened on the
ninth and also ran for ten nights. The Albion's review described it as a good production of a rather bad play: "This
thing, like all of its class, is supremely ridiculous, and the
characters of all description are in caricature; but the parts
are well-fitted, the groups are ably managed, the rehearsals
have rendered the action perfect, the scenes and the magic
changes are prompt and fanciful, the music is good, and the
general effect delightful."[41] The notice attests to Mitchell's
ability to make something out of nothing, or at least, very
little.

    The remainder of March was characterized by a fre-
quent repetition of the season's successful pieces. Only one
additional long-running hit appeared during the waning weeks
of the manager's fourth campaign.

    Through the middle of April, topical burlesque at the
Olympic was conspicuous by its absence. There had been no
burlesques of other productions, actors, or social and political events. But the winter of 1842-43 did not provide any
material suitable for one of Mitchell's timely topical lampoons.
Nothing of interest transpired at the city's other theatres, and
New York was without incident or personality suitable for
ridicule by Mitchell's Aristophanic sense of humor. The
manager, however, was not to be thwarted in his penchant
for burlesque. He rose to the occasion and prepared a burlesque of the most successful theatrical event seen anywhere
in New York during the season: his own production of Amilie.

    In order to refresh his patron's memories on the object

of his new burlesque, he produced the opera it was to ridicule on the night before the debut of the new piece. Thus, Amilie played on 12 April, and the new burlesque, Amy-Lee, opened on 13 April.

The new lampoon marked the playwriting debut of the Olympic's prompter, Ben Baker, who was to contribute several successful farces and burlesques to the theatre's repertory during the next several years. In the burlesque, each member of the company played a role analagous to the one he or she had performed in the opera. This provided the greatest imaginable opportunity for self-indulgent self-parody on the part of a company of actors. Amy-Lee was even more successful than its object had been, and was played on twenty-two consecutive evenings to sellout houses. The format of the piece and the songs contained in it were quite similar to the productions of "the later house of Harrigan and Hart."42

Amy-Lee ran until 8 May. During the last two weeks of the season, Mitchell rotated the most successful pieces from the season's repertory and closed his fourth campaign at the Olympic on 23 May 1843.

This fourth season differed significantly from its predecessors. Except for Mitchell's exercise in self-parody, there were no specific burlesques produced. Early in the season the manager had astonished his patrons by successfully producing a grand opera. Only slightly later they were again amazed to see Mitchell, the low comedian nonpareil, portray the moving title role in Grandfather Whitehead. It truly seemed that there were few types of entertainment beyond the ability of the Olympic's company. While the season may have been less exciting than some of its predecessors, frequent mention of overflowing houses attests to its success. According to Odell, 1842-43 was the low point of the theatrical depression brought on by the specie panic of 1837, and Mitchell was the only theatrical manager in New York City to earn a profit during that year.43

Part of the season's success can be attributed to Mitchell's newfound ability to produce recent British plays in advance of his competitors. At least six extremely popular London farces received their American premieres at the Olympic during the season, and each of them proved at least moderately successful.

It is also apparent that the acting company substantially

improved during the season.   While Mitchell lost the estimable
services of Horncastle, the addition of Taylor, Clarke, and
especially Walcot--all of whom were virtually unknown before
joining the company--proved valuable indeed. Each of these
three performers established enviable reputations during their
first season with Mitchell. Walcot rapidly rose in popular
esteem and rivaled Nickinson as the Olympic's most popular
actor--other than the manager of course. The orchestra, too,
improved significantly with the addition of two members. But
most of all, the fourth season clearly indicates Mitchell's
continuing ability to maximize the effectiveness of both his
company and his physical facilities.

       The Olympic had been consistently praised for the high
quality of both its scenery and its stage appointments since
Mitchell had assumed management of the little theatre in
December of 1839. But frequent notices in the press, particularly during December and January of the season currently
being considered, suggest that he had achieved an even higher
degree of excellence. Moreover, his managerial ingenuity in
casting the operas that he produced during the season and
altering the texts and singing requirements in such a fashion
that the operas' requirements were reduced to the range of
abilities of his stock company was a radical departure from
previous operatic production tradition in the city of New York.
His sound artistic control began to manifest itself in unusual
ways during this season and catapulted the Olympic to an undisputed position as the most successful theatre in the city of
New York.

       While the Olympic was closed for the summer, Mitchell
busily contracted personnel for the next season. Mrs. J. B.
Booth, Jr. was hired to fill the vacancy left by Lydia Singleton,
who had retired from the company to become a bride the preceding April.   Three new inexperienced performers were also
added: Andrew Isaacs, Aaron Lever, and Mrs. Stafford.
An additional new member of the company was George Holland.
He is unusual as one of Mitchell's recruits in so far as he
had been a traveling star and possessed a reputation as one
of the finest low comedians in America.

       Holland had been acting professionally since 1817, and
knew Mitchell from their time together in DeCamp's company
in Sheffield in 1822. Like many other British actors of the
period, Holland had come to America on a starring tour and
decided to remain here. Arriving in New York in 1827, he
played first at the Bowery Theatre, and later in other cities

on the Eastern Seaboard. During 1833 and 1834 he toured
the frontier theatres of the lower Mississippi Valley with
Sol Smith. Subsequently settling in New Orleans in 1836, he
went to work for James Caldwell as secretary-treasurer of
both Caldwell's St. Charles Theatre and the manager's New
Orleans' Gas Works. He remained in the Crescent City as
Caldwell's principal low comedian, stage manager, and book-
keeper until the first St. Charles burned down in March of
1842.

A ventriloquist of extraordinary ability, Holland was a
tremendously popular low comedian, even though he "lost sight
of the artist in being the funnyman, and for the sake of being
funny was needlessly comic."44 Throughout his professional
life, Holland tended to sacrifice consistency of character and
appropriate humor for the cheap laugh and surefire sight gag.

Holland's continuous career in New York, which began
with his association with Mitchell, extended to 1870 and included employment with William E. Burton, J. W. and Lester
Wallack, and Augustin Daly. Through a strange quirk of
history, the eccentric comedian is better remembered for the
circumstances surrounding his funeral than for his forty-three
year American career which stretched from the frontier theatres of the lower Mississippi Valley to Daly's post-Civil War
stock company.

A respected Anglican clergyman refused to conduct
Holland's obsequies from his church because of the deceased's
immoral profession. The clergyman's decision had two important effects: it outraged a large portion of the public;
and it led to Holland's funeral services being conducted at a
"little church arround the corner," which has been the actors'
church in New York since that time.

It seems surprising that Holland, a star of significant
magnitude, would join Mitchell's stock corps unless one remembers that the general economic depression that had
ravaged the country since 1837 made acting a more than
usually tenuous profession. Holland was engaged by Mitchell
for eight weeks, beginning with the opening of the 1843 sea-
son.45 For the next five years this two-month contract was
renewed every time it lapsed.46 With the acquisition of
Holland, Mitchell could legitimately claim two of the country's
finest low comedians as members of his company. Only two
other actors, Sol Smith and William E. Burton, could possibly
be considered equal to Mitchell and Holland as low comedians.

In spite of the good fortune which brought Holland to the
Olympic, however, the company was weakened by the absence
of Mrs. Timm, who was ill and unable to return to the company until well into November.

The fifth season opened on 14 September 1843, with
Le Savoyard and two of Holland's vehicles, Bill of Fare and
Day After The Fair. Of the two pieces, A Day After The
Fair was Holland's comedic tour de force. In it, he portrayed
Jerry, a servant who is sent by his master to buy a country
cottage. He stops along the way at a country fair and when
he arrives to make the purchase for his master, the real
estate has already been sold. He and his betrothed, the maid-
servant Polly, get the new owner to relinquish his claim on
the property by impersonating several different characters who
supposedly haunt the neighborhood. Holland, as Jerry, por-
trays: Sam Wax, a drunken cobbler; Susan Squall, an itinerant
ballad singer; Timothy Thumpwell, a deranged military drum-
mer; Mademoiselle Dumpling, a French songstress, three-
and-a-half feet high; and Octavius Moonshine, a lunatic es-
caped from a supposed nearby mental asylum. His persona-
tions shatter the new owner's nerves, and he is able to obtain the cottage at a bargain price.

With Holland to attract audiences, Mitchell was able
to appear on the stage less frequently and devote more time
to managerial duties. In fact, during the second week of
the season, Holland's established vehicles plus a new extravaganza by H. R. Gratten entitled Diana's Revenge--which
ran for eleven nights beginning 13 September--proved so
popular that the manager did not appear at all for two weeks.

Mitchell had no trouble finding a "novelty" early in
the season and was not forced to rely on revivals from the
past seasons as he had done during the opening weeks of his
previous campaigns. The Spirit of The Times noted, two
weeks into the season, that it had not taken Mitchell long
to produce a hit.[47]

While Diana's Revenge, a revival of Amy-Lee, and
several new farces drew crowded houses during the last two
weeks of September, New York theatregoers were becoming
excited about the impending arrival of England's greatest
living tragedian, William Charles Macready.

Macready had not appeared in this country for seventeen years prior to his tour of 1843-44, and the Americans

were anxiously anticipating his return. An event of such
public interest as Macready's tour provided Mitchell with a
grand opportunity to display his talent for burlesque. In
order to understand the full scope of Mitchell's burlesque of
Macready, it is necessary to be familiar with some of the
eminent tragedian's not-so-pleasing personality traits and
professional quirks.

Macready was not a very pleasant individual. He
disliked actors and was ruthless to those poor unfortunates
who played support for him during his starring tours. Moreover, he had as little respect for the intelligence and taste
of most of his audience as he had for the ability and competence of his supporting actors. He was an aristocrat by in-
clination, although not by birth, and had consciously cultivated
the friendship of such men as Charles Dickens in England. A
mean and taciturn individual, he was also something of a par-
anoiac and showed an inordinate amount of concern for the way
in which the critics reviewed his performances in the cities
he visited on his American tours.

Although he was acknowledged as England's finest
tragedian, many idiosyncracies of his acting style lent themselves to burlesque. He was a stiff intellectual actor, not
at all given to the impassioned moments which had characterized the work of the elder Kean. In an attempt to convey to
his audience a sense that he was actually thinking of what
to say next while in character, he developed a famous pause
between the lines of certain speeches which even his ardent
supporters admitted was a bit long. He was, in short, an
ideal object for burlesque. Furthermore, a hot temper,
which assured that he would be absolutely furious at any
burlesque of him, added to the fun that such a burlesque
would produce.

Macready opened his engagement in New York at the
Park Theatre on 25 September 1843. Remaining there until
11 October, he played his usual round of characters which
included Macbeth, Hamlet, Richelieu, and Virginius. His
performances at the Park were immensely successful, and
the reviews were very flattering.

While Macready was pleasing audiences at the Park,
Mitchell was preparing a new Shakespearean travesty with
the eminent tragedian in mind. Macbeth was custom tailored
for Mitchell by William Knight Northall, a quick-witted New
York dentist who was one of Mitchell's regular patrons.

Since the travesty focused on specific objects of ridicule,
Mitchell took the occasion of its opening, 16 October, to
lampoon Charles Kean's scholarly programs in the Olympic's
playbills which discussed the origin of the Macbeth story and
contained some biographical information on Shakespeare. A
playbill from the Bowery was dutifully cited as Mitchell's
authority for his information.

Although Kean was ridiculed in the playbill, Macready
was Mitchell's prime target in the production. He mimicked
the excesses of the tragedian's style in his own acting, while
the play itself invested Macbeth with some of Macready's
less desirable personality traits. The tragedian's paranoia
about unfavorable press notices is reflected in the character
of the worthy thane who is not remorseful about having
killed Duncan; his only concern is what the press will think
of him. Macbeth, soliloquizing after having murdered the
king, laments: "If the same knife which cuts poor Duncan's
life supported could only cut the throats of common news reporters and thus make dumb the press--its pretty clear this
cut would be the be-all and end-all here."[48]

Macready's acting style was also lampooned in the text
of the play. One of Macbeth's speeches calls for a pause in
the middle of a line during which the entire company sings a
song before the line is finished. This exaggeration of the
famous "Macready pause" no doubt convulsed those members
of the audience familiar with the tragedian's style of acting.
Macready's dislike for his starring competitors was also
lampooned in the text, for the line of Banquo's issue destined
to replace Macbeth as king includes the ballerina, Fanny
Elssler and a "Yankee" actor.

The production was extremely popular, running for
fourteen consecutive evenings before being withdrawn. Although the several barbs at Macready contained in the text
were sharp, it was Mitchell's burlesque of the tragedian's
acting which provided the prime source of amusement. Even
the playwright found this to be the case: "This success was
undoubtedly owing in a great measure to the inimitable acting
of Mr. Mitchell, who performed Macbeth in his own peculiar
style--half tragic, half comic, half Macready and half funny
Mitchell."[49] The press was much impressed with Mitchell's
new travesty. The Spirit of The Times informed its readers:
"We know half a dozen clever people who think it the best
thing ever got up at the Olympic."[50] A strong statement,
considering the accolades earned by many of Mitchell's earlier
novelties.

"William Knight Northall."   The Harvard Theatre Collection.

Holland's popularity, coupled with the success of both Diana's Revenge and The Macbeth Travesty enabled Mitchell to enjoy the strongest September and October he had experienced since assuming management of the Olympic. In previous seasons, he had groped his way to a long-running hit during September and October while relying on revivals of popular pieces from the theatre's ever increasing repertory to draw profitable audiences. But Holland, Diana's Revenge, and The Macbeth Travesty captured the public's fancy from the outset of Mitchell's current campaign. On 28 October, The Spirit of The Times confirmed the management's good fortune by reporting to its readers, "...the receipts of the house have never been, at this season of the year, so great."51

The Olympic's burlesque of Macready's engagement at the Park extended beyond the production of the Macbeth Travesty. While the British tragedian was playing his usual Shakespearean characters, Mitchell took the opportunity to play his "usual Shakespearean characters" and burlesqued the entire touring tragedian tradition in the process. The Olympic's playbill for 20 October proudly announced:

> Mr. Mitchell has much pleasure in announcing to the public that he has, at enormous expense, effected an engagement with himself for a few nights, during which he will appear in a series of Shakespearean characters in the true tragico-comico--illegitimate style. During this engagement he trusts he shall be able to induce himself to appear as Hamlet, Richard #3, and Macbeth. N. B. No sudden indisposition (usual in star engagements) will take place on account of wet weather or any other accidental circumstances. Postscript: In order to prevent too great a depression of spirits of that portion of the sympathetic public, who witness the heart-rending pathos of these thrilling performances, Mr. Holland has in the most liberal manner, consented to be funny every evening 'till further notice.52

The "Shakespearean characters" and the new strength of the company, vested primarily in the person of Holland, were making the Olympic even more popular than it had been. Early in November The Albion saw fit to comment at some length on the uniqueness and good taste of Mitchell's entertainments and praised him as the best manager in the city. Noting the Olympic's phenomenal success at a time when

New York's other playhouses were either changing managements
with dazzling rapidity or closing for extended periods of time,
The Albion's columnist sought to explain the little theatre's
extensive and unique popularity. Describing Mitchell as
"the very paragon of managers, "53   the thought-provoking
commentator notes that many people lamented that the Olympic's repertory consisted of burlesque, short farce, musical
extravaganza, and an occasional opera to the total exclusion
of full-length plays from the established legitimate repertory.
But the reporter shrugged off this complaint from the more
refined segment of New York's theatregoers by noting that
Mitchell was in business and could hardly be faulted for producing the minor forms when he discovered, early in his
management, how lucrative they could be.

        Yet other managements specializing in repertories
similar to Mitchell's had failed. How had he become the
first manager in New York specializing almost exclusively in
short, light entertainments to succeed? The reporter cited
two factors: Mitchell's "scrupulous attention"54 to scenery,
costume, and the other visual details of production; and the
starless stock company which was "fused and amalgamated
by the tact of the master hand. "55 By implication, New
York's other theatres were less successful because they still
relied on traveling stars, frequently shoddy stage appointments,
or both. Mitchell's consistent ability to provide his patrons
with well-produced, well-acted light entertainments had, according to The Albion's columnist, resulted in a theatre in
which "all works pit-pat and harmoniously, "56 while "all
around him has been prostrated by hard times, and the growing
distaste for theatrical amusements. "57

        The Albion's overview, in speaking of the "master
hand" which controlled every element of production and welded
the various members of the company into an acting ensemble,
amplifies the idea suggested by Mitchell's changes of the text
of Fra Diavolo: he was able to be extremely successful at
a time when his competitors were not, by functioning in a
manner strongly analagous to that of the directors who emerged
during the last third of the nineteenth century.

        During the month of November, the Olympic continued
to draw crowded houses. The Albion complimented Mitchell
on the eleventh of that month for the manner in which he and
Holland, as resident stars, shone "harmoniously in the same
horizon. "58 There was no apparent rivalry between the two
comedians and they worked well together, even when appearing
in the same play.

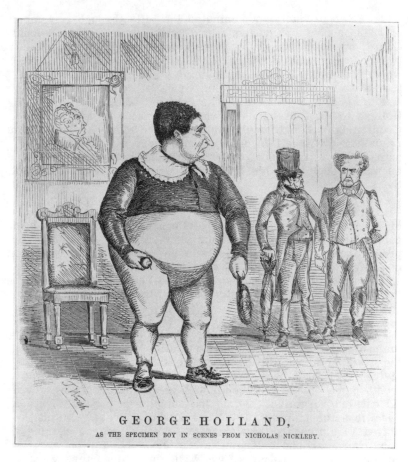

GEORGE HOLLAND,
AS THE SPECIMEN BOY IN SCENES FROM NICHOLAS NICKLEBY.

"George Holland as the Specimen Boy in The Savage and The
Maiden." The Harvard Theatre Collection.

Two productions dominated the bills through November of 1843, a new extravaganza by Planché entitled The National Guard, which played eight times between the thirteenth and the twenty-fourth, and a revival of The Savage and The Maiden, which featured Mitchell as Crummles and Holland as Folair, the Savage. It was played nine times between the eighteenth and the end of the month. The revival, adding the antics of Holland to the long-heralded characterization of Mitchell as Crummles, was extremely popular. The Spirit of The Times reported: "Mitchell is clearing all before him, by some extraordinary powers of compression, he gets three times as many people into his theatre as would fill any other double the size."59

On 27 November Mitchell produced another example of the much-lauded scenic art of Bengough, who had not been contributing as much spectacular new scenery to the Olympic's productions as he had in past seasons. The new presentation consisted of two tableaux vivants from Weir's painting of the embarcation of the pilgrims which had recently been completed for the rotunda of the Capitol building in Washington. This new spectacle proved extremely attractive.

Because of the popularity of Mitchell and Holland in their established vehicles, remunerative audiences attended the Olympic during the first two weeks of December in spite of the absence of new plays. The first new offering of the month came on the fourteenth with another travesty by North-all entitled Virginius. Again the script was prepared with a specific actor in mind, this time Edwin Forrest. Mitchell played Virginius, "a gentleman of Roman firmness bearing a hard character and belonging to the do-nothin-for-one's-country school of patriots."60 Virginius' supporters were "b'hoys" as were Forrest's greatest fans, and each was attached to a volunteer fire company of Rome, just as the actual "b'hoys" were invariably members of one of the volunteer fire companies in New York. Perhaps because the lower-class audience in the Olympic's pit did not care to see their favorite tragedian burlesqued, even by Mitchell, Virginius was not nearly as successful as Macbeth had been. In any event, Mitchell's diminutive height, rotundness, and not-very-strong voice no doubt militated against an effective mimicry of Forrest's robust acting style. The play managed to run for only eight performances and was dropped from the bills on the twenty-second.

That Mitchell was having his most successful fall, even

though he had produced only two new pieces which achieved
anything like a long run, was attested to by his announcement
of the Olympic's first Christmas matinee. The Olympic's
playbill for 23 December 1843 states that the afternoon performance was to be presented, "In compliance with the wishes
of numerous respectable families and in order to accomodate [sic]
many hundreds of persons who would otherwise be unable to
obtain seats owing to the overwhelming rush which invariably
takes place on holiday nights."61

      The Olympic's company played two separate programs
on Christmas: one in the afternoon; and one in the evening.
The only play which was performed in both bills was a new
burlesque, Robinson Crusoe, which premiered on that day.
New York's theatregoers were familiar with the Robinson
Crusoe story in a wide range of native and imported extra-
vaganzas, but the most popular version was no doubt the
Bowery Theatre's melodrama, which served as a vehicle for
the melodramatic touring star J. Hudson Kirby. It was
Kirby's vehicle that seems to have been the object for the
Olympic's holiday burlesque. The afternoon audiences saw,
in addition to the new piece, The Festival of Apollo and
Bathing, while Billy Lackaday and Diana's Revenge filled out
the evening's entertainment. Through the holidays, Robinson
Crusoe served as the theatre's prime attraction while Mitchell
prepared another of Northall's burlesques for production.

      On 8 January 1844, Northall's new play, Old King Cole;
or, Foreign Fiddlers, was performed for the first time. In
it, a contest is held between several immigrant violinists all
anxious to win the prize: the hand of the princess. This
burlesque had as its object the mania for concert violinists
which had been sweeping the country since the fall, the
greatest cause of which had been the tour of the celebrated
Norwegian virtuoso, Ole Bull. Bull had made his American
debut at the Park Theatre on 25 November 1843. Immensely
and immediately successful, he played to capacity crowds
wherever he appeared. As Odell notes, "There can be no
doubt that Ole Bull created a veritable sensation, not only
in New York, but throughout the land. Dramatic stars suffered severely in competition."62 Theatre managers attempted
to cash in on the sensation Bull caused by engaging other
well-known concert violinists. Among the most prominent
was Henry Vieuxtemps. Although his tour was lucrative, it
was not nearly as successful as Bull's.

      Although the new burlesque ran for only a week, it is

symptomatic of Mitchell's ability to seize the topical as a
subject of ridicule. The Albion noted this proclivity in its
review of 13 January: "Mitchell always seizes the prevailing
excitement as a means to fill his treasury--and it was not to
be supposed that the late fiddling mania would escape his keen
eye for the ridiculous."[63] The remainder of January and the
first two weeks of February at the Olympic featured revivals
of popular farces starring Mitchell and Holland. One
new piece, however, did prove attractive. This was
the American premiere of Henry Mayhew's The Wandering Minstrel, an English farce in which Mitchell played
Jem Bags, a role which was to become one of his most popular vehicles throughout the remainder of his acting career.
The new play opened on 22 January and ran for only five
nights before being withdrawn, but it was to prove extremely
popular when revived during later seasons.

     Although Mitchell played a great number of roles in
farces, extravaganzas, and burlesques throughout January,
there was not very much differentiation between his many
characters. The Albion preferred him in such serious roles
as Grandfather Whitehead over his farce and travesty characters, "which have no distinctive marks of difference, save
costume and language. They are all simply Mr. Mitchell
endeavouring to be funny."[64] Mitchell apparently excelled
as a comic impersonator. In those topical burlesques in
which he drew a model from life--Macready, Elssler, Sheriff
--he developed interesting and hilarious individual characters.
But the rest of the time he seems to have been satisfied to
rely on his charm, sense of timing, and ability to mug.
Given a choice between a consistent character and a certain,
if cheap, laugh, Mitchell seems to have consistently opted for
the latter.

     The manager was not the only member of the company
criticized for this proclivity during the winter of 1844.
Other actors were following the manager's lead to such a
degree that The Albion chastised the entire company for the
very broad style of acting which they had adopted: "We would
in all friendship suggest that when a legitimate Farce, Opera,
or Drama, is presented it may be divested of the burlesque
style prevalent here."[65] While the cheap shots taken by the
members of the company may have produced raucous guffaws
among the "b'hoys" in the pit, The Albion indicates that it
was not appreciated by Mitchell's more sophisticated patrons
in the private boxes and dress circle.[66]

"O come out o'the cart! d'ye think I don't know the valley *o'peace
and quietness? I never moves on under Sixpence."*

"William Mitchell as Jem Bags in The Wandering Minstrel."
The Harvard Theatre Collection.

Mitchell's theatre continued to be crowded through the last three weeks of January, even though no new pieces were produced. It seemed that people flocked to the Olympic regardless of what was playing. The Albion reported, "Mitchell seems to think that while the public will crowd nightly to see their old favorites, it would be a wasteful expenditure to treat them to novelties."[67]

It was not until late in February that Mitchell produced a new example of the kind of spectacle for which his theatre had become famous. The new offering, which opened on the nineteenth, was Rossini's opera Cinderella, featuring Mary Taylor as Cinderella and Constantia Clarke as the Fairy Queen. Rossini's opera had received its American premiere at the Park Theatre in 1834. New York's opera buffs saw it again at the venerable playhouse in 1837, 1838, and 1839, but the most noteworthy prior production of the opera, like all of the other operas Mitchell had produced, occurred at Wallack's National Theatre. Wallack's version, which had been produced in March of 1839, proved to be among the most popular attractions of the National's spring season that year. Bengough, who had not painted as much new scenery as he had during preceding seasons, contributed significantly to the success of the opera with eleven new drops. Act One's three scenes consisted of a fairy haunt and magic fountain; a gothic chamber in the baron's castle; and an eastern landscape. Act Two opened with a chamber of the prince's palace which was followed by an exterior of the same palace. The six scenes of Act Three represented: a ballroom in the palace; a landscape adjacent to the palace; a kitchen in the baron's castle; an apartment in the castle; a hall in the prince's palace; and, a magnificent salon in the prince's palace.

During the first three nights of the opera's run the house was so crowded that Mitchell suspended the free list for the first time that season. The new piece ran for seventeen nights and could have enjoyed a longer run, but it taxed the vocal strengths of the company, who were not used to the rigors of operatic production, and was withdrawn "in consequence of the great fatigue attending...[its] frequent performance."[68] The house was literally crammed to capacity during the entire run of the opera which was enthusiastically received as the best piece of its kind that Mitchell had ever produced. The Albion reported that it had "drawn together crowded houses, composed of the fashion and taste of the city."[69]

During the course of the season, a phenomenon of
interest to the Olympic's audiences occurred. While The
Albion had noted back in November that Holland and Mitchell
played to each other well and without any conscious sign of
rivalry for supremacy in the eyes of the audiences, two female members of the company had taken a slightly different
tack. Mary Taylor had slowly but surely risen in the esteem
of the theatre's regular patrons and would have posed a very
real threat to Mrs. Timm, who for three years had reigned
as undisputed queen of the Olympic, had the actresses not
consciously appealed to different segments of the audience.
This construction of rival followings among the theatre's
patrons intensified throughout the season to the point that one
of the city's periodicals commented on it late in March in an
article which provides much information about the acting
styles of the two women. The Brother Jonathan reported:
"If Timm wins the heart of the pittites, Taylor has the white
gloves and boxes in her favor. Timm may have the largest
bouquets, but Taylor has the choicest, Timm draws out the
hi-his of the ground floor by a familiar glance or a well-
timed wink; Taylor captivates the aristocrats of the dress-
circle by the tenderest side-long looks. "70 Timm's broad
familiar style made her the favorite of the "b'hoys" in the
netherworld, while Taylor's more refined and restrained
manner of acting pleased Mitchell's patrician patrons in the
dress cricle and private boxes.

At about the same time the previously quoted article
appeared, Mitchell began the annual benefit nights for the
members of his company. This period usually extended for
about a month, during which three of the six nights each
week on which the theatre was open were devoted to benefits.
On 5 April, a most unusual bill of fare was presented to the
Olympic's patrons for the benefit of Mrs. J. B. Booth, Jr.
On that evening, J. B. Booth, Sr., the only tragedian ever
to play at the Olympic during Mitchell's tenure as manager,
acted Richard II for his daughter-in-law's benefit. She was
also aided by her brother, Ben DeBar, who appeared in his
best-known character, the Artful Dodger, from an adaptation
of Oliver Twist. Mitchell and DeBar had both been fined as
members of London's Strand company for violating that theatre's
limited license in 1834.71 He had also worked with the Olympic's manager at Wallack's National Theatre during the season of 1837-38. Known primarily in New Orleans, where he
had performed a wide variety of comic characters for both
Caldwell and the team of Ludlow and Smith, DeBar was later
to become famous as a manager in both New Orleans and St.
Louis.

During late March and early April, Mitchell offered
his patrons revivals of popular farces and burlesques from
past seasons while preparing a new opera for production,
Mozart's The Marriage of Figaro. An English version of
Mozart's opera had been a staple of New York's operatic
repertory since its premiere at the Park Theatre on 10 May
1824. Appearing during virtually every season between its
American debut and 1839, the opera's most noteworthy production occurred in March of 1839 at Wallack's National Theatre
with Mitchell as stage manager and Bengough as scenic artist. Wallack's celebrated production of the opera was the
last that New York's opera buffs were to see until Mitchell's
revival of it. Opening on 8 April, the opera featured Nickinson as Almaviva, Walcot as Figaro, Holland as Antonio, Mrs.
Timm as Cherubino, Mrs. Booth as the Contessa, and Mary
Taylor as Suzanna. Unlike its operatic predecessors at the
Olympic, the new piece did not feature Bengough's spectacular
scenery but utilized a rather stock garden scene and the neo-
classical chambre à quarte portes. It was, however, unlike
Mitchell's previous operas in another more important respect: it failed miserably and fell from the bills after only
five performances. The Albion kindly damned the production
in its review, noting, "The effort is too great for the company. "72

     In another review which appeared on the same day,
The Spirit of The Times suggested that producing Mozart's
opera at the Olympic was not a good idea because, "the
music is of too refined a character to receive ample justice,
either from his company or his audiences, ... "73 Among the
members of the stock corps, Mary Taylor and Charles Walcot
were the most severely criticized. Taylor was found "totally
at fault in the character of Suzanna, which she marred more
by her acting than her singing, being at least, an indifferent
actress. "74 Walcot played Figaro as a character "whose
chief merit was the activity of his legs, a display of agility
Mr. Walcot would do well to avoid. "75 He must have invested Figaro with an amount of low comic physical activity
inappropriate to the character. Only Holland's Antonio,
"whose drunken song was rapturously encored, "76 was thought
to be an appropriate and successful characterization.

     The Marriage of Figaro is significant as the first of
Mitchell's operas to fail. The Spirit's review suggests that
the audience, presumably the "b'hoys" in the pit, was not
sufficiently sophisticated to appreciate the piece, even if it
had been done well. But more importantly, it marked the

first time that any type of dramatic entertainment selected
for production by Mitchell proved to be clearly beyond the
abilities of his company.

Throughout the spring of 1844, another of the company's
actresses joined the competition between Timm and Taylor for
honors as the fairest of the fair at the Olympic. Constantia
Clarke, an actress of little previous experience who had joined
the stock corps with Mary Taylor at the beginning of the 1842-
43 season, had slowly but surely risen in popular esteem.
While the potential rivalry between Timm and Taylor was not
as hostile as it might have been because they appealed to different classes of the Olympic's audience, Miss Clarke came to
rival Taylor for the primary affections of the theatre's sophisticated patrons. Taylor had the better singing voice, but
Clarke was a better actress. The growing rivalry was intensified by the fact that both actresses excelled in breeches
parts--roles which enabled them to show off their legs and
hips while disguising themselves as young boys. Although
Taylor became popular earlier than Clarke, The Spirit of
The Times opined that by the beginning of May, Clarke was
rising rapidly in ability, reputation, and presumably, popularity.
Reviewing her performance in The Young Scamp, the weekly
journal reported: "Miss Clarke performed Joseph in an
unexceptionable manner, and in the last scene the rapid tran-
sition of the character from the wild, thoughtless boy, to
the sorrow struck, weeping Champion of his sister's rights,
was given in a forcible, natural, and most affective manner--
a piece of pathetic acting we have seldom seen rivalled."27

During the final two weeks of the season, Mitchell relied exclusively on the most popular farces and burlesques
from the earlier portion of the campaign. The season closed
inordinately early--18 May--because the manager had contracted
to move his entire company to Niblo's Gardens and appear under
the auspices of that entrepreneur of ice cream and entertainment for the summer. This marked the first occasion since
the brief summer season of 1840 that the Olympic's company
performed together as a unit during the hot months.

The period from 1842 to 1844 saw many changes at
the Olympic. The acting company had improved significantly
with the addition of Holland, Taylor, Clarke, and Walcot.
It is a tribute to the manager's ability as a trainer of actors
that the last three performers mentioned possessed virtually
no professional reputations before joining the Olympic's company, but rose to prominence quickly during their first season

under Mitchell. Although none of Mitchell's actors have
testified to his part in the development of their talents, several
sources attest to the care with which he rehearsed his actors
and Lawrence Hutton noted, "It was quite a common sentiment
in the days of Mitchell that Mitchell made the brilliant people
who first became prominent at his theatre."78

The manager had also broadened the spectrum of his
entertainments and surprised his audiences with the two excellent operas he staged during the 1842-43 season as well
as with his own performance in the serious Grandfather Whitehead. His ability to best his competitors at the production
of good new farces from England proved an additionally strong
managerial asset.

From 1842 through 1844, Mitchell diversified his
entertainments and established himself as a manager capable
of mounting a wide variety of dramatic productions successfully. His theatre was no longer a burlesque and extravaganza
house. It had become the home of a fine stock company which
presented many different types of entertainments with several
different performers of high calibre sharing the acting burden
that the manager alone had labored under during his first two
seasons.

CHAPTER SIX

The Palmy Days Continue, 1844-46

Mitchell's sixth season at the Olympic opened extremely late because the company did not terminate its "summer" engagement at Niblo's until 7 October 1844. The summer season at Niblo's had been successful, but not particularly noteworthy. Mitchell had merely repeated the large number of popular pieces in the Olympic's ever-increasing repertory of hits. As Odell notes: "The term of Mitchell's at Niblo's had the uneventfulness usually attributed to the happy; but few pieces were needed."[1] An additional week lapsed while the actors rehearsed and the annual refurbishing of the Olympic was completed.

Although the summer season at Niblo's had been financially successful, it had cost Mitchell the services of two of his most valuable employees. Corbyn, who had been the Olympic's treasurer since Mitchell opened the theatre in December of 1839, resigned his post and remained at Niblo's to manage the theatre there through the winter months. His position was filled by B. F. Tyron. Another defector was Mrs. Timm, the Olympic's first popular leading lady, who also stayed at Niblo's. Her departure was to have important repercussions during the ensuing season at the Olympic, for Mary Taylor and Constantia Clarke rapidly became involved in an intense rivalry for the affections of the theatre's pit patrons, the "b'hoys" who had been Mrs. Timm's most ardent fans.

Mrs. Timm was not the only actress to desert Mitchell. Both Mrs. Watts and Mrs. J. B. Booth, Jr. quit the company, and although there were no deserters among the male members, Walcot was two weeks late in rejoining his fellow performers.

The most important new member of the company was

Mrs. Booth's brother, Ben DeBar, who had formerly acted
for Caldwell in New Orleans and Wallack in New York.   A
versatile actor who excelled in comic roles ranging from the
Artful Dodger in Oliver Twist to Joseph Surface in The School
For Scandal, DeBar was a welcome addition to the Olympic's
company.   The company was further bolstered by two young
dancers, the Valle sisters, who danced a brief pas de deux
as part of the evening's entertainment almost nightly through
the first two months of the new season.

Mitchell's sixth season as manager of the Olympic
opened on 14 October 1844, with a new extravaganza by Gilbert A'Beckett entitled The Yellow Dwarf and two farces
which had premiered at Niblo's over the summer: William
Emden's New Inventions--a vehicle for Holland; and, John M.
Morton's The Milliner's Holiday.   Although The Yellow Dwarf
ran for only four performances, the two farces were well received and drew large audiences during the opening week of
the new season.   Porter's The Spirit of The Times reported
the seasonal reopening of the little playhouse on lower Broadway as the "theatrical feature of the week."[2]   Mitchell's patrons had eagerly anticipated the resumption of delights at
their favorite place of amusement.   On the opening night of
the season, they "filled the theatre immediately on the opening
of the doors, and testified their pleasure by loud and pro-
longed cheers for all manner of persons and things...."[3]
The Olympic's continuing success seems to have been taken
for granted, for the reporter matter-of-factly suggested that
the abilities of the company, coupled with Mitchell's excellence
as both a performer and manager, "must insure a continuance
of those favors the public have so liberally showered upon his
enterprise."[4]

It did not take Mitchell very long to show his patrons
that he was still interested in, and capable of, topical burlesque.   On 21 October, he produced a new extravaganza entitled Open Sesame, which was based on the forty thieves
legend.   Although the subject matter and title do not suggest
it, the prime target of the new piece was Hamblin's production
of N. H. Bannister's Putnam, or The Iron Son of '76, which
had premiered the previous 5 August at the Bowery and had
drawn large crowds for almost a month.

Hamblin's production of Putnam, a horse thriller in the
Mazeppa vein, starred the celebrated steed Black Vulture,
"on which Putnam nightly swooped down a vast incline to the
delight of his friends and consternation of his enemies."[5]
The Bowery's playbills advertised Putnam's charge on the black

stallion as "a rapid and dangerous descent from the ceiling
of the theatre down to the very footlights."6

   Mitchell's production of Open Sesame featured Holland
as the hero Hassarac, who remained mounted on a good-
natured donkey named Dapple throughout the course of the
action. An opening night's playbill describes the new entertainment's climax as the "perilous descent of Hassarac,
mounted on his faithful donkey, Dapple, down a stupendous
mass of rock reaching several inches above the stage. A
feat never attempted by any person on the like spirited ani-
mal."7 Putnam's ride on Black Vulture was not the only
element of Hamblin's production ridiculed by Mitchell. The
Bowery's sensational melodramas had long been noted for
their fight scenes. The martial tradition also served the
Olympic manager's keen eye for the ridiculous. The action
of Open Sesame included: "A terrific combat of two by
Hasserac and Abdallah. Nervous ladies are requested to be
under no apprehension as the swords used upon the occasion
are remarkably good-tempered blades."8 Although the
Bowery Theatre had been converted to a circus at the end
of the preceding August, the relationship between Putnam
and Open Sesame would have been apparent to Mitchell's
audience.

   On 28 October, two days after Open Sesame was withdrawn from the bills, Mitchell produced the American premiere of another farce by J. R. Planché. Follies of A
Night, featuring Walcot in the leading role, ran for the entire week and received eleven additional performances during
the season. Although its frequency of production qualifies it
as a moderate success, The Spirit of The Times blasted
Walcot for his performance of the leading role. Noting that
Walcot "entertains too high an opinion of his own abilities
as a comic actor,"9 the reviewer observed that whenever the
performer failed to generate a desired response on the part
of the audience, he "invariably descends to coarse action or
buffoonery--a device too frequently resorted to."10 At that
stage of his career, Walcot seems to have forced his acting
anytime he felt that he wasn't being funny enough.

   Follies of A Night's place in the bills was taken by a
new extravaganza entitled The Magic Arrow on 4 November.
The new offering ran for the entire week and drew large
crowds. The press, however, did not share the enthusiasm
of the Olympic's patrons. The Spirit of The Times opined
that the only thing which saved the piece from universal

condemnation was the music,[11] and The Albion found the
extravaganza lacking in "originality and point."[12]

The Magic Arrow was followed by La Viviandere, a
grand opera which shared its predecessor's critical fate.
Yet even though Mitchell's productions were not getting the
flattering notices awarded those of earlier seasons, they
continued to draw large audiences. The Albion noted on 16
November: "Neither local circumstances nor oppositions seem
to effect the fortunes of Mitchell. The theatre has been
crowded during the week, and this without positive novelty."[13]

Perhaps part of the apparent paradox of large crowds
attending the Olympic to see old pieces and new plays of
questionable quality can be explained in terms of the greater
efforts Mitchell was taking in rehearsing his players and arranging his stage. Although Mitchell had earned an enviable
reputation for his "tact" and the manner in which he carefully and thoroughly supervised every element of production,
the autumn of 1844 marked a new high point in his stage
management. The manager was now rarely appearing on the
stage of his theatre, relying on Clarke, Taylor, Holland,
Nickinson, and DeBar to fill his coffers. Beginning with the
opening of the season, the pride which he took in staging his
productions evidenced itself by a phrase printed at the head
of the bills for every new play: "Produced under the direction of Mr. Mitchell." The Albion found cause to praise
Mitchell for both this theatrical thoroughness and his sense
of the public's predispositions late in November. Noting that
Mitchell's playhouse continued to be crammed nightly even
though no new pieces had been produced, the reviewer mused,
"It is curious to trace the causes of the success which have
so uniformly attended the Olympic, under his management."[14]
Observing that neither the company nor the repertory was
consistently excellent, the commentator attributes the theatre's
ongoing success to the "tact of the management."[15] Frequent accolades to Mitchell's abilities as a manager in the
newspapers and weekly periodicals of the period contain the
word "tact." Perhaps because the director was yet to emerge
as the unifying force in theatrical production, contemporary
critics did not have the word direction in their critical vo-
cabulary. Yet testimonials to Mitchell's tact are certainly
analogous to what is commonly referred to as direction some
twenty years later.

While audiences continued to flock to the Olympic
during the month of November, the competition between

Constantia Clarke and Mary Taylor for the title "Queen of the
Olympic" intensified. Each had developed her own following
among the "b'hoys," and each consciously sought to elicit
vociferous testimonials of approval from her admirers. It
is surprising that Mitchell did not put a stop to this competition, for the often rowdy acclaim that the two actresses stimu-
lated in their respective followings occasionally interrupted
the performances and apparently drove some of the Olympic's
upper-class patrons from their seats in the private boxes and
dress circle. It was this unchecked rivalry which produced
the closest thing to a riot ever to occur at the Olympic on
6 December 1844, the date of George Holland's benefit.

On that night, during a performance of Cinderella, an
inebriated "b'hoy" seated, atypically, in one of the orchestra
boxes, interrupted the course of the action with loud shouts
of "Three cheers for Mary Taylor."16 The sophisticated
patrons in the boxes rose up and demanded that the raucous
youngster be removed from the theatre, while their counterparts in the pit brandished their fists and suggested that the
offender be executed on the spot. Matters rapidly approached
a climax when three or four well-aimed benches from the gallery almost carried out the suggestion of the "b'hoys" in the
pit. Mrs. Timm, although no longer a member of the company, was appearing for Holland's benefit, and came to the
rescue. Never known for her demureness, she sprang from
the stage into the box where the noisy youth was challenging
the entire audience to "come and get me" and dragged him
to the police, who were just entering.17

Perhaps the seriousness of the situation made the com-
peting actresses realize the dangers inherent in attempting to
bolster the ranks of their admirers with claptrap. The rivalry
between them and consequent rowdy demonstrations of allegiance
seem to have abated after the near-riot.

On 9 December, three days after the incident, Mitchell
produced the American premiere of an extremely popular
British farce, Don Caesar DeBazan, by Gilbert A'Beckett and
Mark Lemmon. The piece, set in the time of Charles II of
Spain, concerns itself with a swashbuckling title character who
is the best swordsman in all of Spain. He finds himself condemned to death for breaking the King's royal order forbidding
dueling during Carnival Week. His adversary, Don José, gulls
him into agreeing to marry a peasant girl whom the king
wants titled prior to Don Caesar's scheduled execution. But
Don Caesar escapes death, uncovers a plot by the wicked Don

José to assassinate the king, is awarded the governorship
of Granada, marries the beautiful peasant, and lives happily
ever after. The new play had proven so overwhelmingly
popular in England that it was still running at ten theatres
in London on the evening that it first graced the boards of
an American theatre. Mitchell was not the only manager in
New York anxious to produce the piece. Simpson, manager
of the Park, had announced his preparations in advance of
Mitchell's premiere, and thought that he would be the first
in the field with the new piece on 16 December. But the
Olympic's manager kept his own production plans a secret,
and no one knew that the play was to be presented at the
Olympic until the publication of the bills on the morning of
its debut. Simpson must have been sorely disappointed by
the fact that Mitchell eclipsed the Park's much-heralded
premiere by a week.

Mitchell's production, featuring Walcot as the Don and
DeBar as his faithful companion, ran for twelve performances
before being withdrawn and returned to the Olympic's stage
an additional nine times before the season ended. The Spirit
of The Times praised the production: "Taking the piece as
a whole, it must prove popular, as the manner in which it
is put on the stage is very neat, the scenery new, and the
dresses newly fabricated, and of very beautiful material."[18]
But the critic once again proved that he was no fan of Walcot,
complaining that "his performance of the role was not, taken
as a whole, as spirited and marked as we would desire...."[19]

The Albion had no such reservations about the quality
of Walcot's acting. Indeed, it considered the new play an
"unequivocal success,"[20] and congratulated Mitchell for his
ability to be the "first in the field with this popular drama."[21]
The Olympic's production continued to draw crowded houses
throughout its run, even after Simpson opened his version
at the Park.[22]

On Christmas night, Mitchell brought out the seasonally
customary new extravaganza. But the new piece, Telemachus,
did not prove nearly as attractive as its several holiday predecessors at the Olympic and ran for only six nights. The
Spirit of The Times' assessment of the holiday offering may
explain why it was less popular than its predecessors had
been: "Altogether this little drama abounds in many fair
jokes, and good situations, although it lacks a broad humour
and pointed satire."[23] Nevertheless, the reviewer felt obliged to commend Mary Taylor for her performance of the

title role: "We must congratulate Miss Taylor on the palpable
improvement she evinces in her acting; she performed Telemachus in a highly creditable style as regards pronunciation
and gesture."24

The first two weeks of January saw frequent changes
of bill at the Olympic featuring popular farces of past seasons. On the eleventh, The Albion observed: "Another week
without novelty and yet no great dimunition in the number of
the audiences."25 Mitchell was the only manager in the city
playing to good houses; the other playhouses were either closed
or destitute. The Bowery had been converted into a circus
late in August, and the Park ceased operation as a theatre
from 11 January until 12 March. The Chatham, Mitchell's
only competitor during the ill-paying winter months for several
seasons, closed during February of 1845. The Olympic, then,
was the only theatre in New York to maintain operations
throughout the entire winter. Perhaps because they had no
competition, the members of the Olympic's stock company
became sloppy in their work. In mid-January the usually
fair critic of The Spirit of The Times complained that although the company contained an inordinately high number of
physically attractive actresses, "there is scarce a woman,
with the slight exception of Miss Clarke, who can utter two
consecutive lines without a murder of grammar."26 Noting
that the diction of the company's men was even worse, the
critic sarcastically suggested that, "the audience must hail
with pleasure the slightest symptom of grammatic accuracy."27

Extravaganza returned to the Olympic's stage on 20
January with The Mirror of Truth. Written by Northall, it
was altered extensively after its first few performances. Although it ran for sixteen nights, critical reaction to it was
extremely negative--a probable reason for the extensive re-
visions. The Spirit of The Times found it "a very clumsily
contrived and lamely written ineffective burletta,"28 and
suggested that the only thing which prevented its total failure
was Mitchell's stage arrangements.29 The same journal's
critic returned to the Olympic after alterations were made
in the text, and still did not like the new piece. Finding the
character Rosabella, "one of the most offensive parts ever
presented at this house,"30 the reporter expressed disappointment that the role wasn't completely cut from the extravaganza.
Complaining that the character was rife with "coarseness and
obscenity,"31 the reporter warned: "Vulgarity is a rock upon
which the Olympic Theatre may split. Double Entendre can
be concealed by a hasty utterance, but a low part, like

Rosabella, will inevitably tend to drive respectable people out
of the boxes--in obscenity there is no half way."32

The review implies that Mitchell's extravaganzas and
burlesques frequently contained double entendre. But not
since the Mirror's critic had found Mitchell's portrayal of a
female character--Molly Brown in The Roof Scrambler--of-
fensive five years earlier had any reviewer criticized Mitchell for bad taste. It must therefore be assumed that Mitchell's productions had rarely offended his audiences or the
press.

During the theatrically depressed month of February,
Mitchell produced no new pieces worthy of note. All of the
city's other theatres were closed, and nothing of social or
political interest had transpired for some time. It was impossible, then, for him to develop any topical burlesques.
Yet his carefully staged productions continued to fill the Olympic nightly. The Albion reminded its readers, on 15 February, "of an axiom we frequently endeavour to impress upon
managers, that pieces well selected and produced with care
and attention, are sure to repay the outlay and labour. Mitchell understands this secret perfectly."33 This brief notice
specifies some of the elements of Mitchell's much heralded
"tact" and indicates the chief source of the Olympic's continued success.

Mitchell continued to rely on old Olympic favorites until
11 March. On that date was produced, for the first time, a
burlesque of Balfe's popular opera, The Bohemian Girl entitled The Bohea-Man's Girl. Written by the prompter
Baker, the new burlesque, like most of the Olympic's operatic lampoons, was general in nature and did not ridicule any
particular production of the opera or any specific operatic
performers. It ran for thirteen nights and according to The
Spirit of The Times, "went off in a blaze of triumph."34

Because the Olympic proved to be the only theatre in
New York able to remain open throughout most of the winter,
Mitchell could afford to experiment with his repertory. But
producing comedies more sophisticated than the broad farces,
topical burlesques, and extravaganzas which usually entertained
the theatre's patrons succeeded only partially. Two factors
precluded consistently successful production of longer, more
subtle comedies: the taste of his audience; and the frequent
carelessness of his actors. The Spirit of The Times attributed the failure of Planché's Don Giovanni Travestie, which

opened on 25 March, to a devolution of the audience's taste.
The critic argues that Mitchell had debased his audience's
taste by the constant production of low comic plays to the
point that they seemed reticent to accept anything a bit more
sophisticated. Moreover, the reviewer believed that Mitchell's
repertory could not become more sophisticated due to the
manager's necessity, "to satisfy the cravings of the pit for
low comic action."[35]

    Another new play, John M. Morton's The Corporal's
Wedding, debuted on 5 April. Although it was more in keeping with the taste for low comedy Mitchell had developed in
his audience than Don Giovanni had been, it too failed, primarily as a result of the sloppy performances of the company.
The Spirit of The Times described the new play as "a farce
of some cleverness in design and language,"[36] that had been
"unfortunately and deliberately murdered by the ignorance and
carelessness the actors evinced concerning the author's
words."[37] Only Holland and Constantia Clarke were acquitted
of the general crime committed against Morton's play.

    On 7 April Mitchell brought out a new topical burlesque
which had a double object of ridicule: the competition between
Taylor and Clarke for the affections of the "b'hoys," and a
forthcoming horse race which was generating tremendous enthusiasm among sportsmen all across the country.

    It became known early in March that the national
championship four-mile long horse race would be held early
in May at the Union Course on Long Island. Only two horses
had emerged from the elimination process as competitors
in the final race. Matters were made more exciting than
they otherwise would have been by the fact that one of the
horses, Peytona, was owned by a planter from the Deep
South while the other, Fashion, was the proud possession of
a northerner. The race took on additional meaning as a focal
point for the ever-increasing sectional rivalry that the country
experienced during the 1840's.

    The pending race provided the subject for Mitchell's
new burlesque which was aptly entitled Peytona and Fashion.
By casting Mary Taylor as the northern debutante Fashion,
and Constantia Clarke as the southern belle Peytona, Mitchell
was able to draw upon the rivalry of his two most popular
actresses for the affections of the "b'hoys" and add an extra
element of self-burlesque to the new play. The Spirit of The
Times, which had not been impressed with either Mitchell's

productions or his performers throughout the winter, was
quite taken with the new trifle. Gleefully reporting that
Mitchell's ability "to turn out a regular up and down farce
on the subject of the great race is a little more than we
could happily expect, "38 the critic found that although the
dialogue was "disconnected, " like that of all topical pieces
written and rehearsed rapidly, "the piece has some strong
merit from its ingenuity and local tendency. "39 The production ran for only four nights. The rapidity with which it
was written and produced probably militated against the possibility that it would be a big hit. It no doubt served Mitchell's purpose of providing amusement for his patrons for
a week, however, and it is significant as the first of his burlesques since Boz, three years earlier, which had as its object a nontheatrical event.

On 15 April, Mitchell opened yet another topical burlesque, Antigone. It had as its object New York's first production of that ancient classic, produced at Palmo's Opera
House. This production had been attempted as something of
a sophisticated novelty to attract patrons who had grown tired
of the voices of Palmo's Italian opera company. Staged by
George Vandenhoff, the tragedy featured Vandenhoff as Creon,
F. S. Chanfrau as Haemon, and Miss Clarendon as Antigone.
The singing of the chorus' parts to Mendelssohn's incidental
music prompted an unfortunate piece of staging which made
the "legitimate" production of the play at least slightly ridiculous. The score is extremely difficult, and the chorus
members, outfitted in togas and false, long, white beards,
had been unable to memorize the intricate music for their
odes, so sheet music was placed on music stands in front
of each of them. The spectacle was made additionally ludicrous by virtue of the nearsightedness of several of the
chorus members, who had to reach into their himations,
withdraw their glasses and put them on each time they began
an ode. The result must have been at least curious. 40 Although this attic tragedy was performed nightly from 8 through
18 April at Palmo's, "it was a colossal failure. "41

Mitchell's playbill for 15 April, the one-week anniver-
sary of the classic's opening at Palmo's, announced to the
Olympic's patrons:

ANTIGONE

The piece produced under the immediate direction
of William Mitchell esq. The music, principally

from the most eminent barrell organs, posed, composed, decomposed, by various authors, and arranged
by George Loder esq. The orchestra will be on the
usual (not large, but effective) scale, and led by
Henry Marks, esq. The scene representing the
front of Palmo's Theatre, in Chambers Street, for
a sketch on the spot with a perspective of the 'dog-
gery' next door, out of sight, in the horizon, after a
a vivid recollection, is painted and done brown by
Richard Bengough esq., which eminent artist has
produced the playbills of the time of Antigone, from
the original letters, the chef d'oeuvre of the
literary genius of George Vandenhoff, esq.... The
original tragedy on which the present version is
founded, was written 2295 years before Mrs.
Mowatt's comedy of Fashion was produced at the
Park, by an ancient Greek, named Patrick Sophocles,
Esquire.
The chorus of the present tragedy are supposed to
be the unemployed artistes of the Italian opera, who
have assembled in front of Palmo's for the purpose
of opposing the introduction of the English Drama,
making a quizzical comment on what passes before
them, and thus, as it were standing as intruders
between the poet and the actual audience. 42

    Interestingly, both Vandenhoff, who had staged the
production at Palmo's, and Loder, who had arranged the
music there, contributed to the Olympic's burlesque in the
significant areas of playwriting and musical arrangement.
Like several other of Mitchell's pieces during the season,
Antigone contained an element of self-parody by virtue of the
association of Vandenhoff and Loder with the productions at both
Palmo's and the Olympic.

    Although the new burlesque ran for only a week, it
earned praise as one of the best things Mitchell had ever
presented. The Spirit of The Times, which had been critical
of both Mitchell's repertory and his acting company throughout the winter, delightfully exclaimed: "We have seldom heard
recited a wittier piece of composition than this burlesque, com-
bining the humour of the stage, in good acting points, with a
most excruciatingly comic libretto. "43

    On 30 April, eight days after Antigone was withdrawn
from the bills, the season ended. During the final week,
Mitchell offered his patrons revivals of several of their favorite

farces. The Spirit of The Times, in an article written the
week after the Olympic had closed for the season, warned
Mitchell about the necessity of winning back his fashionable
patrons who had been driven from the theatre by the vulgar
nature of some of the entertainments presented that season and
by the rowdy accolades of the pittites in the Taylor vs. Clarke
competition for the admiration of the "b'hoys." The columnist
noted: "At the opening of Mr. Mitchell's career, his dress-
circle was graced by fashion, his boxes by well-doing respectable people, and his pit was quiet and orderly. But now we
regret to perceive that the disorderly and noisy groundlings,
nightly increasing in strength and uproar, have by a constant series of insult and riot, driven many of the old frequenters of the little house from their wonted seats."44
Suggesting "elevating the tone of the pieces represented at
this house"45 as the most likely solution to the problem of
the capture of the Olympic by the increasingly tyrannical pit
patrons, the reporter wished Mitchell well in his reform
campaign.

Despite the warning of The Spirit of The Times about
Mitchell's need to win back some of his disillusioned fashionable clientele and the same journal's frequent scolding of the
actors for sloppy work, the brief season was an extremely
impressive one for several reasons. Mitchell had produced
three specific burlesques of high quality which were hilariously
topical. During two different periods in the season, the
Olympic continued to draw large audiences--at a time when no
other theatre in the city could even remain open--without producing any new plays. The several compliments extended to
Mitchell's managerial ability by the press, and the great
pride he took in his role as manager by announcing in the
bills that all new pieces were produced under his direction,
suggest that the long-time high quality of Mitchell's arrangements and stage appointments had reached a new pinnacle of
expertise and thoroughness. Yet the frequent notices in The
Spirit of The Times and The Albion criticizing the stock company for its carelessness indicate that Mitchell's attention to
the visual details of production had superseded the care with
which he rehearsed his actors. But the sixth season was as
successful as any of its predecessors, and perhaps even more
so. There was no doubt that "Mitchell was still the master
in the realms of mirth and laughter."46

While the Olympic was closed for the summer of 1845,
the company temporarily disbanded. The theatre was sched-

uled to reopen for the 1845-46 season on 8 September, but delays in the annual cleaning and renovation of the auditorium postponed the season's debut by a week.

There was surprisingly little change among Mitchell's personnel when he opened the doors of his theatre for the new season. All of the nonperforming positions remained in the hands of those who had previously held them; and, no new additions were made to the stock company, even though DeBar left to assume the management of the Chatham Theatre and Walcot was six weeks late in rejoining his fellow players.

On 15 September 1845, Mitchell commenced his seventh season. The bill of fare for the opening night included one piece previously seen at the theatre--The Corporal's Wedding--and two new plays: Northall's adaptation of Planché's extravaganza Graciosa and Percinet, and an anonymous farce entitled Mr. and Mrs. Caudle which featured Mitchell as Mr. Caudle, and Holland, who rarely played transvestite characters, as his spouse.

This opening bill proved unusual. In past years Mitchell inevitably had trouble finding a new hit during the first month of the season, but the first night of his seventh campaign produced two long-running pieces. Graciosa and Percinet, featuring Taylor and Clarke, ran for twelve nights, while Mr. and Mrs. Caudle proved even more popular than the new extravaganza and played twenty nights in succession. With these two new attractive pieces in the season's opening bill, it is little wonder that The Spirit of The Times could report, less than two weeks into the season: "The Olympic has had the most crowded houses ever known at that crowded box, and Mr. Mitchell appears to have lost little of his prior popularity."47

On 29 September, Graciosa and Percinet dropped from the bills in favor of Dick Whittington and His Cat, a Northall adaptation from several British pieces bearing the same title. Featuring Clarke and Taylor at Coney Island, the new extravaganza proved so popular that Mitchell suspended the free list on 2 October, three days after it opened.

With three decided hits produced within two weeks of the opening of the season, the Olympic's popularity was greater than it had ever been. The Spirit of The Times, noting the success of both Whittington and His Cat and Mr. and Mrs. Caudle, reported: "The House is crammed night

after night. "[48]   A week later, the same journal marvelled at
the crowds the Olympic continued to draw without producing
any new pieces: "Mitchell's Olympic continues overflowing.
We with great difficulty crowded in the other night to see
'Mr. and Mrs. Caudle.' "[49]

After three phenomenally popular new plays were produced within two weeks, no new pieces appeared between
27 September--the premiere of Whittington and His Cat--and
27 October.   With a repetition of the new pieces and old
favorites as the source of attraction, the most telling thing
that The Spirit could report of the Olympic during that month-
long period was: "Full Houses--full treasury--four farces,
and not half seats enough. "[50]

November saw several new farces and a new extravaganza on the stage of the little box on lower Broadway.
The tenth of the month marked the first performances of
both All Night Out--a piece custom tailored for Holland by
Baker--and C. W. S. Brook's, Our New Governess.   Both
pieces drew well until the seventeenth when Asmodeus,
or The Little Devil's Disciple eclipsed them in attractiveness
on the first performance of its ten-night run.   The unfailing
ability of Mitchell to produce one hit after another in rapid
succession during the opening two months of the season
caused The Albion to print one of its frequent testimonials to
Mitchell's ability as a manager noting, "that he has been
quietly accumulating a fortune while other managers were
starving. "[51]

Two days after the above appeared in print, Mitchell
brought out another new piece, Charles Selby's The Irish
Dragoon.   Selby's new Irish play featured the Irish Dragoon,
one Paddy Murphy O'Brallaghan, posing as lord of the manor
while his master leaves for a weekend.   The newly elevated
servant manages to gull a beautiful young country lass until
his master returns and spoils his deception.   Featuring Mitchell's resident Irishman of four year's standing, Nickinson,
it ran for the entire week and was repeated an additional
nine times during the remainder of the season.

Toward the end of November The Spirit of The Times,
which had been extremely critical of Mitchell's repertory and
the overall performance of the company during the preceding
season, was moved to comment on the manager's consistent
success in his current campaign: "The Olympic keeps quietly
on its way to fortune, the houses never varying much for it

is nearly always full, and at times more than full, and before
one novelty begins to flag, Mitchell's industry and tact has
another in readiness. "52

So great had been the Olympic's drawing power during
the autumn that the free list had not been reinstated after
its initial suspension on 2 October. Attendance seems to have
increased through the month of November, for on the twenty-
ninth The Albion reported in an exasperated tone, "It has
become absolutely a task of some labour for the press to
obtain admission into this theatre, crowded as it is nightly
even to overflowing. "53

On 1 December Mitchell produced what proved to be
the first failure of the season, an opera entitled The Fairies
Lake. Despite careful and thorough staging and some excellent new scenery by Bengough, the opera proved unpopular
because, according to The Albion, "The pittites miss the
broad fun they are accustomed to enjoy--and the calibre of
the singers is unequal to the music. "54 Another review found
the opera to be satisfactory in every way with regard to
staging and performance, and attributed its lack of drawing
power to severe abridgement, which made the libretto lack
any semblance of continuity. 55

The failure of the opera gives credence to The Spirit
of The Times' observation a season earlier that Mitchell had
debased the taste of his audience by an overreliance on
broad farce. During the season currently being considered,
Mitchell was relying more heavily than ever on the low
comedy of broad farces. But the quality of the acting company may have improved substantially. The performers had
all been at the Olympic during at least one previous season,
and, as most of them were young players of relatively little
experience, it is reasonable to assume that they had been
improving in the practice of their craft. The Spirit of The
Times, a severe but generally fair critic of acting, had
found frequent cause to complain of the company's carelessness during the preceding campaign, often singling out Walcot
for special condemnation. Yet during the ensuing season the
journal found little with which to take issue regarding the
performances of the actors and was even laudatory in some
instances. In a review of My Uncle's Card which appeared
in The Spirit of The Times on 20 December 1845, the critic,
presumably the same one who had found the performers frequently less than adequate during the preceding season, noted
that Constantia Clarke, "in the parts in which she plays, is

certainly not excelled in the United States. "56 Citing Mitchell
and Nickinson for their consistent excellence in the roles they
had been playing, the review concludes with the startling observation that "Mr. Walcot is a delightful actor. "57 Considering the frequent harsh criticism applied to Walcot's performances a mere year earlier either the actor had improved
markedly, the critic had mellowed considerably, or both.

For the first time in his managerial career, Mitchell
did not offer his patrons a new burlesque or extravaganza on
Christmas Day. Instead, Graciosa and Percinet, the season's
initial hit, was presented along with two new farces: Thomas
Mildenhall's The Governor's Wife and an anonymous play entitled The Railroad King. Both were popular recent London
plays which received their American premieres on the holiday.

While the two new farces were packing crowded audiences into Mitchell's small theatre nightly, the city's other
theatres were having their first successful season in several
years. At the Park, long the New York stop for traveling
stars of the highest magnitude, the great attraction of the
early winter was Mr. and Mrs. Charles Kean, who produced
several of their "historically accurate" Shakespearean plays.
One of their productions, Richard III, provided Mitchell with
his first opportunity of the season for topical burlesque. The
Olympic's playbill for 12 January announced that a new burlesque of Richard III was being prepared for production:

> The manager has spared neither pains nor expense
> in the production of this mortal play. Mr. Ben-
> gough, the artist, has been engaged for nearly twenty
> minutes a day during the past week, and the cos-
> tumer has not slept much, except at night, during
> the same period, so great have been the exertions
> in that department.
> N. B.   A roll of red flannel has been imported
> expressly for this occasion.
> N. B.   The Last Dollar changed was for the pur-
> chase of raw material for the agitated face in the
> tent scene. 58

The new burlesque was not Mitchell's long popular
vehicle Richard #3, but a completely different piece, written
by Walcot, and entitled Richard The Third To Kill. The
title suggests the point of the burlesque--the supposed historical accuracy and lavish preparations with which Charles
Kean mounted his Shakespearean productions.

Mitchell must have been optimistic about the new piece's chances for success, as it was announced two weeks before its premiere and he and Walcot had spent much time in preparing it. His optimism proved misplaced, for the new burlesque, despite its topicality, was not very successful. The Albion noted that various segments of the audience disagreed regarding the merits of the play: "Much opposition was exhibited during the progress of the piece, and at its close, but Walcott [sic] is deservedly so great a favorite as an actor that the good nature of the audience finally made the applause drown the disapprobation, and the burlesque has run through the week."59

The Spirit of The Times confirmed the hostile reaction the play received from some quarters of the audience: "...we are forced to confess that 'Richard No. 3 To Kill' did not strike us at all favorably, nor were we along in our opinion of its merits, for some very pertinacious hissing from several different quarters of the house proclaimed the dissatisfaction of a part, at least, of the 'many headed.'"60 In reporting that the play was hissed "from several different quarters of the house," the reviewer indicates that it was not a single segment of Mitchell's audience that found it unsatisfactory. If only the "b'hoys" didn't like the burlesque, the critic would probably have noted that the dissatisfaction was most evident among the theatre's pit patrons.

Although the play did manage to run for ten consecutive evenings, it was only presented four additional times during the remainder of the season. It was, indeed, a failure. As such, it marks the first time that one of Mitchell's carefully prepared, long-awaited, specific theatrical burlesques failed to live up to the expectations of the Olympic's patrons.

On 30 January, with Walcot's lampoon still running, Mitchell brought out another new burlesque aimed at Bulwer-Lytton's extremely popular The Lady of Lyons. Entitled The Lady of The Lions, it was a general burlesque of the play it ridiculed rather than a specific lampoon of any particular production, even though Walcot, as Claude Meddlenot, the hero, burlesqued Macready's style of acting. The piece was even less attractive than Richard The Third To Kill, and ran for only seven evenings.

During the first week of February nothing new was presented on the Olympic's stage, but on the ninth Mitchell brought out the premiere of a recent British play by F. M.

Maddox entitled The Violet. A serious piece, much like
Grandfather Whitehead, it featured the manager, who had
acted only infrequently during the season, in the leading role
of Martin André. Although the audiences had accepted Mitchell's excursion into the realm of serious drama some four
seasons earlier, they may not have done so on the occasion
of The Violet's premiere. The Albion saw fit to criticize
both Mitchell's performance and the audience's reception:
"Mitchell is not Martin André--and yet when we remember
his inimitable delineation of Grandfather Whitehead, we almost wonder the part fails in his hands... But these serious
affairs do not suit the Olympians, actors and audiences are
both at fault. The latter most provokingly laugh when they
should cry--and the actors are comic when they should be
tragic. "61

        A review of the same production which appeared in
The Spirit of The Times, a journal usually much more severe
than The Albion in its criticisms, makes one wonder if both
critics saw the same play: "Here it is that 'The Violet' is
played, in an almost perfect manner. Mitchell is Martin
Andre, Miss Clarke as Blanchette, and Miss Roberts as
Blanche are all capital. "62

        Whichever of the reviews is correct in its assessment of
The Violet and the audience's reception of it, the piece did
manage to run for eight performances. The reason that Miss
Roberts, and not Mary Taylor, played one of the principal
roles is that the latter was absent from the Olympic from
about 1 February until the first week in March, apparently
as the result of a salary dispute with Mitchell. 63

        March and April at the Olympic were characterized
by the American premiere of several British farces, all of
which had been popular on the London stage. On the last day
of February the first of these, J. P. Woller's The Man
Without A Head, was given the initial performance of its
week-long run. It was followed on 2 March by J. H. Sto-
queller's An Object of Interest, which also ran for a week.
The ninth saw the premiere of a new extravaganza entitled
The Flying Horse, which enjoyed six consecutive performances
and was repeated an additional eight times during the two remaining months of the season. Success followed success so
rapidly at the theatre and came to be taken so much for
granted, that the following review from The Albion is typical
of the cursory attention given to Mitchell's new pieces by
the press during the spring of 1846: "Mitchell has produced

a fairy extravaganza founded on the opera of the Bronze Horse,
called The Flying Horse. We have only space to say that
it has proved perfectly successful. It is full of points, is
admirably acted, and beautifully put upon the stage."64

Four additional American premieres of English plays
were produced during the benefit months of March and April.
Considering that the theatre had been more popular than at
any other time in the manager's career, it is not surprising
that the benefits for the actors reaped higher returns than
ever before. The Albion reported that the benefits of the
individual members of the company had all "been bumpers,"65
and that, "Mary Taylor's took more receipts than ever collected
on a single evening at the Olympic."66 Mitchell's ability to
produce the premiere of more new plays than any other manager in New York combined with his meticulous attention to
scenery, costumes, and staging continued to "render the
theatre the most popular in the city."67

While Mary Taylor enjoyed the flood tide of her success at the Olympic, her rival for the affections of the theatre's patrons, Constantia Clarke, was ebbing. She had contracted tuberculosis some years earlier and the disease had
reached such an advanced stage that she was unable to perform throughout most of the spring. She was so ill that on
the evening of her benefit, 28 April, she was unable to speak
at all, and had to appear in pantomime for the pleasure of
her devotées.

During the last five weeks of the campaign, Mitchell
relied almost exclusively on the revival of popular farces of
the current and prior seasons to attract audiences. Only one
new piece, Taming A Tartar, a farce burlesque of Timon
The Tartar, was produced. Opening on 13 May, it ran for
twelve evenings before being withdrawn. A week after its
run terminated, 30 May, Mitchell's seventh season at the
Olympic came to an end.

The Olympic's seventh season marks a new high point
in its popularity among New York's theatregoing public and a
logical extension of some policies Mitchell had developed
during earlier campaigns. He seemed consciously to avoid
the long run and to rely instead on a constant succession of
new farces to please his patrons. Farce had replaced both
burlesque and extravaganza as the Olympic staple, and, if
announcements in the playbills can be taken as accurate,
Mitchell produced the American premiere of no fewer than
fourteen London farces during the 1845-46 season.

The acting company remained amazingly stable during the period from 1844 to 1846. Although they were criticized for carelessness during the spring of 1845, comments on the performances of the various thespians during the following season are all laudatory. This indicates that Mitchell's young actors had seasoned and improved, quite possibly owing to the large number of new plays in which they were required to appear.

During this two-season period the many accolades heaped on the manager regarding his ability to select and mount farces for the Olympic, in addition to those which realized his role in making his performers favorites among the theatregoing population of New York, leave no doubt that Mitchell bore the primary responsibility for making the little Olympic theatre "the most popular in the city."[68]

CHAPTER SEVEN

A Step Backward, 1846-47

During the season of 1846-47, New York's large play-houses continued their policy of relying on a constellation of traveling stars to draw paying houses. Odell notes: "The Park was now inalterably committed to the star system; indeed the company, alone, played to empty benches."[1] Hamblin's Bowery had been destroyed by fire on 25 April 1845. A third theatre with the same name was constructed on the site of its predecessors and opened in August of 1845 under the management of A. W. Jackson. During the two ensuing seasons, Jackson competed with the Park in his selection of repertory and engagements of traveling stars. The Bowery was no longer the home of sensational melodrama which it had been under the regime of Hamblin. The Park and The Bowery managed to remain open throughout the entire season of 1846-47, but Odell suggests that profits at both of the large playhouses were marginal at best.[2]

While the large playhouses were pursuing policies which had been operating for more than two decades, the city's smaller theatres began to operate in a way similar to the one which had brought fame and fortune to Mitchell's Olympic.

Ben DeBar and William Deverna took the lease on the Chatham Theatre in the fall of 1846 and attempted to establish a management similar to and in competition with Mitchell. But the venture failed, the partnership dissolved, and the Chatham was converted into a circus in December of 1846. The Alhambra, a new small theatre in the growing city, also sought to challenge Mitchell's supremacy, but was forced to rely on variety acts and Christy's Minstrels in order to draw profitable audiences. Thus, Mitchell's competition was doing better business than it had in a decade, but the managements which survived were earning small profits and none seemed

able to challenge the Olympic's preeminent position as the
city's most successful theatre.

    Although Mitchell's eighth season at the Olympic began
at the same high level of popularity with which the seventh
season had ended, some changes in the company's personnel
forebode the decline in patronage which the theatre was to
suffer during the ensuing campaign. The most important performer to leave the company was Mary Taylor, the Olympic's
most popular actress, who went to play at the Bowery. Her
desertion was more important than it might appear because
many of the extravaganzas and farces in the theatre's repertory were successful primarily as vehicles for Miss Taylor.
No other actress in the company, with the exception of Constantia Clarke who was often unable to appear because of re-
current attacks of chronic tuberculosis, possessed either the
professional ability or personal attractiveness necessary to
make Mary Taylor's former vehicles highly popular. In
losing his most celebrated actress, Mitchell also lost a
sizeable part of his theatre's repertory. Mary Taylor's
desertion was indeed serious, but it was made less than the
disaster that it might have been by Mitchell's ability to per-
suade his first highly popular actress, Sarah Timm, to re-
join the company.

    Another important member of the staff to leave was
George Loder. He had been the Olympic's musical director
since Mitchell's inaugural season. Loder left to join Corbyn,
Mitchell's first treasurer, in managing the Alhambra Theatre.

    Although Taylor and Loder were the most important
personnel to resign, they were not the only ones to do so.
Three other actors--Fennon, Miss Phillips, and Mrs. Hard-
wick--also left the acting company, but low professional
status made their departure unimportant. The stock company,
however, was considerably smaller than it had been, for its
only addition besides Mrs. Timm was the daughter of John
Nickinson. Although Miss Nickinson was but a teenager and
had no professional experience, she rapidly became one of
the Olympic audiences' favorite performers.

    The seventh season opened on 21 September 1846,
with two Olympic favorites--Lend Me 5 Shillings and Who's
The Composer--and a new extravaganza by Planché entitled
The Bee and The Orange Tree. This latest trifle from the
pen of Planché had been the Boxing Night entertainment at
London's Haymarket Theatre the previous December. In it,

MR. JOHN NICKINSON AND HIS DAUGHTER CHARLOTTE,

AS

Havresac and *Melanie* in "NAPOLEON'S OLD GUARD."

ONLY SIXTY COPIES ISSUED: Reproduced from a rare contemporary print, published in New York in 1845.
T. H. MORRELL,
New York, 1889.

"John and Charlotte Nickinson in Napoleon's Old Guard."
Theatre Arts Library, Harry Ransom Humanities Research
Center, The University of Texas at Austin.

a prince, who has been shipwrecked in a vessel which provides the extravaganza with its title, is rescued from a group
of ogres--who eat railroad speculators, engineers, and sur-
veyors--by a princess and her fairy godmother. The extravaganza contains many satirical slaps at railroad speculation
which would have been amusing to New York's theatre audiences
during the railroad and canal boom of the mid-1840s. This
new piece proved moderately successful and was in the bills
during each of the first ten nights of the season. Mitchell
certainly appeared to be taking up where he had left off at
the close of the previous season with regard to the popularity
of his theatre, for the house was crowded nightly during the
first week.[3]

        The early weeks of each of Mitchell's previous cam-
paigns had been characterized by the production of several
new plays. But the first two weeks of the manager's seventh
season were atypical. After the production of The Bee and
The Orange Tree, only two other new plays were presented.
These new pieces--Edward Stirling's On The Tiles and John
Morton's The Irish Tiger--were both recent London farces
which received their American premieres at the Olympic on
28 September. But they, unlike the majority of their imported
predecessors, proved unattractive and fell from the bill of
fare after only three performances.

        Mitchell must have been unprepared for the cool re-
ception which the two new farces received as he had no other
novelty ready to take their place until 5 October. On that
date, the second new extravaganza of the season, an anonymous
adaptation of Charles Stoman's Cherry and Fair Star entitled
simply Fair Star, debuted. This new spectacle proved highly
popular. The Albion reported, "It is full of points and humour,
admirably played by the actors, and carefully put upon the
stage by the manager."[4] In the same review, the reporter
noted: "Mitchell is reaping another harvest this season. The
houses are nightly crowded to overflowing."[5]

        Although Fair Star proved a popular piece, the Olym-
pic's drawing power during the first three weeks of the season
was indebted primarily to revivals of Seeing Holland, Lend
Me 5 Shillings, and The Widow's Victim, all of which were
hits from earlier seasons. Because of their drawing power,
Mitchell continued to rely on the revival of popular plays
from earlier years to attract remunerative audiences. But
this reliance on the Olympic's established repertory was so
extensive that during the entire month of October, only one

additional new play was produced. This new piece, an anonymous farce written expressly for George Holland and entitled
Used Up, was first presented on 8 October and proved popular
enough to run for six consecutive evenings.

While the theatre's patrons apparently did not mind that
Mitchell was not taking his usual pains in bringing out new
plays for their amusement, the press did. The Spirit of The
Times lamented, during the middle of October, that there had
been, "a falling off in the character of amusements."6 Yet
the public must have continued to flock to the Olympic in
spite of the absence of "novelty" because, The Albion noted
on the last day of October, that "Old pieces well played and
the usual run of excellent houses stand as a regular weekly
summary for the proceedings of this pet theatre."7 The
Spirit of The Times also saw fit to comment on Mitchell's
ability to crowd his theatre without new pieces: "Without producing anything positively new, he is giving a budget of sterling
favorites suited to the capacity of his company and to the
great delight of his usual auditors."8

On the second of November, Mitchell finally provided
something new. Two anonymous farces (authors unknown)--
The Two Dukes and The Mysterious Family--received their
Olympic premieres on that date. Although they ran for a
week, neither of the new farces proved very popular, and
The Albion, in its notice of business at the Olympic during
the first week of November, suggested that if the two new
plays were the best the manager could offer in terms of new
pieces, he would be better off to continue his recent policy
of reviving old favorites: "Mitchell is actively employed as
usual, in the production of novelty, although his established
stock favorites are at times more productive to the treasury
than his so-called novelties."9

On 9 November, John Dunn, a former Olympic actor,
began a two-week engagement with Mitchell's company during
which he appeared most frequently in Ringdoves and The
Lioness of The North--two Olympic hits from earlier seasons.
Like his infrequent predecessors who had played limited engagements with the company, Dunn was not given star billing,
even though he was an extremely popular actor. Not one
new play was produced during Dunn's engagement, but his
addition to the considerable comic strength of the male members of the company caused a continuance of crowded houses.
The Albion pointed out that with the temporary acquisition of
Dunn, there was no doubt that audiences went to the Olympic

because of its actors and not its plays, for Mitchell could boast "a combination of comic talent certainly unsurpassed in this city."[10]

While Dunn was lending his talents to the comic abilities of the Olympic, New York's theatregoers were being treated to Charles Kean's production of King John at the Park.

Kean had begun to produce the rigorously researched and spectacularly lavish versions of Shakespeare's plays which were to characterize his management of London's Princess's Theatre from 1850 through 1859 at the Park Theatre in New York in 1845, with his version of Richard III. Kean's approach was to be as authentic as possible regarding scenery, heraldry, and costuming from the period in which the plays took place. This archaeologically correct approach to the production of Shakespeare's plays gave the theatre some much-needed intellectual legitimacy. In his playbills, Kean dutifully shared his research with his audience to the point that the programs came to resemble pedantic historical monographs.

Featuring Keans' "historically accurate" costumes and scenery, the production of King John cost over twelve thousand dollars and utilized over fifty thousand square feet of detailed and elaborate scenery.[11] Its "magnificence in every detail eclipsed anything of the sort ever seen in America."[12] Despite the tremendous expense and painstaking preparation with which the play was produced, it was not very successful. Opening on 16 November 1846, it limped along until only 5 December when it was replaced by the Viennese Children, a troupe of preadolescent female dancers. They did what Kean and Shakespeare had been unable to do: fill the large Park Theatre to capacity every night for a month. George Vandenhoff, who played Faulconbridge to Kean's King John, remembered the actor-manager's humiliation and disgust at having his lavish and scholarly production fail and be pushed off the Park's stage by the forty-eight little dancers of the Viennese Children:

> Well, what was the result of all this preparation and outlay? The piece ran, with some difficulty, to moderate houses, the best of which did not reach $800, for three weeks; and then to Mr. Kean's great mortification and disgust was superseded by the Viennese Children (enfans [sic] Terribles! in Kean's eyes) who crammed the house to suffocation for the following month.[13]

Kean apparently made no secret of his anger over being replaced by a troupe of little girls and took his production off
to Boston in something of a self-righteous Victorian huff.

Given Kean's seriousness about his lavish productions
and the ironic humor involved in having one of them literally
driven out of town by a troupe of preteen terpsichoreans, it
would have been surprising if Mitchell had not made some
comment on the event from the boards of the Olympic. As
early as 21 November, it became generally known that Mitchell was preparing a burlesque of recent events at the Park.
The Albion reported: "We understand that Mitchell has a
burlesque of King John nearly ready for representation. This
was to be expected--Mitchell never misses 'good points' either
as an actor, or manager."14

Presumably, Mitchell's original intention was merely
to burlesque the production of King John. But the new lampoon was not ready for production by 5 December, the date
on which the Viennese Children replaced the Shakespearean
play at the Park. Consequently, Mitchell had the script
extensively altered to incorporate the conflict between Kean
and the Austrian sweethearts. The Olympic's playbill for 7
December announced: "a number of Very-Nice children are
engaged and will appear shortly."15 In an effort to get his
new burlesque on the boards while the incidents at the Park
were still immediately topical, Mitchell had the revision completed and the piece ready for production within a week of
the previously quoted announcement. On 14 December, King
John vs. The Very-Nice Children received the first of its six
consecutive performances on the Olympic's stage. Walcot
affected many of Kean's mannerisms in his performance of
King John--"with an aversion to children."16 The brief play
consisted of only three scenes: "De Hoops and Pink Muslin,
by 25 Dancers Very-Nice"; "De Backs of the Characters in
King John by the Backs of the Company"; and, the "Departure
of the Legitimate to Boston, and Triumph of the Very-Nice
Children."17 The rapidity with which the three short tableaux
were prepared probably precluded the possibility that Mitchell's
comment on recent events at the Park would enjoy a long run.
Nevertheless, the humorous topicality of the piece amused the
Olympic's audiences for a week and once again demonstrated
Mitchell's ability at pointed burlesque when provided with a
suitable subject.

The week between the closing of Mitchell's burlesque
and Christmas was characterized by the revival of two old

Olympic favorites, Sleeping Beauty and Sketches In India.
This policy of relying on revivals continued on Christmas
Night, when audiences were treated to new scenery for
Mephistopheles, Mitchell's popular extravaganza of three sea-
sons earlier. The perennial popularity of the piece, com-
bined with the new appointments, enabled it to run through
New Year's Eve and serve as the prime source of attraction
throughout the holiday season.

Although the popularity of revivals produced during the
first three months of Mitchell's seventh season attracted remunerative audiences to the Olympic, the fact that the annual
suspension of the free list did not occur indicates that business
was not as good as it had been during earlier campaigns. This
decrease in attendance, no doubt the result of Mitchell's recent inability to produce many popular new plays, is further
attested to by a review in The Albion which, by stating that
"Mitchell has roused up with the holiday season,"18 suggests
an attendance slump in early December.

The manager's policy of relying on revivals of favorites from the Olympic's repertory to the almost total exclusion of the production of new pieces was a self-defeating one.
Sooner or later, he would run out of former hits and attendance, which appears to have fallen off slightly during the
fall of 1846, would plummet. One is forced to ask why,
given the unequivocal success of the policies Mitchell had
developed and established during his first six seasons, was
he pursuing what would eventually become a suicidal course
of action?

Perhaps the primary reason for the decline in the
manager's ability to please his public with new plays through
the fall was the state of his health. Mitchell's personal life
had been extremely trying for over two years because his
wife was approaching the advanced stages of insanity which
finally necessitated her confinement in an asylum and their
subsequent divorce in 1849. As personal matters had wor-
sened, Mitchell, who had always been a convivial man, had
taken more to drink. His increased tippling apparently did
not directly impair his professional abilities. But combined
with the extremely hard pace at which he worked, it produced
nervousness, obesity, and probably hypertension. Matters
came to a crisis on 25 January when the theatre's bills had
to be cancelled and reprinted, owing to the fact that Mitchell
was unable to act in the plays advertised for performance.
While it is impossible to determine exactly what malady befell

the manager, his personal problems, drinking habits, and
obesity, combined with the extremely rigorous work schedule
he had been obliged to follow throughout his career as the
Olympic's manager, suggest that he suffered a mild stroke
or sudden heart attack. Whatever the nature of his illness,
it was severe enough to prevent him from appearing on the
stage until the opening of the following season nine months
later. Moreover, ill health also prevented his customary care
and effort in selecting and rehearsing new plays. This proved
a definite detriment to the theatre's fortunes, for it had been
obvious that the prime cause for the Olympic's success was
the manager's imagination, taste, and hard work. With Mitchell now disabled, his responsibility for the popularity of the
theatre became even more evident, as its attractiveness began to slip slowly away.

The first certain indication that things were not going
well was that the annual benefit season at the Olympic started
in January, two months earlier than usual. This may have
been an attempt on the part of Mitchell to stall for enough
time to recover sufficient health to take active command
again. If that was the case, it did not work, for the fact
that he did not appear on the stage throughout the remainder
of the season suggests that there was little improvement in
his physical condition during the six months following his
debilitation.

A decline in the theatre's popularity is further suggested
by another move on the part of the manager. He hired the
first star to grace the Olympic's boards since his initial season. Ironically, the performer who broke Mitchell's seven-
year long tradition of operating without stars was Mary Taylor,
a former member of the company who had risen to prominence
under Mitchell's management. The playbills for her engagement, which began on 15 March and continued until 24 April,
leave no doubt that she was hired as a star; her name is
printed in bold type at the top of each bill advertising her
appearance. Unlike stars of the first magnitude, however,
Miss Taylor was required to appear nightly, primarily in
farces and extravaganzas that she had made popular during her
earlier seasons at the Olympic.

Mitchell's stratagem worked wonderfully. Not only
did attendance at the Olympic during Mary Taylor's engagement increase to a point reminiscent of the earliest weeks of
the season, but the "beauty and fashion" of the city, who had
slowly been driven from their seats in the private boxes and

dress circle by the rambunctious pittites, returned in large numbers.[19]

The closing weeks of the season were also aided by another incident which was somewhat providential in nature. With the coming of warmer weather, Constantia Clarke, who had rivaled Mary Taylor in popularity during earlier seasons but had been inactive most of the winter because of her tuberculosis, improved markedly in her condition and was able to appear on the stage with her former colleague nearly every night during Mary Taylor's engagement. Mitchell now had his three most popular actresses performing again, for Mrs. Timm had rejoined the company in the fall and had been appearing regularly throughout the season.

During the first week of Mary Taylor's engagement, which began on 15 March, she drew crowded audiences in two of her former vehicles, Telemachus and Diana's Revenge. The Albion noted that the return of Taylor and Clarke to the Olympic's stage had immediately restored the theatre to its former pinnacle of success: "Mitchell has restored all the old attractions of his popular establishment. Miss Taylor and Miss Clarke, added to the excellent company, bring back all of the old associations of the Olympic."[20] The Spirit of The Times' critic was equally delighted by the return of the two lovelies to the Olympic's stage and congratulated Mitchell on his happy fortune.[21]

While Mary Taylor was appearing in two of her former roles in popular extravaganzas, the company was rapidly rehearsing The Child of The Regiment, an opera previously produced at the Olympic under its original title, La Viviandere. Featuring Taylor in the title role, it opened on 24 March and played twelve times within two-and-a-half weeks. The Spirit of The Times found the opera's revival as delightful as its original production at the Olympic: "The 'Child of The Regiment' having lost none of its charms, and Miss Taylor none of hers, has been performed nearly every evening since her engagement to crowded houses."[22] The notice congratulated Constantia Clarke, Holland, and Walcot on their performances in the opera, and predicted great success for the next operatic offering, The Marriage of Figaro.

The Spirit of The Times was wrong. The Marriage of Figaro had failed miserably when first produced three seasons earlier. It was probably revived only because Mary

Taylor had sung Suzanna and the company's personnel had
not changed significantly, so that only a small number of
rehearsals were required to prepare the piece. That the
hasty revival was unsuccessful is attested to by the fact that
its single performance was the one mentioned in The Spirit
of The Times.

The remainder of Mary Taylor's limited engagement
was filled by the revival of another opera which had proven
popular when first presented. On 9 April, Fra Diavolo, a
solid hit of the 1843-44 season, received the first performance of its revival. However, the piece must have been
underrehearsed because it was replaced by The Child of The
Regiment after only one night's performance. But two days
later, Monday, 12 April, it reentered the bills as the prime
attraction. After enjoying a nine-day run, it dropped from
the evening's entertainment on 24 April only because Mary
Taylor's engagement concluded on that date. A review of
the revival which appeared in The Spirit of the Times indicates that it was every bit as attractive as The Child of The
Regiment had been.[23]

On the date of Mary Taylor's last performance the
same journal reported that the Olympic's audience had re-
acquired the heterogeneous quality which had characterized
the theatre during earlier seasons. Noting that "The boxes
of the Olympic are always crowded, "[24] the reporter marveled
at the constant support given to Mitchell's enterprise by his
pit patrons: "The boys, indeed, have so continuously occupied
this pit that they feel perfectly at home, and adopt measures
for comfort, convenience and fun, with which no man, scien-
tific, diplomatic or authoritative dare to interfere."[25]

With the departure of "our Mary," Mitchell lost the
drawing card which had crowded the Olympic during the six
weeks of her engagement. Consequently, the season closed
one week later on 1 May. During the six performances remaining after Taylor's departure, the prime source of attraction was a burlesque of The Child of The Regiment entitled
The Child of The M.P.'s which featured Holland and Constantia Clarke. Although it proved unattractive, it, as an
example of Mitchell's ever-increasing proclivity for self-
burlesque, did manage to draw substantial audiences during
the final evenings of the manager's eighth campaign.

The season had been an unfortunate one for Mitchell.
During the first three months, he managed to continue to ride

the crest of popularity which had developed continuously since
his assumption of the theatre's management. But his inability
to bring out any new topical burlesques or to produce successfully any popular recent British farces took its toll, and attendance fell off during the month of December. Since the Olympic's phenomenal success had been vested primarily in the person of Mitchell, both as an actor and as a manager, it is
not surprising that the severe debilitation which made it impossible for him to act, and presumably minimized his
managerial functions, decreased the theatre's popularity. Yet
the weakened manager's pragmatic resourcefulness enabled
him to salvage what would no doubt have been a disastrous
spring by hiring his most popular former actress, Mary
Taylor, for a six-week engagement. Providence also helped
the indisposed manager during the spring of 1847, for the
fair weather caused a temporary improvement in Constantia
Clarke's chronic ill health and enabled her to perform frequently.

The season was characterized by a paucity of topical
burlesque as well as a dearth of good, new imported pieces.
The only example of the kind of topically specific burlesque
upon which a good deal of Mitchell's reputation rested was
his ridicule of the greater popularity of the Viennese Children
than Kean's lavish production of King John, which was produced early in December, six weeks before the manager was
suddenly taken ill.

This lack of both topical burlesque and good new
British plays, combined with Mitchell's ill health, certainly
made the season less interesting than any of its predecessors.
But perhaps even more significantly, although the Olympic
continued to be well attended, occasional notices in the press
and the fact that the free list was not suspended indicate that
the 1846-47 campaign was less remunerative than earlier
campaigns. The season, both artistically and financially,
appears to have been a step backward.

CHAPTER EIGHT

The Last of the Palmy Days, 1847-48

From 1847 on, the general state of the American
economy and the particular attractiveness of theatrical speculation steadily improved.   When Mitchell opened the Olympic
for his ninth season on 13 September 1847, he had some new
competitors.   The Broadway Theatre was ready for business
and soon eclipsed the Park as both New York's most popular
upper-class playhouse and the city's standard stop for traveling stars of the highest magnitude.   Fashionable New Yorkers
were preparing to open their own private entertainment palace,
the Astor Place Opera House.   Its difficult early history will
be discussed later in this chapter.

The city's older playhouses were to have difficult seasons.   The Park, under the management of an aging and
weary Edmund Simpson, continued to provide its audience
with a steady stream of visiting stars.   But competition from
the upstart Broadway Theatre fettered Simpson's best efforts
and the Park closed from mid-December until mid-March.
When Simpson reopened the venerable playhouse, he was unable to compete with the city's other theatres and retired as
the Park Theatre's manager in May of 1848.   The Bowery
also suffered from competition from the new Broadway Theatre.
Jackson's management limped along unspectacularly until
March, when he abdicated in favor of T. S. Hamblin, who
reinstituted the policy of sensational melodrama and occasional
stars that had characterized his earlier career as the Bowery's
manager.   Among the smaller theatres, only the Chatham
managed to operate throughout the entire season, but only
because F. S. Chanfrau became its manager in the spring of
1848 while still a member of Mitchell's stock company.   Thus,
while New York's theatres fared slightly better than they had
in over a decade, none of them were able to challenge Mitchell's position as manager of the most successful theatre in
the city of New York.

The Olympic's personnel had again changed significantly.
Two of Mitchell's most popular and useful actors, Charles
Walcot and John Nickinson, had left their benefactor. Nickinson went to play at the Park and Walcot, who took the ailing
but temporarily improved Constantia Clarke with him, started
a series of touring engagements which took him to virtually
all of the established theatrical centers of the country.

To fill the void left by Nickinson and Walcot, three
actors with little previous experience were hired. Two of
them, George Arnold and Peter Cunningham, became useful
performers but never achieved great popularity with the
Olympic's audiences. Walcot proved particularly difficult to
replace, since he had been, excepting Mitchell, the company's
best imitator of other actors. When the manager's ill health
made it doubtful that he would be able to perform frequently,
it became an absolute necessity to find someone capable of
taking Walcot's share of the burden in imitating the styles
and affectations of other performers often demanded by Mitchell's topical burlesques. For that purpose a young actor
named Frank S. Chanfrau was engaged. Chanfrau had debuted
at the Bowery in 1843. As a stock actor at the Chatham
during the 1844-45 season and at the Park during the 1846-
47 campaign, he had become best known for his ability to
mimic other actors. Like most of Mitchell's young recruits,
he had little claim on the public's favor prior to joining the
Olympic's stock company.

While it was uncertain that the male members of the
company would prove as effective as they had in the past,
the Olympic's list of actresses was definitely strengthened
by the return of Mary Taylor. She had discovered, much
as Mrs. Leslie Carter was to find more than half a century later, that her success was almost totally contingent
on the manager under whom she first became popular.
"Our Mary" returned to the fold, though not as a star in
residence, for she received no preferential treatment regarding either frequent benefits or bold advertisements in the
theatre's playbills.

During the summer months, the theatre had undergone
its usual scrubbing and painting. Preparations were completed
early in September for commencement of the season on the
thirteenth of that month. Mitchell, who had been nursing
himself back to good health over the summer vacation, had
evidently improved markedly and was able to resume ener-
getic and active control of the affairs of the theatre. The

season's opening night audience saw Mitchell in one of his
most popular roles, Timothy Tapewell in Saratoga Springs,
plus the American premiere of Planché's Paphian Bower,
which had served as Madame Vestris' Boxing Night attraction
at the London Olympic in 1832 and had run for seventy-seven
performances there. Although fifteen years old, Planché's
extravaganza was new to New York's audiences and proved
attractive enough to play for twelve consecutive evenings before being withdrawn from the bills. The Albion noted that
the first week's business seemed to predict for the manager,
"even more than his usual continuance of unimpaired success,"[1]
and that on the season's opening night, "the reappearance of
Mitchell, after his severe illness, was converted into an
ovation."[2]

With the return of both Mary Taylor and Mitchell to
the boards of the Olympic's stage, the audience rapidly regained the heterogeneous quality which had helped to make
the Olympic the most unusual and successful theatre in New
York. In noting, "The boys are in ecstasies, and have gone
down three years in juvenile appearance; the middle-aged
men look healthier and smile oftener, and the old decrepit
people have dropped their sticks to walk boldly and erect to
the box office,"[3] the reviewer from The Spirit of The Times
implies that a mixed audience had found its way back into
the little band-box of a theatre on lower Broadway.

Halfway through the second week of the season, with
Paphian Bower still drawing crowded houses, Mitchell opened
another of Planché's works, The Jacobite, which received
its American premiere on 22 September.

New plays and the reappearance of Mitchell were not
the only reasons for the early-season success of the Olympic.
The manager's extremely good judgment in hiring Chanfrau
soon became evident. The Widow's Victim, which had been
one of Walcot's most popular vehicles, was revived at the
same time The Jacobite was produced and proved to the manager and audiences alike that Chanfrau was indeed an able
young actor. By the end of the second week of the new campaign, Chanfrau regularly played the lead in those pieces
which had previously been successful at the Olympic, primarily
because of Walcot's abilities as a mimic.

Continually crowded audiences did not lure Mitchell
into repeating his mistake of the early months of the previous season by relying exclusively on the revival of popular

pieces from the theatre's repertory. Novelty followed novelty
with dazzling rapidity through September and October. On
27 September, J. S. Coyne's How To Settle Accounts With
Your Washerwoman received its American premiere and ran
for the entire week.

Coyne's one-act farce had premiered at London's
Adelphi Theatre a mere two months prior to its production
at New York's Olympic Theatre. Mitchell's ability to obtain
and produce the play within two months of its London debut
attests to his renewed managerial vigor. The new piece provided Mitchell with an excellent vehicle in the character of
Whittington Widgetts, a tailor who has promised to marry his
laundress, Mary White, to settle accounts for twenty-nine
unpaid laundry bills. But Widgetts' head has been turned by
Cheri Bounce, a ballerina with whom he has arranged an
intimate champagne supper in his apartment. The laundress
finds a note from the ballerina to Widgetts in his soiled
linen and decides to revenge herself by leaving a suicide note
and immersing a dummy dressed in her clothes in Widgetts'
water butt. But matters become hilariously complicated when
Widgetts' servant inadvertently burns the suicide note while
cleaning and Mary has to abort the hoax to keep Widgetts
from being accused of her murder since no one will get close
enough to the body in the water butt to establish its identity
as a dummy. The role gave Mitchell much scope for comic
anguish and became one of his popular vehicles.

Opera was first produced on 6 October when The
Night Dancers, scored by E. Loder with libretto by G. Soane,
played for the first of its seven evenings. By the time it
was produced, two other popular London farces--E. Stirling's
Kissing Goes by Favour, opening on 1 October, and Alfred
Wigan's Luck's All, first seen on the fourth of the month--
had been given their American debuts. An extremely busy
manager, Mitchell premiered more recent London pieces
during the first three weeks of the season than he had during
the entire previous year.

In an article which praised Mitchell for a return to
those policies responsible for the Olympic's rise to prominence, The Spirit of The Times observed, "Some new and
successful pieces have been produced lately, and the old
regime by which the theatre won its way to public favor has
been restored."4   Citing good, new pieces well produced as
the cause of the Olympic's resurgent popularity,, the columnist
suggested: "The patrons of the house are almost immoveable,

"Sarah Timm and Mary Taylor in The Night Dancers." The
Harvard Theatre Collection.

and anomalous as it may seem, this house has permanent
boarders enough to maintain, if fed by variety."[5]

New farces were not the only testimonial to the manager's vigor in catering to his public, for on 20 October another extravaganza from the pen of Planché, entitled The New
Planet, premiered at the Olympic.

Planché's new offering had debuted the previous April
at London's Haymarket Theatre. Concerning itself with the
recently discovered planet Neptune, the extravaganza focused
on the problem of the new planet's name. Portrayed by a
voluptuous young woman, the solar system's most recent
addition had been horribly misnamed by her discovering as-
tronomer. The cast of characters consists of the solar
system's other planets and the standard Greek gods. During
the course of the action, Venus and Juno get into a fight.
Mercury becomes harlequin during the transformation scene
and conducts the lovely Neptune on a welcoming tour of London
by night, during which they visit the Polytechnic Institute,
Egyptian Hall, and other noteworthy sites about the city. The
extravaganza concludes with a committee meeting of the other
planets, who decide that although Neptune's name is inappropriate, it would simply be too much trouble to change it.

The piece was adapted for Mitchell's theatre by Northall in such a fashion that it concentrated on the topic most on
the minds of Americans during the autumn of 1847: the war
with Mexico. Rather than conducting the new planet on a
tour of New York's most interesting sites, Mercury as Harlequin takes Neptune on something of a fact-finding mission
to the war zone. Myth and contemporary history mixed
curiously in front of four newly painted drops by Bengough
which represented: The Capture of the Sabine Women; General
Taylor being crowned by Fame and supported by Justice and
Mercy; The Maid of Saragozza; and, a Market-place in Mexico.[6]
The altered import proved a hit and ran for twenty consecutive evenings--the longest run any play had enjoyed at the
Olympic since the phenomenally popular Mr. and Mrs. Caudle
two seasons earlier. In its review of the new extravaganza,
The Albion noted the textual alterations: "The piece is announced as from the pen of J. R. Planché, but it must have
undergone a complete revision from the original, for it is
local in its character and dialogue."[7]

While The New Planet was on the boards, The Spirit
of The Times carried an article which suggested that the

antics of the "b'hoys" in the pit, if occasionally obstreperous,
contributed significantly to the amusement of the theatre's more
sophisticated patrons. 8 Moreover, the columnist suggested
that the "b'hoys" were generally astute if somewhat unsophisti-
cated critics: "The juvenile portion of the community at this
day are wonderfully precocious, and not only patronize the
drama, but indulge in criticisms which actors might appreciate
and improve by."9 Going to the theatre had become the
favorite recreation of the newsboys and apprentices of the city's
Lower East Side, and the reporter marveled that "It is not
at all uncommon to meet on corners groups of boys full to
the throat with quotations from various dramas..."10

It was also during the run of The New Planet that
Mitchell produced the first of the season's topical burlesques.
The play, with the unlikely title of Chinese Junk, represented
Mitchell's explanation of a phenomenon which had been causing
much interest in the city since midsummer.

Sometime during July, a Chinese Junk appeared off
Castle Gardens and remained moored there until well into
November. Although no one knew it at the time, the ship
was manned by a crew of Chinese sailors who wished to
immigrate. The ship laid at anchor for a long time without
having any apparent reason for being there and gave rise
to much speculation regarding who owned it and what it was
for.11 The most consistent and apparently logical explanation
concerning the ship suggested that it was a speculation of
P. T. Barnum's which would be part of his fall exhibit at
Barnum's Museum. It was this rumor that Mitchell capitalized on in Northall's Chinese Junk, a burlesque which received the first of its twenty consecutive performances at
the Olympic on 1 November.

In the piece, the hero is a thinly disguised caricature
of Barnum named Theophilus Catchall, esq.: "A whipper up
of unconsidered trifles, but as the saying is, he is a man,
'A take in for all in all. We shall not look upon his like
again.'"12 The action involved Catchall's attempt to rouse
the Chinese to revolt in order that he might rule that mysterious land of the East. The manner in which his goal was
to be accomplished consisted of loading the Chinese Junk with
his "worn out curiosities"--much in the manner of Noah--and
sailing off to China, where his array of attractions would
enable him to pass himself off as a deity to the populace.
The playbill of 1 November lists the passengers on Catchall's
oriental ark:

General T. Thumb;	a great traveller in a small way. He visited all the courts of Europe and though so small he frequently put the English sovereign in his pocket.
Ole Ole Ander;	A shaking Quaker but no great shakes.
C. Serpent esq.;	The author of a periodical tail of the sea not to be continued.
Santa Anna Leggett;	A retiring gentleman, fully unprepared, with the truth that discretion is the better part of valour.
The Mysterious Lady;	A great lady for any place where Miss Tree would be required.
Joyce Heth;	A very dry nurse. 13

Reviewing the production on 6 November, The Albion found it very amusing: "The piece is sufficiently pointed and humourous to create a hearty laugh,--and the manager's and author's end is thus fully answered. The author has seized the idea that got into circulation of the Junk's being a speculation of Barnum's. "14

With both Chinese Junk and The New Planet in the bills, the Olympic could boast its most attractive set of offerings in over a year, and crowded audiences continued to be the manager's reward for increasing his efforts to please his patrons.

On 15 November, with Mitchell's burlesque of Barnum still drawing well, a new one-act farce by J. S. Coyne entitled This House to Be Sold, Property of the late Wm. Shakespeare, Enquire Within, was produced. The play had received its London premiere at the Adelphi Theatre on 9 September 1847. The rapidity with which Mitchell obtained and rehearsed the new piece for production at the Olympic amply demonstrates that it did not take very long for recent hits from London's theatres to cross the Atlantic and find their way onto the boards of the Olympic. As the lengthy title indicates, the new piece was inspired by the then recent sale of Shakespeare's birthplace. Like most of Mitchell's other "novelties" of the fall, the new trifle proved extremely popular and was performed on fifteen consecutive evenings. In it, Holland played Chatterton Chopkins, a dilettante with more money

than sense who purchases the Bard's birthplace. Spending the
first night in the poet's chamber of his new home, Chopkins
falls asleep and is visited by the shade of Shakespeare, which
The Albion praised as "exceedingly well embodied by Mr.
Cunningham."[15] The Bard's ghost is accompanied by major
characters from many of his plays including Hamlet, Othello,
Shylock, Falstaff, Polonius, Romeo, Macbeth, Lady Macbeth,
Desdemona, and Juliet. Shakespeare and his characters
complain bitterly yet comically about the displacement of the
legitimate drama by ballet and opera. Because the poet can
no longer find work for his creations, he discharges them and
they go their separate ways. Othello joins a minstrel troupe
as an Ethiopian Serenader, Desdemona finds employment at
Astley's Circus as a bareback rider, the Macbeths are forced
to take in laundry, and Hamlet runs away to join the army.
Chopkins awakens from the dream so frightened that he decides to give the house to his countrymen as a national shrine.
The Albion's critic found the new farce delightful and reported
that "the whole thing is well conceived and is admirably put
upon the stage."[16]

        This House to Be Sold ran in conjunction with Robin-
son Crusoe The Second--an extravaganza which opened on
12 November--until the twenty-seventh of the month. During
the two ensuing weeks, Mitchell relaxed a bit, and did not
present any new pieces. Still, the people came to his theatre
in droves. The Albion complained: "The critic's labour at
this house is becoming comparatively a sinecure. It is only
to record a succession of crowded houses attracted nightly
to a repetition of old established stock pieces. While this
continues, Mitchell will keep his repertoire of novelties fast
locked--wisely retaining them for future exigencies."[17]

        While the Olympic's audiences were being entertained
by revivals of some of their favorite stock pieces, Mitchell
was rehearsing another of Northall's topical burlesques. The
new piece had as its object of ridicule the unfortunate early
history of New York's newest and most elite temple of the
drama, the Astor Place Opera House.

        With the return of economic prosperity, New York's
mercantile aristocracy found themselves in an extremely
comfortable position; they were wealthier than they had ever
been before. A concomitance of their new wealth and power
was a desire to establish New York as a rival cultural center
to the capitals of Europe. To this end a committee of the
city's leading citizens formulated plans for the construction

and management of a new opera house. Located in Astor
Place, the new theatre was to be the private possession of
the elite seasonal subscribers, all of whom were to be carefully scrutinized regarding their wealth and social standing in
the community.

The new temple of sophisticated dramatic entertainment was ready for occupancy by a company early in November. Seating eighteen hundred patrons, its opulent decorations
far surpassed anything ever seen in any theatre in this country.
In order to preserve the insularity of the sophisticated community from the "rabble" of the city, certain measures, at
best unusual and at least undemocratic, were taken regarding
admission.

The "free list, " which was honored by every other
theatre in the city and provided gratis admission to members
of the press, actors and managers from other theatres, and
some fashionable and influential opinion leaders from the
realms of politics and literature, was not to be honored at
the new temple of the muses. Furthermore, admission was
to be available only to those who had subscribed for the entire season, and, as mentioned previously, subscribers were
carefully screened before their applications for season tickets
would be considered. Not surprisingly, these policies rankled
New York's growing middle class and the "democratic" mechan-
ics of the Bowery who had developed a taste for opera as
the result of the productions of Mitchell and Palmo.

The committee in charge of the opera house optimisti-
cally assumed that there would be no problem in recruiting
eighteen hundred season subscribers from the elite citizens
of New York, but they were sadly mistaken, for only five
hundred persons had subscribed by the date on which the opera
house was to open. As James Gordon Bennett sarcastically
noted: "Now as this movement was considered highly important
in the fashionable annals of New York...instead of their being
tens of thousands of this self same upper class, it appears
that when the subscribers were required to pay in advance,
the number shrunk to five hundred."[18]

The governing committee was not discouraged, however,
for they assumed that the opening production of the season
would be a resounding success and thereby induce great numbers of the right kinds of people to apply for season subscriptions. Nothing could have been further removed from the
actual course of events than the hopes of the committee. The

company engaged to open the opera house was mediocre at best, and the opening production, the American premiere of Ernani, an opera by Verdi and Piave based on Hugo's play Hernani, proved unpopular.

The failure of the expected surge for subscriptions after the opera's opening night, 22 November, caused the management to destroy its first barrier against the commoners: the free list was instituted as part of the opera house's policy, much to the amusement of those New Yorkers who had been annoyed by the conceits of their wealthy and fashionable fellow citizens.

The glee with which the news of the introduction of a free list at the opera house was received among New Yorkers is probably best represented by the following item from the editorial column of Bennett's Herald:

> Now all these salutary rules are rescinded, and probably the next move of the managers, Sanquirico and Co., will be to send agents all about town, and not only to offer free tickets, but actually even white kid gloves. Consequently, every man sporting moustaches will be in danger of being arrested by the opera police, of being carried to Astor Theatre, invested with white kids, and there be imprisoned and confined and punished a whole long tedious night with having to listen to a dull Opera, in order that the house may make a fashionable appearance.[19]

Even the introduction of the free list, however, did not increase sophisticated support for the opera house. Problems were compounded by the failure of the second production, the popular La Sonnambula. It was miserably produced and proved even less attractive than its predecessor. Matters were rapidly going from bad to worse in Astor Place, and despite the intent of the board of directors to insulate the subscribers from the lower classes, they were forced to develop a plan by which they could expect to meet expenses. Therefore, they opened the house to the general public on Saturday nights at a price of admission competitive with the Park and Palmo's. But New York's less affluent opera buffs had been so insulted by the pretense of the board of directors that they boycotted the opera house. On 5 December, when La Sonnambula was offered to the public at large for the first time, the eighteen hundred-seat theatre was attended by only one hundred sixty paying patrons.[20]

Within a short time, it became obvious that the "opera season" was an impossible failure. Consequently, the house became available for the production of legitimate plays for the amusement of the general public, and the displaced Italian opera company went on tour to Philadelphia and Boston.

The humor inherent in the events which caused the "fashionable" members of the community to humiliate themselves with their own conceit is readily apparent and provided Mitchell with a marvelous occasion for topical burlesque.

While the Olympic's audiences were witnessing a revival of popular farces and extravaganzas during late November and early December, the manager was rapidly rehearsing a new burlesque from the pen of Northall entitled, aptly, Uproar House in Disaster Place. "Produced under the direction of Wm. Mitchell,"21 the new burlesque opened on 13 December and ran for twelve consecutive performances. It concerned itself with the attempt of three people to found a fashionably elite opera house and closely paralleled the actual events which had caused the "disaster" in Astor Place.

The principal character and mastermind of the fictitious opera house was A La Mode, "King of the realm of Fashion, a gentleman who does not wear his clothes, but lets them wear him."22 A La Mode's principal aide de camp was a thinly disguised caricature of Count D'Orsay, the Prince of Victorian Dandies, named Count Daresay: "Minister to A La Mode, a gentleman of such deep learning that nobody can discover its depth."23 Their principal benefactor was Mrs. Millionaire--"Rich in everything but taste, refinement, and education."24

Producing a theatrical comment on the incidents surrounding the difficulties at the new Opera house was a dangerous undertaking, for its effect was contingent on maintaining the very fine line that separates ludicrous burlesque from stinging satire. Apparently, Mitchell was up to the task, for The Albion commented on the good taste with which he handled the potentially troublesome subject: "The subject is a delicate one to handle so as to avoid personalities which might be impertinent and offensive, and considerable tact is exhibited by the author in arranging his materials. The hits are occasionally pointed and telling, too serious and truthful, perhaps, for an extravaganza, but they are harmless and in tolerably good taste."25

The Albion was not the only journal to think that

Mitchell's production did not contribute to the already-strained relations between different segments of New York's citizens caused by the incidents in Astor Place. The Spirit of The Times suggested that the burlesque was so harmless, yet so funny, that it would actually help to heal the emotional wounds inflicted upon the various socioeconomic classes of the community by the opera house fiasco: "Mitchell will reap a harvest from public dissensions and will at the same time contribute much to the restoration of good humour."26

On 20 December, with Uproar House still running, Mitchell produced the American premiere of yet another popular play by J. R. Planché, The Pride of The Market. Unlike many of Planche's other offerings which Mitchell produced at the Olympic, The Pride of The Market was not a one-act farce or an extravaganza, but a three-act comedy of manners. Set in Paris during the reign of Louis XIV, the play contains a romantic intrigue in which a decadent chevalier kidnaps a beautiful market wench and sequesters her in his apartment at Versailles while trying to seduce her. Her virtuous third-estate fiancé discovers the plot and rescues her while showing the chevalier the error of his ways. The play contains no low comic characters or situations, and is more sophisticated than most of Planché's pieces that received their American premiers under Mitchell's direction.

Mitchell's amazing ability to produce one hit after another through the fall and early winter caused The Albion to comment on his talent in an article which appeared on Christmas Day. Noting that since the beginning of the current season he had produced "a constant succession of novelties, adapted to the tastes of his audiences,"27 the reporter suggested: "If ever there was a manager who understood the great secret of success, in New York, that man is Mitchell. With a company scarcely rising above mediocrity, yet by a judicious application of their talents, occasionally appearing to be great, he contrives to fill his little box nightly with delighted audiences."28 Things had changed in New York theatres during the eight years Mitchell had been in business. Audiences no longer favored traveling stars supported by inept stock companies in tiresome pieces from the standard repertory. They had come to favor Mitchell's approach: a constant succession of new plays lavishly produced and performed by an ensemble company without either stars or incompetents.

On 3 January, Mitchell produced his first "novelty" of the new year, the American premiere of J. M. Morton's

phenomenally popular Box and Cox. Featuring the manager
and Holland in the principal roles, the piece ran for a week
and was presented frequently throughout the rest of the season.
The critic for The Spirit of The Times reported: "It is one
of the most amusing pieces we have ever seen; and from its
commencement to its termination, is a series of the most
ludicrous and mirth provoking events we have ever had the
pleasure to observe."[29]

     With the coming of the new year and the benefit season
at the Olympic, fewer new pieces were produced. Nevertheless, people continued to fill the theatre in spite of the sudden,
inexplicable depression in theatre attendance which closed the
Park and reduced the Broadway's income to the point that it
could barely meet overhead expenses. The Albion commented
that, "Mitchell is certainly a petted child of fortune in his
managerial character. Let whoever will fall, the attractions
of the little Olympic buoy him up."[30]

     The Olympic's first "local peculiarity" of the new year
was produced on 12 January. For some time, signs reading
"Where's Eliza?" had been seen on buildings throughout the
city. No one could determine what the signs meant, but
Mitchell produced an anonymous piece entitled Where's Eliza?
and thereby capitalized on the curiosity that the inexplicable
signs had created. Although the piece failed and was withdrawn after only two nights, it once again demonstrated Mitchell's ability to draw on matters of public interest as material
for his "local peculiarities." The Spirit of The Times reported: "Our readers in this city, no doubt, saw placards
posted in various parts of the city, bearing the significant
words, 'Where's Eliza?' What is the meaning we cannot well
determine, but Mitchell thought he could, and did. If you
wish to know, go to the Olympic."[31]

     Sometime during January, the pittites, who had been
on their good behavior since the near riot of Holland's benefit
two seasons earlier, became unruly again. Frequent inter-
jections and even interruptions of performances by the "b'hoys"
caused The Albion to demand that Mitchell do something to
discipline his less sophisticated patrons. In reviewing the
history and nature of the Olympic, the journal noted that many
people "have always looked upon the Olympic as a sort of
pet establishment, not subjected to strict criticisms on its
performances, nor severity of stricture upon the general
character of its entertainments."[32] Acknowledging that
Mitchell's "avowed purpose was to amuse his patrons at all

hazards, "33 the columnist admits that the manager had been
preeminently successful with his myriad of comic entertainments. But the problem, according to The Albion's reporter,
was that Mitchell "has imperceptibly created quite a peculiar
audience for his house. He has so educated this audience
that it is now as knowing, and as wise, as its instructor. "34
Noting that, "The Pittites of the Olympic are a part and par-
cel of the performances of his house, and manager and actors
are on perfect terms of understanding together, "35 the journalist complains that the behavior of the Olympic's pit patrons
had gradually gotten out of hand and become a nuisance to
the theatre's other audience members. The columnist called
for Mitchell to discipline the "b'hoys, " and "return to a more
decorous observance of those rules which should always separate the actor...from identification with his audience. "36

     Although the exact nature of the "b'hoys" bad behavior
on the above-mentioned occasion has been lost to history, a
probable reconstruction of the incident and its causes is possible. Mitchell and other members of the company frequently
offered pointed ad-lib asides to the pit, and the "b'hoys" often
responded in kind when called upon to do so. It appears that
the patrons of the pit slowly but surely became engaged in an
attempt to be as funny and as pointed as the actors, without waiting to have their comments solicited. It is easy to imagine
how annoying this could prove to the upper-class patrons of
the boxes and dress circle. Mitchell must have realized that
matters were getting out of hand, for during the week of 23
January, he made a speech to the pittites enjoining them to
remember that there were other paying visitors who were
more concerned with what transpired on the stage than in the
pit. He probably also resorted to his infrequent threat of
raising prices of admission to the netherworld if the "b'hoys"
did not begin to conduct themselves in a more acceptable
fashion. Whatever the exact nature of his address to the
pit, it served its purpose. A column in The Albion, probably written by the same journalist who had complained of
the "b'hoys" behavior and urged Mitchell to take appropriate
disciplinary actions, noted: "Mitchell has shown his diplomatic
skill to perfection, the belligerent Pittites are reduced to
submission, and all goes 'Merry as a Marriage-bell.' "37

     With the coming of February, two or three nights a
week were given to the theatre's personnel for their benefits.
It was on one such occasion that Mitchell produced what was
to become the most famous play ever presented under his
auspices, A Glance At New York in 1848. Although the play

was written by Ben Baker, the Olympic's prompter, Frank S.
Chanfrau must be considered equally responsible for its creation.

      Chanfrau, as previously noted, was a consummate
mimic.   During the fall, he became fascinated by the dress
and mannerisms of the "b'hoys" in the Olympic's pit.   He
knew the type, for he had been born and raised on the Bowery
and had even been a volunteer fireman in the famous "Old
Maid" company.   The idea of creating a character drawn from the
ranks of the "b'hoys" appealed so strongly to the young actor
that he approached Baker, who had written several pieces for
the Olympic, and asked him to write a sketch with a "b'hoy"
as the main character.   Baker, too, thought the idea a good
one, and completed the sketch early in the new year.   But
when Mitchell saw the new piece, he was not anxious to produce it, for although he considered the characters good, he
found the action not at all to his liking and was afraid that
the play would be unsuccessful.[38]   Because of Mitchell's
dissatisfaction with the play, Chanfrau and Baker decided to
wait until the evening of Baker's benefit, 15 February, to
present it.   Traditionally, beneficiaries at the Olympic had
the option of selecting the bill for their benefit nights and
even of recruiting the aid of performers not attached to the
theatre's staff.   Although Mitchell had reservations about the
play's potential success, they were not strong enough to cause
him to prohibit its production on the evening of Baker's benefit.   In fact, Mitchell even helped to prepare the play for its
premiere, for it, like all of the Olympic's new offerings,
was "Produced under the direction of Mr. Mitchell."[39]

      Chanfrau, as Mose, was the prime attraction of the
new play and his characterization was the result of both his
background and long careful observation of the Olympic's
pit audience.   Mose Humphrey, one of the largest and loud-
est of Mitchell's regular customers who had been the toughest
street fighter on the Bowery until beaten by Chanfrau's older
brother Henry,[40] may have served the actor as a specific
model.   The performer's background, observation, makeup,
and costume--including a red flannel shirt, suspenders, plug
hat, boots, "soap lock" coiffure, and omnipresent "seegar
butt"--enabled Chanfrau to create a convincing and realistic
character.   His physical appearance and mannerisms were
so true to life that on the night of the play's first performance,
Mitchell, who saw him waiting in the wings to make his en-
trance, mistook him for an actual "b'hoy" who had wandered
backstage and ordered the actor put out of the theatre before
he realized that it was Chanfrau.[41]

A few minutes after Mitchell's embarrassing mistake
the curtain went up and the pittites saw their mirror image
on the stage. With Chanfrau's first line, "I ain't goin to
run wid der machine no more, " the "b'hoys" cheered and the
Olympic had the greatest hit in its history. The play's popularity was so immense that on 8 March, three weeks into its
run, Mitchell suspended the Olympic's free list for the first
time in two years. Reviewing the new hit on 19 February,
The Albion informed its readers: "The present sketch may
be called a dramatic version of our police reports, as it
exhibits the various modes adapted by the sharpers about
town to delude the unwary. "42 The reviewer described Mose
as, "inimitably played by Chanfrau. It is really a character
both in the creation by the author and the embodiment by the
actor. As may by supposed it is received with shouts of delight by the thousand originals of the pit. "43

The Albion's review and an examination of the original
promptscript indicate that, in addition to chronicling some of
the more acute social problems which were plaguing the growing city of New York by 1848, the play treats the traditionally
shrewd rural yankee character most frequently portrayed by
Hackett, Hill, and Marble as unequipped to compete with
urban confidence men and in need of the protection of Mose
in order to survive in the city.

In the opening scene, George, an upstate New Yorker,
has just arrived in the city. The rival claims of the turf of
Mose and Jonathan are made perfectly clear by Harry, George's
urban cousin: "Here you can see all sorts of life. How much
better it is to live here, than in your stupid village in the
backwoods, with no society but that of bumpkins and old
women. "44 George is immediately gulled into buying a solid
gold watch at a bargain price by Mike and Jake, two "sharpers. "
In the next scene, George is again victimized by a now-
disguised Mike and Jake. This time, the unwary yank is
duped into giving ten dollars advance on an expected reward
for a wallet full of bank notes the three "find" together: the
classic pigeon drop. Before Mose arrives to lead George
safely through the maze of swindlers, he gives Jake and Mike
a dollar for admission to Battery Park, changes counterfeit
money, and buys worthless goods at an auction. George does
not fare well in Gotham. Mose's role in the play is to guide
George safely through his first day in the city; the country boy
needs the city boy in order to survive.

The production seemed as contemporary and topical as

"F. S. Chanfrau as 'Mose'." The Harvard Theatre Collection.

the script to the reviewer from The Spirit of The Times, who
found Chanfrau's Mose the most realistic character ever seen
on the stage of a New York theatre:

> Mr. Chanfrau personates one of [the] fire B'hoys
> under the name of 'Mose' in a most capital manner,
> and it is really difficult to divest yourself of the
> conviction that he is a Simon Pure. In all the details
> of the character from the use of a seegar through
> the various changes of habit and manner, the per-
> formance is the very embodiment of the creature
> designed to be represented. We cannot speak too
> highly of the astonishing accuracy with which Mr.
> Chanfrau plays his part, and we advise our friends
> to go and see a character often heard of, but owing
> to his peculiar habits, rarely seen by the larger
> and better community.45

By the date on which the above quoted article appeared in
print, 11 March, Chanfrau and Baker had taken a lease on
the Chatham Theatre, where they were preparing another Mose
play for production while Chanfrau continued to act his role
in A Glance At New York at the Olympic. From 15 April
through 11 May he appeared nightly in two different Mose
plays at two different theatres.

On 22 February, the night of Levere's benefit, A
Glance At New York had been withdrawn from the bills, but
it was reinserted on the next evening. It was again absent
on 21 March, when Dan Marble appeared in two of his popular Yankee vehicles for Mrs. Seymour's benefit. Although
the play proved phenomenally successful, it was altered during the week prior to 18 March. Baker lengthened it and
wrote in the part of Lize, "one of the gals," for Mary Taylor.
In doing so he provided the play with a romantic interest between Lize and Mose, while creating a strong vehicle for the
Olympic's most popular actress, Mary Taylor. With the new
additions, the play proved even more popular. From 15
February--the date of its debut--until 11 May, A Glance At
New York in 1848 was absent from the evening's bills on
only two occasions. It was produced seventy-four times out
of a possible seventy-six evenings, thereby enjoying the longest run of any play in New York prior to Barnum's production
of The Drunkard in 1850.

Halfway through the play's phenomenal run, The Albion
made a suggestion to would-be dramatists which contained an

unusual amount of historical foresight. Calling the marvelous
success of "Mr. Baker's local sketch"[46] to the attention of
aspiring playwrights, the columnist argues that realistic dramatic situations and recognizable characters from contemporary
life "are the true materials on which to form the superstruc-
ture of a native American drama. "[47]

With the unprecedented popularity of Baker's play, Mitchell had no trouble filling the Olympic nightly during the
remainder of the season, and it is not surprising that he produced only four new pieces between the date on which Mose
first graced the boards and the close of the campaign.

The manager's ninth season at the Olympic was certainly a marked improvement over its predecessor. Mitchell
had apparently regained his health, for he acted with greater
frequency than he had for several years. Both the constant
succession of novelties he presented prior to the premiere of
Baker's play and the satisfactory manner in which he disciplined
his unruly pit patrons during January attest to a renewal of
managerial vigor.

The season would probably have been extremely suc-
cessful even if A Glance At New York had not been produced.
Fifteen British farces and extravaganzas premiered on the
Olympic's stage during Mitchell's ninth campaign, and topical
burlesque, represented by Chinese Junk and Uproar House In
Disaster Place, also proved immensely attractive.

In many ways, the season marked a return to policies
which Mitchell had not been pursuing for several seasons.
Frequent changes of bill gave way to a return of the long run.
Eight pieces achieved initial runs of ten performances or
longer, and ten plays were seen twenty times or more during
the season. There were only two week-long periods during
which one of Mitchell's several long-running hits was not providing the theatre's prime source of attraction.

With the full houses and glowing praise the theatre
enjoyed during the first three months of the season and the
meteoric success of A Glance At New York during the late
winter and spring, there is no doubt that Mitchell more than
regained the public support he had lost during his previous
campaign. The season of 1847-48 was indeed a grand one--
the last grand one that Mitchell was to manage at the Olympic.

CHAPTER NINE

The Decline and Fall of

William Mitchell, 1848-50

While the Olympic was closed during the summer of 1848, two new theatres were opened in New York. They were to have a profound effect upon the public patronage that Mitchell had enjoyed for nine seasons.

The first was Chanfrau's Chatham. "Mose" had leased that theatre and opened it in March of 1848, but was unable to devote his total energies to it until he had completed his season-long contract with Mitchell in May of that year. The Chatham became the new home of Mose, and the star siphoned off many of the "b'hoys" from Mitchell's pit during the summer months. Thus, when the Olympic reopened for business in the fall, many of Mitchell's devoted pittites were in the habit of going elsewhere for their theatrical bill of fare and needed to be wooed back to their former home.

The second competitor was more important. William E. Burton had purchased Palmo's Opera House on Chambers Street during the spring of 1848, renovated and redecorated it, and opened it as Burton's Theatre on 10 July 1848.

Burton and Mitchell had much in common: both were British; both were among the leading four low comedians of their day; and, both had the uncanny ability to detect and develop talent in performers of little previous experience.

Burton had previously attempted to establish himself as a theatre manager in New York at the National Theatre during April of 1841. After recruiting a strong stock company, he promised to rival both the Park and the Bowery, but his theatre was destroyed by an arsonist on 19 May 1841. He quit the field of management and resumed his career as a touring star and magazine editor.

The new manager's plans for operating his theatre
were similar to the policies which Mitchell had developed
during his tenure at the Olympic. A good stock company,
performing without the aid of traveling stars, was to appear
in two or three short farces, burlesques, and extravaganzas
nightly. In fairness to Burton, it should be noted that he was
not consciously copying Mitchell's successful policies, for he
had developed the procedures which were to guide his Chambers Street Theatre during the preceding three years as manager of the Arch Street Theatre in Philadelphia.

In spite of Burton's independent development of policies
similar to those of Mitchell, the newcomer's initial success
was directly indebted to the Olympic. Two of Burton's most
important personnel during his first season at Chambers Street
--Loder and Northall--had been important members of
Mitchell's production staff and had developed their abilities
under Mitchell's guiding hand. Moreover, the taste of New
York's theatregoers for the type of entertainments Burton
produced during his initial season at the Chambers Street
Theatre had been well developed by Mitchell during his nine
seasons as the Olympic's manager.

There were other significant changes in New York's
theatrical life during the season of 1848-49. Hamblin had
succeeded Edmund Simpson as manager of the Park Theatre
and sought to manage it and the Bowery Theatre with a
single large stock company, the members of which would
alternate between the two playhouses as needed. This joint
enterprise was slowly failing when the Park was destroyed
by fire on 16 December 1848. But the newer Broadway
Theatre had already eclipsed the venerable playhouse as the
home of the most lustrous stars playing in New York and,
without competition from the older playhouse, enjoyed a
successful season. Hamblin then concentrated both his efforts and his stock company on the Bowery and resorted to
the sensational melodramas and occasional stars that had
characterized his leadership of that theatre for more than a
decade.

When Mitchell opened the Olympic for the tenth season on 18 September 1848, he soon became aware that competition from Burton, and to a lesser degree Chanfrau, had
decimated the Olympic's audience. The fashionable and sophisticated frequenters of Mitchell's boxes and dress circle
had gotten into the habit of visiting the theatre on Chambers
Street over the summer, and Mitchell was forced into

the position of trying to win back a large portion of his former audience. Even the pit was not as crowded as it had once
been, for many of the "b'hoys" were to be found making themselves at home in Chanfrau's Mose-palace, the Chatham.

        Luring back his former patrons was a difficult task for
Mitchell. Some important defections from the Olympic's stock
company made it extremely difficult for Mitchell to compete
with such actors as Burton and John Brougham, who were
nightly packing crowded houses into the new enterprise in
Chambers Street.

        The most important actor to leave the Olympic's com-
pany was Chanfrau. Because Walcot had left the company a
season earlier, the only highly popular actors remaining--
other than Mitchell himself--were George Holland and John
Nickinson, who rejoined the company during September of
1848. The company was now without a mimic of the calibre
of Chanfrau and Walcot, and could not play many of the pieces
in the established repertory that relied on the leading performer burlesquing other well-known actors. Yet the company
suffered even more with regard to lost female talent. The
fickle Mary Taylor had again taken leave of Mitchell, and
Mrs. Timm had retired. Of Mitchell's three most popular
actresses, only the chronically ill Constantia Clarke remained.
In order to fill the vacancies left by Taylor, Timm, and
Chanfrau, Mitchell hired Mary Gannon and William H. Reynolds. These new acquisitions soon proved, as many of their
predecessors had, that Mitchell possessed an astute ability for
discovering and developing talented young actors.

        When the Olympic's tenth season under Mitchell's
management opened on 18 September 1848, the prime source
of attraction was Bengough's panorama of Broadway. The
Albion praised the new scenic spectacle as "the most
beautiful specimen of panoramic painting we have witnessed in
this country; the correct drawing and artistic execution throughout being worthy of all praise."[1] The Spirit of The Times
also acclaimed Bengough's panorama, but suggested that the
prime reason for Mitchell's reliance on the wordless spectacle
as the season's opening attraction was his realization that his
performers needed thorough and extensive rehearsals before they
could be expected to compete favorably with the new company
at the theatre on Chambers Street: "The company appears to
have lost much of its original strength, and the newcomers
are far from making up for the deficiency experienced by the
defection of 'Our Mary,' Miss Clarke [her ill health had
prevented her from appearing], Walcot, cum multis alius."[2]

One week into the season, on 25 September, Mitchell
produced two examples of the kind of "novelty" for which the
Olympic had long been famous. The first, an anonymous import from England entitled Nature and Art, proved a miserable
failure and was withdrawn after two evenings, while the second,
a burlesque of Lola Montez's vehicle for acting her life story,
gave the recently acquired Mary Gannon an opportunity to display her talents. The Spirit of The Times flatteringly reported
that "to the merits of a very clever actress she joins the
talents of a more than fair danseuse, and what she lacks in
the former capacity, she makes up for in the latter qualifica-
tion for an Olympic pet."3

Although Mary Gannon immediately established herself
as a popular and strong addition to the stock company, the
Olympic's ability to attract its usual good houses in the face
of strong competition from Burton was impaired, primarily
because of new indications of the manager's ill health. Mitchell seemed to be actively and energetically managing the
affairs of the Olympic, but he was apparently not well enough
to act frequently and appeared only twice during the first two
weeks of the season. Given the keen competition the Olympic
was receiving from Burton, Mitchell would have added his own
attractiveness as an actor to his theatre's bill of fare had
he been physically capable of doing so.

On 2 October with the initial performance of Hero
and Leander--an extravaganza based on Shakespeare's Midsummer Night's Dream--it became obvious that the Olympic
was in trouble, with regard both to the quality of its entertainments and the audiences which those entertainments were
able to draw. The Spirit noted: "Mitchell's Olympic has
thus far been comparatively deserted; the pit being the only
part of the house in any manner well filled. A very clever
mythological burletta, 'Hero and Leander,' was produced on Monday last, and was well received; but in all respects it is inferior
to the fairy extravaganzas hitherto produced at this house."4
But the columnist hoped for better things from the Olympic
in the near future: "It is understood that several persons in
England, engaged for this establishment have not yet arrived,
and until their advent among us, the management is confused
with regard to the production of novelties."5

The impending arrival of new recruits from London
remained merely a rumor, for no immigrants joined the
company during the season. Yet the general belief that Mitchell's stock company was to be improved by the importation

of English actors was a persistent one. The Albion, too, commented on the small audiences Mitchell had been drawing and hoped for better things with the arrival of the company's supposed new members: "The Olympic is not doing its usual flourishing business. Several of the old favourites of this house are missed, and Mitchell's new recruits are not yet arrived from London."6

While Mitchell was desperately trying to win back his fashionable patrons with Hero and Leander, Burton was amusing the former frequenters of Mitchell's boxes and dress circle with the kind of piece upon which a good deal of the Olympic's reputation had been established. A new burlesque by Northall, entitled New York In Slices, received praise reminiscent of that lavished upon the Olympic's "local pecularities" in earlier seasons: "It is well written, and the local hits are pointed and witty. Of its class we consider it one of the best."7

It was during the month of October that Mitchell began to make inroads into Burton's popularity and to attract some of his departed patrons back to their old place of amusement. Fortunately, Hero and Leander improved after its first few performances and ran for two weeks. Then, on 6 October, a new burlesque, aimed primarily at one of Mitchell's favorite targets--W. C. Macready--and secondarily at some of the Olympic's competitors, was produced.

Macready had appeared in Boston late in September of 1848. Because he had made no arrangements to play at any theatre in New York, the managers of the city's larger theatres dashed off to Boston in an attempt to secure his services for their respective establishments.

It was this competition among several of New York's theatrical impresarios that provided impetus for Who's Got Macready, or A Race to Boston. Opening on 6 October, the new burlesque featured Nickinson as Macready, Clark as Mr. Park, Reynolds as Mr. Broadway, Conover as Mr. Astor Place, and Arnold as the auctioneer. The action concerned itself with the auctioning of Macready's services to the bidders from New York. Although the press condemned the play--The Albion described it as "anything but successful"8 --it ran for a week and was partially responsible for the larger audiences which were beginning to attend the Olympic.

Attendance increased steadily during the first two weeks of October and reached a seasonal high with the production of

a Planché extravaganza, Theseus and Ariadne, which received
its American premiere on the sixteenth of the month. In its
review The Spirit of The Times found both the extravaganza--
which was in the bills nightly for two weeks--and the performances of the stock company very attractive. Describing it
as "one of the most amusing pieces of the season,"9 the
columnist commended Conover for a performance that was
"peculiarly comic,"10 and noted that, "the rest of the characters were well represented."11 The Albion confirmed The
Spirit of The Times report, noting, "It is altogether the most
successful extravaganza of the season."12

        Even with the success of Theseus and Ariadne, the
Olympic had still not regained the level of popularity it had
enjoyed in the past seasons, for a week after the new extravaganza opened The Albion noted: "The great competition
in theatrical and other amusements, somewhat interfere [sic]
with this old established resort...."13 Nevertheless, Mitchell slowly but steadily wooed back many of his former
patrons through the remainder of October. Season attendance
reached a new high following the production of a condensed
version of the ballet, La Esmerelda, on 30 October. This
vehicle provided Mary Gannon with an opportunity to demonstrate her considerable talents as an actress and dancer. It
ran for twelve evenings and earned an extremely favorable
review from The Spirit of The Times which indicated that
the new actress's talents were helping to fill the void resulting from the departure of Mary Taylor, the retirement of
Mrs. Timm, and the chronic illness of Constantia Clarke:
"Mitchell has most assuredly an attractive card in this useful appendage to his company, for a good looking young actress
is ever a good feature in a farce, but when she superadds
the advantage derived from singing and dancing, she should
be deemed perfectly irresistible by the 'b'hoys' anywhere,
and most especially at the 'little Box.' "14

        A week after the premiere of La Esmerelda, Mitchell
strengthened the steadily growing attractiveness of his bills
with the American debut of another Planché farce, The
Queensbury Fete. The new piece was something of a hit,
running for two weeks and drawing a favorable review from
The Albion: "A very excellent piece from the pen of Planché
has been playing at this house during the week with unequivocal success."15 Through the remainder of November, the
two new pieces helped Mitchell gain ground in his battle with
Burton and on 9 December The Albion reported: "Mitchell is

keeping the tenor of his ways, and is quietly drawing back
most of his old patrons. During the week the houses have
been good, attracted by the excellence of entertainments."16

Yet attendance did not increase as much as the manager had hoped, and he seemed unable to find and produce the
"novelties" necessary to regain his position as the city's fore-
most theatre manager. In an effort to obtain additional time
to locate and rehearse some new pieces, Mitchell started the
benefit season at the Olympic on 1 December, six weeks
earlier than was customary. But this ploy, a self-admission
of his inability to compete favorably with Burton, was obvious
to The Spirit of The Times. The columnist reported that
there had been nothing new at the Olympic in quite some time,
and complained that Mitchell "seems either to have been
touched by some magician's wand, or to have swallowed
chloroform, he appears to be dozing away the better part of
the season, and no longer summons the crowds who hitherto
were thronged about the high priest of Momus."17

A "magician's wand" had touched the Olympic's manager. Burton was producing the kind of carefully staged
entertainments which had made the Olympic famous and Mitchell's ill health had prevented him from acting--after the
first week of the season--or from managing the theatre's
affairs with his customary gusto. The captain was sick and
could not muster sufficient energy to guide his floundering
ship through the stormy seas of new competition.

Through the first three weeks of December, the entertainments at the Olympic were mediocre and the audiences
were small. But on the twenty-first, Mitchell produced a
highly popular anonymous local burlesque entitled Gold Fever
which ridiculed the California gold rush, then at its high
point. The new lampoon was in the bills nightly until New
Year's eve and was judged to be carefully rehearsed and
attractively staged by The Albion.18

While Gold Fever was drawing good houses, Walcot
returned to the Olympic on 29 December for one evening in
a new burlesque which he had written based on the steadily
intensifying animosity between Forrest and Macready, which
had reached new heights with Forrest's hissing of Macready's
pas de mouchoir piece of business in a performance of Hamlet
at Edinburgh. The play, entitled Le Mouchoir et L'Epée,
featured Conover as Macbeth--imitating Forrest's style of

acting--and Walcot as Hamlet--affecting Macready's mannerisms
A synopsis of the action in the playbill for its sole night of
performance reads:

> Mons. Rosbif has an adopted daughter by the name
> of Melpomene, who though supplanted in general
> admiration by her livelier neighbors, is still courted
> by one constant suitor, Mons. Hamlet, who, like
> Mademoiselle, in genial black, mourns the neglect
> exhibited to the remains of a once general favourite,
> Mons. Shakespeare. At the interesting period of
> one of Le jeune Hamlet's visits to Mademoiselle,
> foreign music announces an approach and a rival.
> Mons. MacBeth, having long courted Mademoiselle
> à la distance, now presents his claims in plaid,
> clad propria, in firm belief that young Hamlet has
> not a leg (like his) to stand on. It is agreed
> that a trial dance shall decide between the rivals.
> A mysterious agent is employed by Mons. Macbeth
> to aid him in his efforts.[19]

The play was performed on only one evening and was not
reviewed in any of the city's daily or weekly newspapers.
Yet it seems to represent a devolution of good taste and
common sense on the part of Mitchell, for Forrest was
idolized at the expense of Macready to an audience composed
primarily of Forrest's most stalwart admirers, the "b'hoy."
The play may well have contributed to the "b'hoys" ill feelings
toward Macready, which were to erupt at the Astor Place
riot five months later.

Although Mitchell's inability to compete consistently
with Burton for the patronage of those New York theatregoers
who favored light amusements was becoming increasing apparent, the manager was still paying careful attention to
those details of production which had contributed significantly
to the Olympic's success. The Albion observed, early in
January, that the defection of popular veterans from the stock
company and stiff competition from Burton presented Mitchell
with "a severe ordeal to pass through this season."[20] Yet
the manager's careful attention to the details of production
were enabling the Olympic to continue operating "quietly and
with more than moderate success. The admirable style in
which pieces are got up at this establishment call [sic]
forth the approbation of every frequenter of the Olympic."[21]
But careful staging was not enough to enable Mitchell to come
from behind in his contest with Burton. A week later The

Albion noted only that "The Olympic holds its own in the
struggle of rival competition,"22 while "Burton's has been
crowded during the week."23

Finally realizing that his stock company was unable
to match the excellence of the new one on Chambers Street
and being too enfeebled by his chronic illness to acquire and
adequately rehearse the number of new pieces necessary to
enable the Olympic to rival the enterprise of the younger,
healthier Burton, Mitchell resorted to employing traveling
stars. The playbills of 15 January announced that Walcot
had been engaged for a limited period, along with C. Von
Bonhurst, "the celebrated banjo player from the south."24

During Walcot's temporary return to the theatre at
which he had first become popular, Mitchell produced two new
pieces: a farce by Edward Stirling entitled The Haunted Man
and one of the several extravaganzas based on The Tempest
entitled The Enchanted Isle. Both plays opened on 15 January
and the farce enjoyed a week-long run, while the extravaganza
was in the bills for nine consecutive evenings. Through the
week of 20 January The Enchanted Isle drew large audiences
to the Olympic even though Burton was offering his patrons
the same piece. Apparently, Burton's production boasted
better acting while Mitchell's was visually more attractive.
The Albion, in comparing the two productions, reported:
"In the race of competition with the Olympic, Burton occasionally gets the start, but Mitchell makes up by his 'solid
foundation' and other equally valuable qualities. The public
will benefit by this rivalry; for novelty and perfectness of
stage detail will be insured at both houses."25

Mitchell's business had temporarily improved and continued to do so even after Walcot left on the twenty-third of
January. The reason for the surge in attendance was Charles
Selby's farce, The Witch of Windemere, which opened on 22
January and provided George Holland with his first new vehicle
of the season. Holland's performance, aided by the temporarily improved Constantia Clarke, made the Olympic's production very successful. The Albion complimented Clarke
and Holland for the manner in which they had "delighted the
Olympians of the pit nightly by their admirable acting."26
Mitchell also bore responsibility for the Olympic's increased
attendance, for the reviewer reported: "The Piece is beautifully put upon the stage by the manager, and with the new
extravaganza and other stock pieces, Mitchell is doing a
really excellent business."27

During the first two weeks of February, Mitchell relied exclusively on revivals of popular pieces from the theatre's repertory. Only two plays, Tom Smart and The
Married Rake, were repeated on consecutive evenings. The
bills were changing with a rapidity unusual at the Olympic.
Yet the old favorites drew fairly well. The Albion noted,
"The Olympic has been prosperous during the week with its
admirably got up stock pieces. "28

Business continued to improve throughout February
largely because of Mitchell's production of the Brough Brothers
popular extravaganza, Camaralzaman and Badoura, on 12
February. Its gorgeous scenery and costumes combined with
excellent performances by the stock company to draw the
largest audiences the Olympic had held to that point in the
season for a dozen consecutive evenings.29   A week later
The Spirit of The Times reported that the new extravaganza
was continuing to prove popular and had "attracted very good
houses. "30

Although larger audiences were attending the Olympic
during February, Mitchell hired another star. His only previous stars since his inaugural season had been Taylor and
Walcot, former members of the company who had returned
to appear in plays which they had made popular while they
were stock actors at the Olympic. But Mitchell's new star
was a radical departure from his managerial tradition. Beginning on 28 February, Dan Marble, the celebrated Yankee
comedian, began a week-long engagement in his popular
vehicles. During his stay at the Olympic, the evening's bills
consisted of two Yankee plays and an extravaganza until the
evening of his benefit, on which three Yankee plays were
performed. With the coming of Marble, the bills were, for
the first time, chosen by the star and not the manager. This
unprecedented move of Mitchell's indicates his inability to
compete successfully with Burton in the production of stock
farces, extravaganzas, and burlesques. The change in policy
was both desperate and drastic. As Odell has suggested,
"Mitchell's, dependent on outsiders, was hardly Mitchell's. "31

Ironically, Marble's engagement was greatly enhanced
by the production of a new extravaganza two days before his
first appearance. The new spectacle, written by Planché and
entitled The King of The Peacocks, was well within the tradition of spectacular extravaganza that Mitchell had been developing for ten years. Bengough's new scenery represented:
(1) Pleasure gardens and the Chateau de la Beaute in the

verdant valley; (2) the old world's end with a view beyond the
bounds of probability; (3) the gates of the city and the palace
of the king of the peacocks; (4) the home park in verdant
valley; (5) the deck of the Chinese Junk; (6) the plume chamber
in the palace of the king of the peacocks; and, (7) the royal
kitchen. Opening on 26 February, the new spectacle played
nightly until Marble's benefit on 8 March.

      Mitchell's stratagem worked wonderfully. With the
popularity of the new extravaganza and the novelty of a Yankee
star, the Olympic drew large crowds. The Albion commented:
"Mr. Dan Marble has proved an attractive 'star' at this house,
and aided by the new burlesque, he has continued to draw good
houses during his whole engagement.... The Olympic pittites
relish him highly."32

      Since the first of the year, Mitchell had been competing
keenly with Burton by producing good extravaganzas and judi-
ciously hiring star performers. While these policies had not
restored the Olympic to its former position as the most popular theatre in the city, they had at least enabled the sick
manager to maintain operations. But on 17 March, eight
days after the conclusion of Marble's engagement, disaster
struck Mitchell; George Holland took his farewell benefit
from the Olympic.

      Holland, from the outset of his employment with Mitch-
ell six seasons earlier, had rivaled the manager as the
Olympic's most popular actor. When Mitchell began to appear less frequently during the 1845-46 season and was subsequently debilitated by his illness during January of 1847,
Holland had assumed the brunt of the acting burden in new
farces and definitely became the manager's most useful actor.
With strong competition from Burton during the season of
1848-49, Mitchell could ill afford to lose Holland. Although
the exact reasons for the veteran comedian's departure are
not known, he may have been irritated at Mitchell's recent
policy of hiring stars whom he was forced to support. Or
perhaps he realized that the Olympic was floundering and that
he could better serve his own interests by moving to another
theatre. Whatever his reasons, the result of Holland's departure was devastating to Mitchell and recognized as such
by The Albion: "He will be sadly missed unless Mitchell
buckles on his armour, and enters the list with all his old
spirit."33

      Mitchell did "buckle on his armour," and reappeared

on the Olympic's stage on 19 March for the first time since
the opening week of the season. He acted in two of his most
popular vehicles--Saratoga Springs and The Aldgate Pump.
His chronic ill health, however, prevented him from re-
establishing himself as the company's prime drawing card,
and, after appearing nightly through 22 March, he was again
forced to give up acting. He was simply too ill to perform.
In order to provide an immediate attraction, a hasty arrangement was concluded with "Yankee" Hill, who began a week-
long engagement in his highly popular roles on 28 March.
But even the Yankee wryness of Hill could not produce large
audiences, and his engagement was only "tolerably successful;"3
Hill left on 4 April and was succeeded on the next evening by
another "star" attraction--The Lee family of acrobats. Their
engagement, which lasted through 12 April, marked a new
low point in Mitchell's fortunes and a further departure from
the policies he had followed over a period of ten years.

        After the acrobats left, the eight remaining nights of
the season were given to various members of the company
for their benefits, presumably because business was so bad
that Mitchell was unable to pay his actors their salaries.35
The season ended on 21 April with Mitchell's benefit when
he appeared in three of his most popular vehicles: The
Savage and The Maiden, The Parson's Nose, and Boots at
The Swan.

        The manager's tenth campaign had been a disastrous
one. Throughout his career, he had been without significant
competition in the production of short light farces, extravaganzas, and local burlesques. But in the summer of 1848,
Burton, certainly one of the best low comedians in the country,
brought a very strong company to his recently acquired theatre on Chambers Street and pushed the sick Mitchell hard
throughout the season. Even though the Olympic lost a large
number of its more fashionable patrons and its former high
level of popularity, Mitchell stood his ground effectively until
the middle of March when Holland's departure forced him to
rely on the aid of outside performers.

        Although the enfeebled manager had suffered a severe
setback, he let it be known that he was going to battle Burton
with every means at his disposal during the next season.
The Albion reported, a week before the close of the season,
"He intends opening next season with a powerfully augmented
company and a return of the old Olympic spirit."36

        In preparation for the 1849-50 season, Mitchell did

indeed "powerfully" augment his company. Both Charles
Walcot and Mary Taylor returned. By adding the talents of
these two performers to those of Nickinson, who had rejoined
the company during November of the preceding season, Mitchell now had three of his most talented and useful performers with him when the Olympic reopened in September of
1849.

       In spite of the return of Walcot and Taylor, the com-
pany was not as strong as it might have been due to the departure of Mary Gannon and the total incapacitation of Constantia Clarke. Mitchell's health posed an additional problem.
It must have deteriorated even further because he rehired
Ben Baker, the former prompter who had left with Chanfrau
at the end of the 1847-48 season, and promoted him to the
rank of acting manager, thereby relieving himself of much
of the burden of rehearsing the performers in new pieces.

       Mitchell's eleventh season opened on 10 September
1849, with No!, a popular farce from the theatre's large
repertory; Boots at the Swan, one of Mitchell's most popular acting vehicles; and two new pieces--The Lawyer's Practice and a new extravaganza by Walcot entitled Brittania and
Hibernia. Business was excellent during the season's first
week, primarily because Walcot's new piece proved extremely
popular and Mitchell was able to appear in two of his favorite
pieces. It now appeared that Mitchell was equipped to match
the popularity of Burton, for The Spirit of The Times noted:
"A tremendous audience filled this theatre to overflowing on
Monday night, when it opened for the season. The manager
has secured an excellent company, and they will come in for
a large share of the public favor and patronage."[37]

       The Albion was also mightily impressed by the strength
of the newly augmented stock company and suggested that the
return of Mitchell's most popular performers and errant patrons portended a return of the golden days of the little theatre: "The house has been literally crammed to overflowing
every night during the week, and the performances have been
received with demonstrations of applause equal to the Old
Olympic's best days."[38]

       Mitchell was certainly off to a good start during the
first week of the new season, and things got even better.
The fact that no other theatre was mounting operatic productions during the fall of 1849 provided Mitchell with an
opportunity to demonstrate his long-heralded managerial tact

by producing a revival of the popular opera Fra Diavolo on
22 September. This revival, which featured Mary Taylor and
Charles Walcot in the principal roles, drew huge audiences to
the Olympic nightly during its week-long run. The Albion
reported, "Fra Diavolo was produced on Monday evening with
complete success, and has been played every night during the
week to literally crowded houses. "39 A week later The Spirit
of The Times noted that the attractiveness of the opera and
the return of two of the Olympic's most popular performers
had restored Mitchell's enterprise to a high level of popularity:
"This little place of amusement is in the tide of popular favor.
The faces familiar to its early patrons, with two or three
exceptions, are again gathered for the public weal, and the
caterings are nearly as good as of yore. "40

        Following Fra Diavolo, Mitchell revived other popular
operas. On the first of October, Cinderella received the
first of its six consecutive performances, and on the tenth,
The Child of the Regiment enjoyed the first performance of
its ten-night revival. By relying primarily on the revival of
popular operas, Mitchell was able to guide his theatre successfully through the first month of the new campaign. The
few new pieces which were produced, however, proved unattractive, and it soon became general knowledge that although the
manager was occasionally able to act, he was too ill to maintain the high quality production of new pieces which had characterized the Olympic's bills in the past seasons. The Spirit
of The Times reported, in late October, "We are told that
Mr. Mitchell does not enjoy good health and has not the
energy, therefore, which is required to keep up the system
of novelties. "41

        During the first week of November, Mitchell was with-
out an opera and provided amusement with his own acting.
Although the crowds attending the Olympic continued to be
large, it was becoming increasingly obvious that the manager
was relying exclusively on the reputation of the theatre and
revivals of hits from earlier seasons. Yet this inevitably ter-
minal policy continued to be lucrative. The Albion noted, on
3 November: "The successful opera revivals still continue
their attraction; and Amilie is nearly ready to be added to
the list. Mitchell is drawing around him many of his early
patrons by the judicious arrangement of the present season. "42

        Amilie was revived on 5 November and proved as pop-
ular as its predecessors, extending Mitchell's good business
for another two weeks and further indicating his total reliance

on pieces from past seasons. The Albion informed its readers, "The opera has drawn crowded houses during the week,
and will doubtless continue its attraction for a long period. "[43]

     By this time it must have become evident to Mitchell
that he was unable to compete with Burton in the production
of new pieces. The necessary result of the manager's
policy of relying exclusively on hits from the past was obvious:
sooner or later he would run out of popular pieces to revive.
And this is precisely what happened. When Amilie finished its
run on 15 November, Mitchell had no other popular opera to
take its place in the bills, so he resorted to presenting The
Child of the Regiment and the burlesque Amy-Lee on alternate evenings for a week. Attendance fell off rapidly, and
benefits began on 21 November, suggesting that patronage at
the Olympic was not enough to enable the manager to meet
his financial obligations to his company. He decided that
he could no longer operate the Olympic as a lucrative enterprise, and it became known, early in December, that the
current season was to be Mitchell's last as manager of the
little Olympic. [44]

     No one knew exaclty when Mitchell would close the
Olympic. It seemed, however, that his sole purpose for
maintaining operations was to provide employment for the
members of his company because at least three nights of
each week continued to be devoted to benefits through the
middle of January.

     From 11 January until 14 February, no benefits were
taken at the Olympic. During that period Mitchell, whose
health had apparently improved, acted frequently. Beginning
on 21 January he appeared nightly on ten evenings in one
or more of his long-popular vehicles. His frequent appear-
ances on the stage of his theatre continued into February,
for by the twelfth of that month, he had acted an additional
six times, and he continued to perform at least weekly during the remainder of the month.

     Perhaps because the primary attraction during late
January and February was the frequent appearance of Mitchell
in his long-popular vehicles, proceedings at the Olympic were
not reviewed in the journals and newspapers. Yet The Albion
noted in mid-February, "There continues a quiet steady attraction here, that yields a profitable return. "[45]

     The frequent appearance of Mitchell and the absence

of any new plays indicated that the season would not continue
into April or May. This was confirmed on 2 February when
The Albion announced: "We understand that Mr. Mitchell
will shortly retire from the active management of this theatre,
...He has realized a competency as the fruits of his labours,
and retires just as the returning flood of public opinion seems
to reach once more the healthier waters of the legitimate
drama."46

    The notice is the only contemporary account which
suggests that in addition to competition from Burton, Mitchell
was hampered by a change in public taste away from the
burlesques, broad farces, and extravaganzas which had always
been the Olympic's main source of attraction. That the
appeal of "novelty" had declined is further indicated by the
fact that Mitchell's successful revivals during the season
were all operas. Very few extravaganzas and no topical
burlesques were dusted off and freshened up. Thus, the
manager was probably as aware as anyone that his previously
most successful types of entertainment no longer had the
appeal they once did.

    Mitchell's performances continued to attract respect-
able crowds to his theatre, even though it was common
knowledge that he had given up his battle with Burton and
decided to quit the field of theatrical management. In the
middle of February The Albion reported that although the
Olympic was certainly no longer the theatre in the city of
New York, Mitchell was still able to maintain profitable
operations. 47

    Three days before the above appeared on 13 February,
Mitchell produced the last popular extravaganza of his managerial career, Charles Dance's The Magic Horn. It ran
nightly through 23 February. For the twelve evenings after
its run concluded, old favorites from the Olympic's eleven-
year repertory drew remunerative audiences for the benefit
of several of the Olympic's actors. On 7 March 1850,
William Mitchell ended the season, abandoned his eleven-
year management of the Olympic Theatre, and retired to
private life.

    On the closing day of Mitchell's management, The
Spirit of The Times printed the theatre's eulogy and concisely
stated many of the manager's contributions to the theatrical
life in New York during his eleven seasons as manager of
the little theatre on lower Broadway:

Mr. Mitchell's health will not, we are informed,
permit him to assume the management for another
season, even if he could procure an extension of
his lease, which we are also informed cannot be
obtained.

The Olympic will no doubt close forever. Its
opening was signalized by novelites founded on local
incidents, the floating literature of the day, and
burlesques upon operas, the whole forming a series
of representations new to the Knickerbockers. Mr.
Mitchell, then in his prime, and an actor of great
merit, won his way to patronage and favor not only
by his performances, but by the unequalled fascination of the stage effects produced by him. His
pieces, however trifling in incident, have always
been produced admirably, and better in respect to
consistent and harmonious appointments--striking
and effective tableaux, than in any theatre in the
city. He established and maintained prices of
admission, which opened his theatre to the million,
and when in health always anticipated his brethren
in the production of foreign vaudevilles adapted to
the New York stage. He has contributed much to
the enjoyment of the people of this city, and has
always secured a company, which taken together,
has been better than at any of the theatres in our
opinion. We need not say that we regret the closing of the Olympic. There are many reminiscences
connected with it, which make it grateful to us,
and we shall ever think of it with pleasure. 48

Although the brief final season was moderately successful, Mitchell, plagued by ill health, must have known
that Burton's theatre was going to eclipse the Olympic by
the end of the 1848-49 season. Yet he reopened despite the
failing popularity of his enterprise. Either he sincerely
sought to redouble his efforts and earnestly engage Burton
in a rivalry for the patronage of those New York theatregoers
inclined to favor light amusements, or he merely sought to
save face by managing one last successful season. The latter seems the most likely explanation for the brief final campaign. Very few new pieces were produced, and the theatre's
attractiveness was almost totally contingent on favorite performers from earlier seasons appearing in revivals of popular operas which had first been produced at the Olympic
five or six years earlier. Nevertheless, the season enjoyed

some success, and Mitchell continued to draw respectable
audiences until his abdication of the theatre's management
on 9 March 1850.

   With the closing of the Olympic, most of its actors
went to Burton's and then to Wallack's; and William Mitchell,
New York's high priest of Momus for a decade, retired.
Plagued by his chronic ill health, he lived in New York for
the remaining six years of his life and died in abject poverty
in 1856.

CHAPTER TEN

The Olympic Theatre's Legacy

From the outset of Mitchell's management of the Olympic in December of 1839 until Burton wooed many of the theatre's patrons away during the summer of 1848, Mitchell's was the most popular and successful playhouse in New York during what Odell describes as the most distressing decade in the history of the American theatre.

The Olympic's success must necessarily be measured financially, for if the theatre had not proven a lucrative business enterprise, it certainly would have ceased to exist. Unfortunately, no account books concerning Mitchell's theatre have survived. Yet information contained in playbills and newspapers, combined with Mitchell's actor-contracts, make it possible to estimate the theatre's operating costs and profits.

The sole particular statement concerning gross receipts at the theatre is contained in the New York Herald of 3 December 1848, which states that ticket sales amounted to about $200 when the house was full. While it would usually be dangerous to take this single statement as accurate, information concerning benefits contained in Mitchell's contracts with his actors tends to support the figure given by the Herald. Olympic benefits were of two types: the company's best-paid and most-popular actors received a clear third of the night's receipts on the evening of their benefit, while less important members of the stock company were given half the receipts after $100 was subtracted for operating expenses. Thus, a clear third benefit must have been more profitable than half the receipts over $100. If so, the theatre could not possibly have held $300 worth of patrons, for at that figure the beneficiary's sum would have been the same whether a clear third of the receipts or half the receipts over $100 was awarded. If the theatre grossed $200 on a good night, those beneficiaries

who received a clear third would have earned about $15
more--approximately a week's salary--than those less-popular
performers who were given half the receipts above $100.

The benefit agreements are also the prime source for
estimating the theatre's operating costs. Although T. Allston
Brown has stated that it cost $80 nightly to operate the Olym-
pic,[1] the $100 figure "for expenses" stipulated in the contracts
seems a more realistic figure, for $50 nightly was required
to maintain the acting company while additional expenses for
scenery, rent, costumes, and advertising could quite easily
have amounted to an additional $50.

It seems, then, that the manager's profits were approximately $100 nightly when the theatre was full. But it
was not always full, even during the period when Mitchell's
theatre was the most popular in the city. Thus, Brown's
estimate that Mitchell's annual profits were about $10,000[2]
prior to the opening of Burton's theatre in 1848 seems reasonable. However, either Mitchell lost large amounts of
money during his final two seasons, lived very extravagantly,
or both. When he died in 1856, he was penniless.

The low overhead and consistently high-gross receipts
that enabled Mitchell to maintain the Olympic as a paying
proposition for the first nine of his eleven seasons as the
theatre's manager were a result of his specific managerial
policies. These policies, at least early in the manager's
career, were as much a synthesis of procedures which other
managers had unsuccessfully practiced as they were personal
innovations on the part of Mitchell.

Operating a theatre in New York which specialized in
light comic entertainments was not new with Mitchell, for
the Olympic had been built for Willard and Blake with that
idea in mind. But Mitchell succeeded where Willard, Blake,
and their successors had failed primarily because he adopted
Wallack's policies of employing a good stock company and
carefully embellishing his productions with elaborate scenery
and tasteful costumes.

Mitchell's initial policies were soon implemented by
some innovations. At the end of his first week in business,
Mitchell reduced his prices of admission so that New York's
theatregoers, who were suffering the ravages of general
economic depression brought on by the specie panic of 1837,
might more easily afford to attend the Olympic. This strata-

gem worked wonderfully, for not only did attendance increase,
but the reduction of prices attracted audience members from
most of the socioeconomic classes in the city and made the
Olympic the only theatre in New York during the 1840's which
could boast a truly broad base of popular support.

Just as the policy which attracted patrons from many
classes of New York's citizens came about almost accidentally,
so did Mitchell's reliance on the efforts of his stock company
to the exclusion of traveling stars. He clearly did not open
the Olympic with the idea of relying exclusively on the stock
company, for he hired George Mossop as a star during the
second week of his first season. Yet when it became obvious
that the efforts of the stock company in The Roof Scrambler,
rather than Mossop in his Irish vehicles, were the theatre's
prime drawing card, Mitchell decided not to hire any more
stars. During the next eight years no one at the Olympic
was given star billing, although Mitchell's popularity as an
actor during his initial five seasons tended to make him
something of a resident star.[3]

With the perhaps unexpected and phenomenal success
of The Roof Scrambler, Mitchell realized the potential popularity of burlesque. Although few topical lampoons had been
produced in New York prior to Mitchell's management of the
Olympic,[4] the little theatre succeeded in large measure because
of the popularity of the many burlesques which the manager produced. During eleven seasons Mitchell staged thirty-two
topical burlesques which ridiculed subjects ranging from the
affectations of Macready and the popularity of Fanny Elssler
to the rival claims of the "hard" and "soft" money men
during the election campaign of 1840. These burlesques have
earned Mitchell some importance among cultural and social
historians. Constance Rourke has noted:

> Mitchell caught and punctuated every current wild
> obsession, romantic or merely comic, every theme
> which the current American fancy had taken up with
> its familiar extreme fervor. He revealed all the
> characteristic native capacity for plunging head-
> long into new enthusiasms. He was, in fact, bur-
> lesquing the American public as well as its pre-
> occupations.[5]

Mitchell's policies regarding the stock company developed over several seasons and made the Olympic's company
"the first distinctive stock company of modern times in

New York. "[6] Its distinction was owing in large part to the
anomaly that although the company had, from time to time,
members who excelled in particular kinds of roles, Mitchell
was the first manager to abolish the time-honored lines of
business which had been practiced since the Restoration in
England and since the earliest days of theatrical enterprise
in this country. Moreover, it was not any single member of
the troupe, but the ensemble of the whole company, welded
together by Mitchell's guiding hand, which was responsible
for the theatre's popularity. Paul Preston's reminiscences
of Mitchell's company makes the point nicely:

>It was the main merit of the Olympic to rely upon
>the actual abilities of the company as a congregated
>mass and not upon the name of a single individual
>to sustain the popularity of the house.
> That the Olympic company was decidedly clever
>cannot be denied, for the members comprising it
>were above mediocrity in their talent, yet their
>efforts, tending to a common end directed by a
>general supervisory head, gave merited repute to
>individual artistes through success in a concentrated
>action. None of the Olympic actors or actresses
>were above the medium grade in professional ability;
>nevertheless, all were immensely popular through
>the nicety with which they were dove-tailed into
>mutually sustaining performances. [7]

A concomitant of Mitchell's ability to weld his stock
company into a "mutually sustaining" working unit was his
ability to detect and develop talent in young actors with little
previous experience. During his management, he launched
into long and prosperous careers several actors who were
virtually unknown before joining the Olympic's company.
Among the most famous of the young performers who developed their talents under his tutelage were Mary Taylor,
William Reynolds, John Nickinson, Charles Walcot, Sr.,
Mary Gannon, and Frank S. Chanfrau.

An excellent resident acting company and topical burlesques were not the only reasons for Mitchell's success.
The large number of plays seen on the Olympic's stage for
the first time in America also contributed significantly to
the theatre's popularity. Of the five-hundred fifteen theatre
pieces produced during Mitchell's management, two hundred
thirty of them, or about 45 percent, were seen for the first
time in this country at the Olympic. These figures indicate

that Mitchell produced the American premiere of more British
farces and extravaganzas than any other manager in the United
States during the 1840s.

Farces, extravaganzas, and satirical lampoons new to
the New York public and acted by a strong corps of performers
were indeed powerful attractions. But the manner in which
they were mounted on the Olympic's stage made them even
more popular than they otherwise would have been. Richard
Bengough, Wallack's former scenic artist, served as Mitchell's
resident scene painter throughout the latter's career as the
Olympic's manager. The theatre's offerings were greatly enhanced by Bengough's scenery. Certainly the frequent accolades in the press attest to Bengough's ability at painting perspective drops. Ironically, a shortcoming of the theatre was
responsible for the new scenery which embellished most of
Mitchell's burlesques and extravaganzas. The narrowness
of the stage precluded the use of wings and demanded only a
small amount of canvas in order to fill the entire back wall
with a drop. Thus, Mitchell could frequently afford to provide Bengough with the material necessary to create new
scenery for a production. Mitchell's selection of repertory,
careful attention to production, ability to forge the best stock
company in New York from actors who, considered individually,
were not outstanding suggests that the phrase, "Produced under
the direction of Mr. Mitchell," which appeared at the head
of the Olympic's playbills was justified: Mitchell was America's first director. He initiated a trend toward careful staging
and a strong stock company which was to characterize, in turn,
Burton's management, the return of Wallack, and even the
early years of Augustin Daly.

The attractiveness of his productions enabled Mitchell
to present many of his offerings on a large number of successive evenings. It was not uncommon for new pieces to
run for twenty consecutive evenings, and two of Mitchell's
plays--The Savage and The Maiden and A Glance At New
York in 1848--enjoyed the longest runs of any plays presented on the New York stage prior to Barnum's production
of The Drunkard in 1850. Mitchell contributed significantly
to the development of the long run.

In addition to developing a taste for good stock companies and careful staging on the part of his audience, Mitchell was also an early force in the development of local
color realism in the American theatre through his production
of A Glance At New York in 1848.

Mitchell had developed a taste for the topical by his frequent production of specific burlesques. Because much of the humor of those burlesques relied on the ability of the Olympic's actors to imitate effectively other actors and well-known personages, certain members of the company--Mitchell, Walcot, and later Chanfrau--had to be comsummate mimics. The step from topical burlesque and ridiculous mimickry to the early realistic drama is a small one. It requires only that the topical subject matter be serious and not ludicrous, and that the actor imitate the characteristics rather than the affectations of his model. This is precisely what happened in A Glance At New York. Baker anticipated Zola's dictum concerning the proper subject matter for the drama to such a degree that the play was described as "a dramatic version of our police reports,"8 and Chanfrau invested the character of Mose with details unusually realistic for that period: "In all the details of the character from the use of a seegar through the various changes of habit and manner, the performance is the very embodiment of the creature designed to be represented."9

While the play and its representation would no doubt be considered highly artificial by contemporary standards, it was certainly realistic to New York theatregoers of the 1840s. Moreover, its creation and performance marks a logical extension of both the taste for the topical Mitchell's burlesques had developed in the Olympic's audiences and the ridiculous mimickry that those burlesques demanded from his actors.

Because Mitchell's theatre prospered at a time when New York's other theatres lost money by relying on stars and not paying sufficient attention to either the stock company or to stage arrangements, it becomes surprising not that Burton entered into direct competition with Mitchell in the summer of 1848, but that he was the first manager to guide his theatre along policies similar to those which Mitchell had established. Mitchell, whose ill health prevented him from managing the affairs of the Olympic with the energy he had employed during earlier seasons, lost much of his popularity to Burton. But even if Burton had not competed with Mitchell, the Olympic's manager could not have prospered for very much longer due to the change in public taste which was making broad farces, burlesques, and extravaganzas less popular than they had previously been. The decline in the popularity of those types of entertainments is attested to by Burton's shift to longer, more sophisticated comedies and Shakespearean revivals after Mitchell closed the Olympic.

A move towards realism, a significant step in the development of the long run, the assumption of a position as director of a theatre company, the forging of the first American stock company not founded on lines of business, and careful attention to the visual elements of theatrical production --these are the significant items of William Mitchell's legacy to the American theatre. But the true greatness of the Olympic is lost to history, for no one is alive today to tell us how he sat in the "little box" at 444 Broadway during the extremely lean years of the 1840s and laughed until he cried.

NOTES

Chapter One

1. Contemporary accounts of the opening of the theatre merely mention that it was about the size of its London counterpart, and no figures regarding the seating capacity of London's Olympic are available. The estimate of the New York Olympic's seating capacity is based on the following: (1) admission prices, under Mitchell's management, were 50¢ for the dress circle, 25¢ for the gallery, and $12\frac{1}{2}$¢ for the pit; (2) a notice in the New York Herald of 3 December 1848 states that the Olympic had been playing to full houses at a nightly gross of $200; (3) an Olympic playbill for 12 January 1846 jokingly advertises for 100 gentlemen to purchase seats for the dress circle, suggesting that figure as the dress circle's seating capacity; (4) another playbill, dated 27 December, 1840 boasts that approximately 5,000 playgoers had attended the theatre in four evenings.

If $200 represented gross sales on an evening when the theatre was nearly full, and the 100 seats in the dress circle produced $50 at the box office, the rest of the theatre would have produced $150. The gallery--actually a series of boxes that surrounded the entire auditorium--probably held 300 patrons and produced $75 in receipts, and the pit, with its $12\frac{1}{2}$¢ admission would have produced an additional $75 if it accommodated 600 persons. These estimates are compatible with the available information and suggest that there were 600 seats in the pit, 100 in the dress circle, and 400 in the gallery. There were also a "few" private orchestra boxes, probably four, which rented for five dollars an evening, but they are negligible in estimating the house's capacity.

2. Lawrence Hutton, Plays and Players (New York: Hurd and Houghton, 1875), p. 19.

3. Ibid., states, "The Narrowness of the building prevented the use of 'flats' and confined the entire scenic display to 'drops,' a fashion that has been adopted by the buildings of some of our more modern and pretentious houses."

4. Quoted in George C. D. Odell, Annals of The New York Stage (15 vols.; New York: Columbia University Press, 1928), IV, 245.

5. The New Yorker, IV, September 23, 1837.

6. Quoted in Odell's Annals, IV, 132.

7. The Olympic's other managers prior to Mitchell were: John Nickinson (10 March 1838-22 March 1838); William Earle (24 March 1838-3 May 1838); Mrs. T. S. Hamblin (7 May 1838-12 May 1838); Charles Thorne (23 July 1838-15 October 1838); and D. D. McKinney (8 May 1839-19 June 1839).

8. The Albion: A Journal of News, Politics, and Literature, I, 21 May 1842, p. 248. (Hearafter cited as The Albion.)

9. Information on Mitchell's English career is taken from William K. Northall, Before and Behind the Curtain; or, Fifteen Years Among the Theatres of New York (New York: W. F. Burgess, 1851), pp. 40-42.

10. The Knickerbocker, or New York Monthly Magazine, XII, October, 1838, p. 380: "Judicious stage-management, beautiful scenery, and the best stock company in the United States have elevated the National Theatre to a high place in the regard of all theatre-goers."

11. Odell's Annals, IV, 211.

Chapter Two

1. George C. D. Odell, "Theatrical Stock Companies of New York," Theatre Annual, I, (1951), p. 8.

2. Olympic playbill announcing the opening of the theatre, no date.

3. Odell's Annals, IV, 401.

4. Olympic playbill, December 14, 1839.

5. See Northall, pp. 53-54, for a first-hand account of the discouraging business at the Olympic during Mitchell's first week of management.

6. Odell's Annals, IV, 54.

7. The Spirit of The Times: A Chronicle of the Turf, Agriculture, Field Sports, Literature, and the Stage, IX, January 11, 1840, p. 540. (Hereafter cited as ST.)

8. Olympic playbill, December 20, 1839.

9. Ibid., December 23, 1839.

10. ST, IX, January 11, 1840, p. 540.

11. New York Mirror: A Weekly Journal of Literature and the Fine Arts, XVII, December 28, 1839, p. 214. (Hereafter cited as NYM.)

12. Ibid.

13. Ibid.

14. ST, IX, January 11, 1840, p. 540 speaks of "... a fashionable attendance ... and actors from other companies."

15. Ibid., December 28, 1839, p. 516.

16. Northall, pp. 37-38.

17. Ibid., pp. 77-78 states: "Unfortunately actors and actresses are too frequently tried, judged, and condemned by people strangers to the idiosyncracies of an actor's life. This is one of the evils of permitting strangers behind the scenes,..."

18. This popular opera was produced at least seven times prior to Mitchell's burlesque.

19. ST, IX, January 4, 1840, p. 528.

20. The play, written in 1734, was ascribed to Benjamin Bounce. The real author is Henry Carey. Like Fielding's Tom Thumb with which it is almost exactly contemporaneous, it is a burlesque of the heroic tragic tradition.

21. Olympic playbill, January 6, 1840.

22. Ibid.

23. Lawrence Hutton, Plays and Players (New York: Hurd and Houghton, 1875), p. 24.

24. Odell's Annals, IV, 406.

25. Olympic playbill, January 22, 1840.

26. ST, IX, January 25, 1840, p. 564.

27. Ibid.

28. Ibid., February 1, 1840, p. 576.

29. NYM, XVII, February 8, 1840, p. 262.

30. Olympic playbill, January 27, 1840.

31. Ibid.

32. Ibid.

33. Ibid.

34. Odell's Annals, IV, 408.

35. NYM, XVII, February 1, 1840, p. 254.

36. ST, IX, February 8, 1840, p. 588.

37. NYM, XVII, February 1, 1840, p. 254.

38. The Knickerbocker or New York Monthly Magazine, XV, February, 1840, p. 174.

39. Olympic playbill, February 13, 1840.

40. Ibid., February 14, 1840.

41. ST, IX, February 15, 1840, p. 600.

42. NYM, XVII, March 14, 1840, p. 302.

43. ST, X, April 4, 1840, p. 60.

44. Ibid., April 11, 1840, p. 84

45. Ibid.

46. Odell's Annals, IV, 411.

47. Quoted in Odell's Annals, IV, 372.

48. Ibid., p. 351.

49. Ibid., p. 363.

50. Ibid., p. 373.

51. Olympic playbill, May 11, 1840.

52. Ibid., May 14, 1840.

53. A plot outline is contained in ST, X, May 16, 1840, p. 132.

54. Ibid.

55. Olympic playbill, May 21, 1840.

56. Odell's Annals, IV, 410.

57. NYM, XVII, May 23, 1840, p. 382.

58. Don C. Seitz, The James Gordon Bennetts (Indianapolis: Bobbs-Merrill and Company, 1928), p. 15.

59. Ibid., p. 81.

60. Ibid.

61. New York Herald, June 4, 1840.

62. Ibid.

63. Olympic playbill, June 13, 1840.

64. Ibid., June 15, 1840.

65. Ibid., June 16, 1840.

66. Ibid., June 15, 1840.

Chapter Three

1. ST, X, September 12, 1840, p. 396.

2. Olympic playbill, September 7, 1840.

3. Ibid.

4. Ibid.

5. Ibid.

6. Ibid.

7. Ibid., September 8, 1840.

8. ST, X, September 12, 1840, p. 396.

9. Olympic playbill, October 15, 1840.

10. Ibid., October 21, 1840.

11. Although Horncastle rejoined the company in January of 1841, both Buy It Dear and The Cat's In The Larder were produced at the Olympic while he was a member of the National Theatre's company.

12. Odell's Annals IV, 440.

13. ST, X, November 7, 1840, p. 432.

14. Olympic playbill, December 24, 1840.

15. Ibid., December 27, 1840.

16. Odell's Annals, IV, 440.

17. Ibid.

18. Olympic playbill, January 11, 1841.

19. Ibid.

20. ST, X, January 16, 1841, p. 552.

21. Ibid.

22. Ibid., February 20, 1841, p. 612.

23. Ibid.

24. Ibid., XI, March 6, 1841, p. 12.

25. Odell's Annals, IV, 503.

26. Frances Hodge, "Charles Mathews Reports on America,"
QJS, 36 (1950), pp. 492-499; p. 494.

27. Una Pope-Hennessey, Three English Women In America
(London: Ernest Bern Ltd., 1929), p. 23.

28. See Ibid., p. 178.

29. Oliver Warner, Captain Marryatt: A Rediscovery (London: Constable, 1953), p. 117.

30. Quoted in Ibid., p. 126.

31. ST, XI, March 20, 1841, p. 36.

32. Ibid.

33. Olympic playbill, April 12, 1841.

34. Ibid.

35. Ibid., April 19, 1841.

36. Joseph Ross, The Image of America in Mazzini's Writing
(Madison, Wis.: University of Wisconsin Press, 1953), pp. 20-21.

37. ST, XI, May 22, 1841, p. 144.

Chapter Four

1. Olympic playbill, September 13, 1841.

2. Ibid.

3. Unidentified, undated clipping, Mitchell folder, Harvard Theatre Collection.

4. Ibid.

5. Ibid.

6. ST, XI, October 2, 1841, p. 372.

7. Odell's Annals, IV, 674.

8. Ibid., p. 128.

9. New York Herald, October 11, 1841.

10. ST, XI, October 9, 1841, p. 384.

11. Olympic playbill, October 12, 1841.

12. Ibid.

13. Ibid., October 25, 1841.

14. The play was first announced as in rehearsal on September 27, almost a month prior to its premiere.

15. The Albion, I, January 1, 1842, p. 11.

16. Ibid.

17. William Forbes Adams, Ireland and Irish Immigration to the New World From 1815 to the Famine (New Haven: Yale University Press, 1932), p. 418.

18. Ibid., p. 377.

19. The Albion, January 15, 1842, p. 48.

20. Ibid., February 5, 1842, p. 68.

21. Ibid.

22. ST, XI, February 5, 1842, p. 584.

23. Olympic playbill, February 10, 1842.

24. The Albion, I, February 19, 1842, p. 92.

25. Olympic playbill, February 10, 1842.

26. Ibid.

27. The Albion, I, February 19, 1842, p. 92.

28. Ibid., February 26, 1842, p. 104.

29. Ibid., March 5, 1842, p. 116.

30. Ibid., March 12, 1842, p. 128.

31. Ibid.

32. Ibid.

33. Ibid.

34. W. Clyde Wilkins, Charles Dickens in America (New York: Charles Scribner's Sons, 1912), p. 111.

35. Odell's Annals, IV, 541.

36. Wilkins, p. 111.

37. Charles Dickens, American Notes (London: 1842; reprinted London: Oxford University Press, 1957), pp. 95-96.

38. Unidentified, undated clipping, Mitchell folder, Harvard Theatre Collection.

39. Wilkins, p. 115.

40. ST, XII, April 2, 1842, p. 60.

41. Unidentified, undated clipping, Mitchell folder, Harvard Theatre Collection.

42. Ibid.

43. Ibid.

44. The Albion, I, May 21, 1842, p. 248.

45. Ibid.

46. Ibid.

47. Ibid.

48. Ibid., June 4, 1842, p. 272.

49. Ibid.

50. Ibid.

51. Ibid.

52. Olympic playbill, June 6, 1842.

Chapter Five

1. Unidentified, undated clipping, Mitchell folder, Harvard Theatre Collection.

2. Odell's Annals, IV, 547.

3. Olympic Contract Book in the Harvard Theatre Collection.

4. The Contract Book lists this as his salary for the following season of 1843-44.

5. The Albion, I, September 17, 1842, p. 447.

6. Ibid.

7. Odell's Annals, IV, 293.

8. ST, XII, October 15, 1842, p. 396.

9. Ibid.

10. Ibid.

11. Ibid.

12. Ibid.

13. Ibid.

14. The Albion, I, October 15, 1842, p. 500.

15. Ibid., October 29, 1842, p. 524.

16. Ibid., November 12, 1842, p. 548.

17. Ibid.

18. Ibid., November 26, 1842, p. 572.

19. Ibid., II, January 21, 1843, p. 36, states: "Mitchell cannot sing."

20. Odell's Annals, IV, 603.

21. George Vandenhoff, Leaves From An Actor's Notebook

(New York: D. Appleton and Co., 1860), pp. 191-194.

22. Odell's Annals, IV, 634.

23. Ibid., 647.

24. The Athenaeum (London), October 1, 1842, p. 853.

25. The Albion, II, March 4, 1843, p. 116.

26. Placide first played the role on 24 April 1843, at The Park Theatre. Odell states that it rapidly became one of his most popular vehicles, perhaps even the role for which he was best known (Annals, IV, 618).

27. ST, XII, December 10, 1842, p. 494.

28. Olympic playbill, December 29, 1842.

29. The Albion, II, January 7, 1843, p. 12.

30. Ibid.

31. Ibid.

32. Ibid., January 21, 1843, p. 36.

33. Ibid.

34. Ibid.

35. ST, XII, January 28, 1843, p. 578.

36. Ibid.

37. The Albion, II, January 28, 1843, p. 48.

38. Ibid., March 4, 1843, p. 116.

39. Ibid.

40. Ibid.

41. Ibid., March 18, 1843, p. 140.

42. Odell's Annals, IV, 661.

43. Ibid.

44. William L. Keese, A Group of Comedians (New York: Dunlap Society, 1901), p. 62.

45. Letter from George Holland to Benjamin Webster, dated February 27, 1845, Harvard Theatre Collection.

46. T. Allston Brown, History of the New York Stage (3 Vols. New York: Dodd Mead & Co., 1903), I, 278.

47. ST, XIII, September 16, 1843, p. 348.

48. W. Knight Northall, Macbeth Travesty (London: Dick's Standard Plays, N.D.), p. 14.

49. Ibid., preface.

50. ST, XIII, October 28, 1843, p. 420.

51. Ibid.

52. Olympic playbill, October 20, 1843.

53. The Albion, II, November 4, 1843, p. 547.

54. Ibid.

55. Ibid.

56. Ibid.

57. Ibid.

58. Ibid., November 11, 1843, p. 560.

59. ST, XIII, November 25, 1843, p. 468.

60. Olympic playbill, December 14, 1843.

61. Ibid., December 23, 1843.

62. Odell's Annals, V, 9.

63. The Albion, III, January 13, 1844, p. 24.

64. Ibid., January 20, 1844, p. 36.

65. Ibid., February 3, 1844, p. 59.

66. Ibid.

67. Ibid.

68. Olympic playbill, March 8, 1844.

69. The Albion, III, February 24, 1844, p. 96.

70. Quoted in ST, XIV, March 30, 1844, p. 60.

71. John S. Kendall, The Golden Age of the New Orleans Theatre (Baton Rouge: LSU Press, 1952), p. 287.

72.   The Albion, III, April 13, 1844, p. 184.

73.   ST, XIV, April 13, 1844, p. 44.

74.   Ibid.

75.   Ibid.

76.   Ibid.

77.   Ibid., May 4, 1844, p. 120.

78.   Hutton, Plays and Players, p. 29.

Chapter Six

1.   Odell's Annals, V, 75.

2.   ST, XIV, October 19, 1844, p. 408.

3.   Ibid.

4.   Ibid.

5.   Odell's Annals, V, 27.

6.   Quoted in ST, XV, April 5, 1845, p. 64.

7.   Olympic playbill, October 21, 1844.

8.   Ibid.

9.   ST, XIV, November 2, 1844, p. 432.

10.   Ibid.

11.   Ibid., November 9, 1844, p. 444.

12.   The Albion, III, November 9, 1844, p. 544.

13.   Ibid., November 16, 1844, p. 556.

14.   Ibid., November 23, 1844, p. 568.

15.   Ibid.

16.   ST, XIV, January 4, 1845, p. 540.

17.   See Ibid., for a full acount of the incident.

18.   Ibid., December 14, 1844, p. 504.

19. Ibid.

20. The Albion, III, December 14, 1844, p. 603.

21. Ibid.

22. Ibid., December 21, 1844, p. 615.

23. ST, XIV, December 28, 1844, p. 528.

24. Ibid.

25. The Albion, IV, January 11, 1845, p. 24.

26. ST, XIV, January 18, 1845, p. 564.

27. Ibid.

28. Ibid., January 25, 1845, p. 576.

29. Ibid.

30. Ibid., February 1, 1845, p. 588.

31. Ibid.

32. Ibid.

33. The Albion, IV, February 15, 1845, p. 84.

34. ST, XV, March 15, 1845, p. 32.

35. Ibid., March 29, 1845, p. 56.

36. Ibid., April 5, 1845, p. 68.

37. Ibid.

38. Ibid., April 12, 1845, p. 80.

39. Ibid.

40. Odell's Annals, V, 27.

41. Ibid.

42. Olympic playbill, April 15, 1845.

43. ST, XV, April 19, 1845, p. 102.

44. Ibid., May 3, 1845, p. 116.

45. Ibid.

46. Odell's Annals, V, 129.

47. ST, XV, September 27, 1845, p. 368.

48. Ibid., October 11, 1845, p. 392.

49. Ibid., October 18, 1845, p. 404.

50. Ibid., October 25, 1845, p. 416.

51. The Albion, IV, November 22, 1845, p. 564.

52. ST, XV, November 29, 1845, p. 476.

53. The Albion, IV, November 29, 1845, p. 576.

54. Ibid., December 6, 1845, p. 584.

55. ST, XV, December 13, 1845, p. 500.

56. Ibid., December 20, 1845, p. 542.

57. Ibid.

58. Olympic playbill, January 12, 1846.

59. The Albion, V, January 31, 1846, p. 60.

60. ST, XV, January 31, 1846, p. 584.

61. The Albion, V, February 14, 1846, p. 72.

62. ST, XV, February 14, 1846, p. 608.

63. Ibid., XVI, February 28, 1846, p. 12.

64. The Albion, V, March 14, 1846, p. 132.

65. Ibid., April 4, 1846, p. 168.

66. Ibid.

67. Ibid.

68. Ibid.

Chapter Seven

1. Odell's Annals, V, 249.

2. Ibid., p. 267; p. 276.

3. The Albion, V, October 10, 1846, p. 492.

4. Ibid.

5. Ibid.

6. ST, XVI, October 17, 1846, p. 392.

7. The Albion, V, October 31, 1846, p. 528.

8. ST, XVI, October 31, 1846, p. 392.

9. The Albion, V, November 7, 1846, p. 540.

10. Ibid., November 14, 1846, p. 552.

11. Odell's Annals, V, 252.

12. Ibid.

13. George Vandenhoff, Leaves From An Actor's Notebook (New York: D. Appleton and Company, 1860), p. 239.

14. The Albion, V, November 21, 1846, p. 564.

15. Olympic playbill, December 7, 1846.

16. Ibid., December 14, 1846.

17. Ibid.

18. The Albion, VI, January 2, 1847, p. 12.

19. ST, XVII, April 24, 1847, p. 108.

20. The Albion, VI, April 10, 1847, p. 180.

21. ST, XVII, April 3, 1847, p. 72.

22. Ibid., April 10, 1847, p. 84.

23. Ibid., April 17, 1847, p. 96.

24. Ibid., April 24, 1847, p. 108.

25. Ibid.

Chapter Eight

1. The Albion, VI, September 18, 1847, p. 456.

2. Ibid.

3. ST, XVII, September 18, 1847, p. 386.

4. Ibid., October 16, 1847, p. 404.

5. Ibid.

6. Olympic playbill, October 20, 1847.

7. The Albion, VI, October 23, 1847, p. 516.

8. ST, XVII, October 23, 1847, p. 416.

9. Ibid.

10. Ibid.

11. The vessel was finally impounded by customs authorities and towed away in late November.

12. Olympic playbill, November 1, 1847.

13. Ibid.

14. The Albion, VI, November 6, 1847, p. 540.

15. Ibid., November 20, 1847, p. 564.

16. Ibid.

17. Ibid., November 27, 1847, p. 575.

18. New York Herald, November 27, 1847.

19. Ibid., November 29, 1847.

20. Ibid., December 4, 1847.

21. Olympic playbill, December 18, 1847.

22. Ibid.

23. Ibid.

24. Ibid.

25. The Albion, VI, December 18, 1847, p. 612.

26. ST, XVII, December 18, 1847, p. 512.

27. The Albion, VI, December 25, 1847, p. 619.

28. Ibid.

29. ST, XVII, January 14, 1848, p. 536.

30. The Albion, VII, January 8, 1848, p. 24.

31. ST, XVII, January 15, 1848, p. 560.

32. The Albion, VII, January 22, 1848, p. 48.

33. Ibid.

34. Ibid.

35. Ibid.

36. Ibid.

37. Ibid., January 29, 1848, p. 60.

38. T. Allston Brown, History of The New York Stage (3 Vols. New York: Dodd, Mead, and Company, 1903), I, 284.

39. Olympic playbill, February 15, 1848.

40. "Mose the Fire B'hoy," News From Home, November 1949, p. 2.

41. Brown, I, 284.

42. The Albion, VII, February 19, 1848, p. 96.

43. Ibid.

44. A Glance At New York in 1848, Manuscript promptbook, Harvard Theatre Collection.

45. ST, XVIII, March 11, 1848, p. 36.

46. The Albion, VII, April 15, 1848, p. 192.

47. Ibid.

Chapter Nine

1. The Albion, VII, September 23, 1848, p. 464.

2. ST, XVIII, September 16, 1848, p. 372.

3. Ibid., September 23, 1848, p. 384.

4. Ibid., October 7, 1848, p. 396.

5. Ibid.

6. The Albion, VII, September 30, 1848, p. 478.

7. Ibid., October 14, 1848, p. 500.

8. Ibid.

9. ST, XVIII, October 21, 1848, p. 420.

10. Ibid.

11. Ibid.

12. The Albion, VII, October 21, 1848, p. 512.

13. Ibid., October 28, 1848, p. 524.

14. ST, XVIII, November 4, 1848, p. 444.

15. The Albion, VII, November 11, 1848, p. 548.

16. Ibid., November 18, 1848, p. 560.

17. ST, XVIII, December 9, 1848, p. 504.

18. The Albion, VII, December 30, 1848, p. 632.

19. Olympic playbill, December 29, 1848.

20. The Albion, VIII, January 6, 1849, p. 8.

21. Ibid.

22. Ibid., January 13, 1849, p. 20.

23. Ibid.

24. Olympic playbill, January 15, 1849.

25. The Albion, VIII, January 20, 1849, p. 32.

26. Ibid., January 27, 1849, p. 44.

27. Ibid.

28. Ibid., February 3, 1849, p. 56.

29. Ibid., February 17, 1849, p. 80.

30. ST, XIX, February 24, 1849, p. 24.

31. Odell's Annals, V, 474.

32. The Albion, VIII, March 10, 1849, p. 116.

33. Ibid., March 17, 1849, p. 128.

34. Ibid., April 7, 1849, p. 164.

35. Odell's Annals, V, 478.

36. The Albion, VIII, April 14, 1849, p. 176.

37. ST, XIX, September 15, 1849, p. 360.

38. The Albion, VIII, September 15, 1849, p. 440.

39. Ibid., September 22, 1849, p. 452.

40. ST, XIX, September 29, 1849, p. 384.

41. Ibid., October 27, 1849, p. 420.

42. The Albion, VIII, November 3, 1849, p. 524.

43. Ibid., November 10, 1849, p. 536.

44. Ibid., December 8, 1849, p. 584, states: "We regret to hear the report that Mitchell is about relinquishing the management of this long established temple of Momus."

45. Ibid., IX, February 16, 1850, p. 80.

46. Ibid., February 2, 1850, p. 56.

47. Ibid., February 16, 1850, p. 80.

48. ST, XX, March 9, 1850, p. 36.

Chapter Ten

1. T. Allston Brown, History of the New York Stage (3 Vols. New York: Dodd, Mead and Co., 1903), I, 286.

2. Ibid.

3. From the conclusion of Mossop's engagement in 1839 un-

til Mary Taylor's temporary engagement in 1848, only Mitchell's
name ever appeared in large type at the head of the playbills.

4.   Leland Croghan, "New York Burlesque 1840-1870, A
Study in Theatrical Self-Criticism" (Unpublished Ph.D. dissertation,
School of Education, New York University, 1968), p. 25.

5.   Constance Rourke, American Humour: A Study of The
National Character (New York: Harcourt Brace and Co., 1931),
p. 121.

6.   George C. D. Odell, "Theatrical Stock Companies of New
York," Theatre Annual, I, (1951), p. 8.

7.   Paul Preston, "The Olympean Gods and Goddesses," New
York Clipper, N.D. Clipping in the Harvard Theatre Collection.

8.   The Albion, VII, February 19, 1848, p. 96.

9.   ST, XVIII, March 11, 1848, p. 36.

BIBLIOGRAPHY

Books

Adams, William Forbes. Ireland and Irish Immigration to the New World From 1815 to the Famine. New Haven: Yale University Press, 1932.

Asbury, Herbert. The Gangs of New York: An Informal History of the Underworld. New York: Alfred A. Knopf, 1928.

Brown, T. Allston. History of the New York Stage. 3 Vols. New York: Dodd, Mead and Company, 1903.

Dimmick, Ruth Crosby. Our Theatres Today and Yesterday. New York: H. K. Fly, 1913.

Dickens, Charles. American Notes. London: Oxford University Press, 1957 (originally published London, 1842).

Hewitt, Barnard. Theatre U.S.A., 1665 to 1957. New York: McGraw-Hill, 1959.

Hodge, Frances. Yankee Theatre: The Image of America On Stage, 1825-1850. Austin: University of Texas Press, 1964.

Hornblow, Arthur. A History of the Theatre in America. 2 Vols. Philadelphia: J. B. Lippincott Company, 1919.

Hutton, Lawrence. Curiosities of the American Stage. New York: Harper and Brothers, 1891.

_____. Plays and Players. New York: Hurd and Houghton, 1875.

Ireland, Joseph. Records of the New York Stage. 2 Vols. New York: T. H. Morrell, 1866.

Keese, William L. A Group of Comedians. New York: Dunlap Society, 1901.

Kendall, John S. The Golden Age of the New Orleans Theatre. Baton Rouge: LSU Press, 1952.

Moody, Richard. The Astor Place Riot. Bloomington, Ind.: Indiana University Press, 1957.

Morris, Lloyd. Curtain Time: The Story of the American Theatre. New York: Random House, 1953.

Northall, William Knight. Macbeth Travesty. London: Dick's Standard Plays, n.d.

_____. Before and Behind the Curtain; or, Fifteen Years' Observations Among the Theatres of New York. New York: W. F. Burgess, 1851.

Odell, George C. D. Annals of the New York Stage. 15 Vols. New York: Columbia University Press, 1927-1949.

Pope-Hennessey, Una. Three English Women in America. London: Ernest Bern Ltd., 1929.

Ross, Joseph. The Image of America in Mazzini's Writing. Madison, Wis.: University of Wisconsin Press, 1953.

Rourke, Constance. American Humour: A Study of the National Character. New York: Harcourt Brace and Company, 1931.

Seitz, Don C. The James Gordon Bennetts. Indianapolis: Bobbs-Merrill, 1928.

Vandenhoff, George. Leaves From an Actor's Note Book. New York: Appleton and Company, 1860.

Wallack, John Lester. Memories of Fifty Years. New York: C. Scribner's Sons, 1912.

Warner, Oliver. Captain Marryatt: A Rediscovery. London: Constable, 1953.

Wilkins, W. Clyde. Charles Dickens in America. New York: C. Scribner's Sons, 1912.

Wilson, Garff B. Three Hundred Years of American Drama and Theatre: From Ye Bare and Ye Cubb to Hair. Englewood Cliffs, N.J.: Prentice-Hall, 1973.

Articles

Anonymous. "Mose The Fire B'hoy," News From Home (November 1949).

Hodge, Frances. "Charles Mathews Reports on America," QJS, 36 (1950), pp. 492-499.

Johnson, Claudia D. "Burlesques of Shakespeare: The Democratic Americans' 'Light Artillery'," TS, 21 (May 1980), pp. 49-63.

Odell, George C. D. "Theatrical Stock Companies of New York," Theatre Annual, I (1951), pp. 7-26.

Preston, Paul. "The Olympian Gods and Goddesses," New York Clipper, N.D. (Clipping in the Harvard Theatre Collection.)

Rinear, David L. "Burlesque Comes to New York: William Mitchell's First Season at the Olympic," 19th Century TR, 2 (Spring 1974), pp. 23-34.

_____. "From the Artificial Towards the Real: The Acting of William Farren," Theatre Notebook, 31 (No. 1), pp. 21-28.

_____. "F. S. Chanfrau's Mose: The Rise and Fall of an Urban Folk-Hero," TJ, 33 (May 1981), pp. 199-212.

Newspapers and Weekly Periodicals

The Albion: A Journal of News, Politics, and Literature. New Series: New York: Vols. 1-9, 1842-1850.

The Daily Herald. New York: 1840-1850.

The Knickerbocker; or New York Monthly Magazine. New York: Vols. 9-20, 1839-1850.

The New York Mirror: A Weekly Gazette of the Fine Arts. New York: Vols. 17-20, 1839-1842.

The New Yorker. New York, Vol. 4, 1839.

The Spirit of The Times: A Chronicle of the Turf, Agriculture, Field Sports, Literature and the Stage. New York: Vols. 9-20, 1839-1850.

Unpublished Materials

Baker, Ben. A Glance At New York in 1848. Manuscript prompt-book. Harvard Theatre Collection.

Croughan, Leland. "New York Burlesque, 1840-1870; A Study in Theatrical Self-Criticism." Diss. NYU, 1968.

Johnson, Rue. C. "The Theatrical Career of William E. Burton." Diss. Indiana University, 1968.

Olympic Contract Book.   Harvard Theatre Collection.

Olympic Playbills, 1839-1850.   Harvard Theatre Collection.

Letter from George Holland to Benjamin Webster, 27 February 1845.
Harvard Theatre Collection.

INDEX

(Underscored numbers refer to pages with photographs.)

Barnum, P. T.   157, 169, 193
Bathing 111
La Bayadere or The Maid of Cashmere   45, 46, 64, 88
Beauty and The Beast 96-97, 98
The Bee and The Orange Tree 140, 142
The Beggar's Opera 77
Behin, Monsieur 33
Bengough, Richard 13, 22, 29, 41, 42, 45, 46, 51, 55,
     56, 57, 58, 62, 63, 66, 67, 68, 78, 86, 88, 89, 94,
     96, 110, 114, 116, 129, 133, 134, 156, 173, 180, 193
Benjamin, Park 37, 38
Bennett, James Gordon 37-38, 39, 40, 65, 160, 161
Bernard, W. B.   97
"b'hoys" (also, "pit patrons"; "pittites") 17, 23, 24-25, 51,
     61, 62, 110, 112, 115, 116, 119, 123, 127, 130, 135,
     148, 149, 157, 164-65, 166, 167, 171, 173, 176, 178,
     181
Biddle, Nicholas 6, 7
Bill or Fare 103
Billy Lackaday 111
Billy Taylor   23, 24
Blackburn 83, 86
Blake, William Rufus 3, 4, 7, 190
Blessington, Countess of 57
Bluebeard 97
Bob Bang 62
The Bohea-Man's Girl 126
The Bohemian Girl 126
Booth, Mrs. J. B., Jr.   101, 115, 116, 119
Booth, Junius Brutus, Sr. 1, 115
Boots At The Swan 91, 182, 183
Boucicault, Dion 64, 92
Bowery Theatre (NY) see The American Theatre, Bowery
Box and Cox 164
"Boz" see Dickens, Charles
Boz, or The Lion Lionized 76, 77, 80, 128
British travelogue writers   51-54
Brittania and Hibernia   183
Broadway Circus 3
Broadway Theatre (NY)   156, 164
Brook, C. W. S.   132
Brother Jonathan (periodical)   115
Brough brothers 180
Brougham, John 87-88, 94, 173
Brougham's Lyceum 88
Brown, T. Allston 190
Browne, James S.   13, 18, 19